Advance Praise for

The Senior Cohousing Hand

Dive right into this book and be enriched by the insights and the wisdom you will find there. I'm not kidding. Go. Now. Your future is waiting for you.

— Bill Thomas, MD, from the Prologue

Charles Durrett has written a book inviting an exciting eldership. ...
Wouldn't it be great if every step of life had such thoughtful design?

— Patch Adams, MD, from the Foreword

The key to living a long, healthy life is community — having a group of people who know and care about you with whom you socialize at least once a week. This book shows you how seniors all over the world are combating isolation and loneliness by building healthy communities.
Viva the community! Long life! Honey in the heart!

— Eric Utne is the founder of *Utne Reader*.

Quality of life is more and more important in the last part of our life, and there is no need to live out our later years alone or lonely.
Aging in place — in community — is an opportunity waiting for development; and cohousing — the most creative housing option for seniors — is one that we can make happen for us NOW, if we, as Chuck Durrett says, "Go forth and be one with [our] own future."

— Bolton and Lisa Anthony, Senior activists, and founders of Second Journey

As a long time developer of housing and a resident of Silver Sage Cohousing, I can't imagine any way to live that makes more of our opportunities for quality of life and living lighter on the planet. Chuck's book captures all that and enables our potential as proactive seniors.

— Jim Leach, Housing Developer and Senior Cohousing resident

THE *A Community Approach to Independent Living*
Senior Cohousing
HANDBOOK *Second Edition*

Charles Durrett

Prologue by William H. Thomas, MD
Foreword by Patch Adams, MD

NEW SOCIETY PUBLISHERS

Cataloging in Publication Data:
A catalog record for this publication is available from the National Library of Canada.

Cover design by Diane McIntosh.
Cover photos: Man with sunflower © iStock/Alex Raths. All others courtesy of
Charles Durrett.

Printed in Canada.
First printing April 2009.

Paperback ISBN: 978-0-86571-611-7

Inquiries regarding requests to reprint all or part of *Senior Cohousing* should be
addressed to New Society Publishers at the address below.

To order directly from the publishers, please call toll-free (North America)
1-800-567-6772, or order online at: www.newsociety.com

Any other inquiries can be directed by mail to:

New Society Publishers
P.O. Box 189, Gabriola Island, BC V0R 1X0, Canada
(250) 247-9737

New Society Publishers' mission is to publish books that contribute in fundamental
ways to building an ecologically sustainable and just society, and to do so with the least
possible impact on the environment, in a manner that models this vision. We are committed to doing this not just through education, but through action. This book is one
step toward ending global deforestation and climate change. It is printed on Forest
Stewardship Council-certified acid-free paper that is **100% post-consumer recycled**
(100% old growth forest-free), processed chlorine free, and printed with vegetable-
based, low-VOC inks, with covers produced using FSC-certified stock. Additionally,
New Society purchases carbon offsets based on an annual audit, operating with a car-
bon-neutral footprint. For further information, or to browse our full list of books and
purchase securely, visit our website at: www.newsociety.com

NEW SOCIETY PUBLISHERS

To Rosem

Contents

Prologue

William H. Thomas, M.D.

Professor and Distinguished Fellow, The Erickson School

I've been rich and I've been poor — and believe me, rich is better.
                                    — Sophie Tucker

Wealth. Riches. Affluence. Capital. Prosperity. Net worth. Security is one of the tent poles of well-being. Everybody wants it, everybody needs it, but what is it, exactly?

The easy thing is to link wealth with money. After all, who could be more secure than a billionaire? A billionaire who had been a successful movie producer, aviator, engineer, founder of a medical research institute, airline mogul, and winner of the Congressional Gold Medal would be especially secure in his old age — don't you think? Maybe, maybe not.

Howard Hughes died a recluse: a drug addict with hair, beard, finger-nails, and toenails all grown to grotesque lengths — despite the fact that he always kept a barber on call. He was estranged from his family, surrounded by strangers. One of the richest people in the world on the day of his death, the autopsy recorded evidence of severe malnutrition (he weighed only 90 pounds), and x-rays revealed broken hypodermic needles still embedded in his arms. Was Howard Hughes rich?

Then there is that nice girl from Albania who moved to India and settled into the life of a schoolteacher outside of Calcutta. There she experienced what she would later refer to as "the call within a call." "I was to leave the convent and help the poor while living among them. It was an order. To fail would have been to break the faith." She began this missionary work in 1948, venturing out into the slums, tending to the needs of the destitute and starving. Despite expressions of support from the Indian government, she had no income and had to resort to begging for food and supplies. Her congregation, the Missionaries of Charity, received official sanction from the Vatican in 1950. Along the way, Mother Teresa won the Nobel Peace Prize and the Presidential Medal of Freedom. At the time of her death, the Missionaries of Charity had over 4,000 sisters, an associated brotherhood of 300 members, and over 100,000 lay volunteers, operating 610 missions in 123 countries. Was Mother Teresa poor?

Real wealth is derived from a blend of financial and social capital. Social capital? While it is vital to our everyday lives (and happiness), the concept of social capital remains something of a mystery to most Americans. Financial capital is something we can understand easily because it is value reduced to numbers. Television networks, newspapers, authors, advisors and wealth gurus are all ready and eager to help us "put our financial house in order." We cannot say the same for social capital, which is, simply, "the net value of all of the voluntary reciprocal personal relationships that are part of our everyday lives." In other words, it pays to have — and to be — a darn good neighbor. Since few of us are likely to follow in the footsteps of either Howard Hughes or Mother Teresa, it makes sense to think about a balanced approach to wealth that provides us with both the financial and social capital we need if we are to find a "life worth living."

This is where senior cohousing comes into play. When you think about it, cohousing can be understood as a wealth-creation strategy that allows people to develop affordable housing enriched with an abundance of social capital. When people come together with the intention of being darn good neighbors and with the expectation of having darn good neighbors, their lives are made better in a myriad of ways that financial capital has a hard time duplicating. Unlike communes, in which people merge their personal finances with the economy of their community, cohousing strikes a balance that honors privacy and autonomy even as it encourages relationship-building and shared governance. Cohousing is, in my mind, the most approachable, most replicable strategy for the creation of intentional communities available to us today.

Thanks to Chuck Durrett, cohousing has grown from a purely European phenomenon (it got its start in Denmark) to an increasingly viable option for elders in America. The future, I believe, is better and brighter than ever. My optimism is based, in part, on the success the earlier edition of this book has already achieved. It is a valuable tool that will help the tens of thousands of people who are looking for another way to live to find what they are looking for. There is a new "old age" out there, waiting to be discovered. It is an elderhood rich in developmental potential, and it will lead us to new ways of understanding our communities, our families, and ourselves.

I remember getting my copy of the first edition of this book. I seized upon it and devoured its message hungrily. Its message was suited perfectly to its time. The second edition is even better, and I am sure that it will help even more people understand what senior cohousing is and how it works.

So what are you waiting for? Dive right into this book and be enriched by the insights and the wisdom you will find there.

I'm not kidding. Go. Now. Your future is waiting for you.

Foreword

Patch Adams, M.D.

I have never liked nursing homes. Even the best and most expensive are not what elders want. How could a senior citizen be a revered elder in these sad institutions? I've often thought, "Am I the only one ashamed that we care so little for our parents that we shove them in these most expensive of scrap heaps?" I've clowned in 1,500 nursing homes and feel tragic parallels with the 1,500 orphanages I've also been in. In both places, there is a huge hunger for love, attention, and fun. In both places, I always wished I could take the residents home with me. Have we so disconnected from human community and intelligence that society no longer sees the need for this unmined wisdom? I see the ads calling for, and encouraging, a carefree life — and connecting the word "burden" with those who need care. My mother made everything in me I like about myself. It was a privilege to have her spend the end of her life with us. I love that I could give back to her and that my children could be with her when she died.

I've lived communally for 37 years, and living communally has made everything easier for me in my life. I think that we primates have been communal for 80+ million years. We thrive in companionship. Loneliness is the worst experience a human can have. I think because we've been tribal for so long that loneliness is the experience of being without a tribe. I think depression is never an illness; rather, it is a symptom of loneliness. There are reasons so many elders are labeled as depressed. The truth is, they are lonely and longing for meaning within the tribe. Most people are not prepared to return to being part of a tribe. Alas, it is a skill most of us have lost. Senior cohousing is an intelligent midwife assisting a return to tribal life.

Chuck has written a book inviting an exciting eldership. Intelligent design. Wow! Wouldn't it be great if every step of life had such thoughtful design? So once the seed is planted —"I will not go to a nursing home"— then what? Read this book and shake your foundation. An exciting part of your engagement with senior cohousing is that, at the same time you cover your needs, you are pioneering extremely important social engineering. This book is your launching pad; your hunger for a better world and a lush imagination will make your model specific to you. Do not go out to pasture.

Acknowledgments

I want to thank all of the extraordinary people who put their heart into this project. To Magnus Soby, an architect who came from Denmark to the US to help with three months of this effort in our office. I also want to thank Chris Kennedy Pierce (a dedicated senior activist and professional), Brad Gunkel, Matthew Eghtessadi-Reed, and Yvonne Kanis.

To the Danes, who start significant movements like cohousing in the first place.

To the seniors who gave so generously of their time, their homes, and their community: Olaf Dejgaard (71, retired architect); Tua Møller (retired statistician for the Ministry of Health); Else Skov (retired secretary); Niels Vonge (retired four star general, Danish Army); Arne Ravan (75, retired high school principal); Inga (76, office administrator); Birthe (71, started, owned, operated, and retired from her own chocolate shop); Leif Behrend (69, factory owner); Ole (67, retired); Dan (68, retired seaman); Jørn Ole (68, retired math teacher); Hans Tovborg and Inga Søreson (72, retired auto executive, and 61, retired teacher); Kirsten Mitchel (77, retired radio and TV producer); Karen Permein 70, retired landscape architect); Ib and Grethe Jan-Mittet (75, retired teacher, and 75 ½ retired teacher); Eigil Nicolaysen (73, retired pharmacist); Anne-Lise Nicolaysen (pharmacist's assistant); Virginia

Thresh, Butch Thresh, Barbara Kronmal and Kirk Davis, Wina Simpson (from the Lodge in Grass Valley, CA), and many, many more.

Special thanks to the Danish housing experts, in particular, Hans Skifter Andersen, Martin Rubow, and of course, Jan Gudmand-Høyer (who has given his life to building more healthful social arrangements and more beautiful physical arrangements). And thanks, too, to Max Pedersen, who generously allowed material to be used from his book *Nybyggere — I Den Tredje Alder*, Kate Vial, Henry Nielsen, who incorporated "Aging Successfully in Place" into Study Group I, Erik Skoven, and the other seniors living in intergenerational and senior cohousing communities over the last 35 years — they are the real experts.

Thanks to the many Americans interested in senior cohousing who have offered suggestions about what they wanted to see in a book and about how to build great communities for seniors: Arthur Okner, Colette and Bob Brugel, Jim Leach, Nick Meima, Sue Hellwig, Phyliss Cole, Galen Cranz, all of those who attended seminars, shared at senior cohousing seminars, and attended various cohousing conferences, the entire Silver Sage Senior Cohousing group, the entire Wolf Creek Lodge Senior Cohousing group (OK. Active adults. Whatever.) And to all of those seniors around the country with whom I have had the great pleasure of designing senior and intergenerational communities.

And to my neighbors at Nevada City Cohousing with whom I have lived for three years and who indeed made life a little easier and always more entertaining. Lots of folks helped, lots of folks were essential, but this second edition wouldn't have been possible without the help of the following people: Marysia Miernowska, a natural and very capable community organizer, she primarily authored the case studies of Glacier Circle and Elder Spirit with the help of Dene Petersen; Laurie Taylor, a gerontologist who cares immensely about seniors and their well-being through proper housing, played a huge role in organizing this edition; Jesse Churchill, a young architect intern who seems to really appreciate that great environments don't happen because architects create them, but because cultures create them; Jean Nilsson, who not only played a significant role in the design chapter, but has read through the book in its entirely and given me great feedback along the way. Jean is a real talent as an architect, one who understands that for environments to succeed, we have to very specifically design them. I want to thank Anne

Glass. Her contribution "Why Aging in Community?" (Appendix A) gives a very sophisticated understanding of the "senior dilemma," and I am forever indebted.

This book was also made possible through the foresight of Chris Plant of New Society Publishers, who saw that if community would ever be available to seniors in the US at any significant scale, the word would really have to get out.

To William Thomas M.D., Patch Adams M.D., and Rabbi Zalman Schachter-Shalomi for their wisdom and encouragement. And to all of the people who incessantly encouraged me because, as they said time and time again, "The time for senior cohousing has come."

And finally to my lovely, lovely one, Kathryn McCamant, who chose not to write this time, but is always a thoughtful reviewer, and who held it all together through the duration, and who, with her company Cohousing Partners, is actively out there helping seniors realize their dream of living in — as the Danes would say, "in a place with goods in it."

Introduction

From the moment I first entered a cohousing community, it was apparent that I was in a special place. While attending the University of Copenhagen in 1980, I discovered cohousing on my one-mile walk to and from the train station each day. I walked by single-family homes, apartments, and clustered housing. There was never anyone in between the houses; there was no chatting, no visiting — and there were no people. But there was one cluster of brick houses where I saw a lot of activity between the houses. People were stopping with laundry basket in hand to talk to their neighbors. In the evening, there might be three or five people sitting around a table with a cup of tea or a beer. On the weekends, two or three people were in a parking area looking under the hood of a car. One day I stopped and knocked on someone's door and asked, "What's going on here?" The woman explained how this group decided to purchase a property themselves and to play an integral role in

Although this is a book specifically about *senior* cohousing, many of the photos in this book show *intergenerational* cohousing. The reason is two-fold. Firstly, it is to give you some idea of what life for seniors can be like in multi-generational cohousing. Secondly, when senior cohousing got started in Denmark, it was the multi-generational cohousing model that served as inspiration for seniors considering new ways of creating great lives for themselves.

The author visiting Munksøgård senior cohousing in Denmark and listening to stories of life before cohousing compared to life after moving in to cohousing.

the design and development of their own neighborhood. Over the year, I learned more. In 1984, Kate and I went back for an intensive 13-month research project. We visited 185 projects, studying 46 in detail. We lived in several of them, and while cooking dinner and during late-night conversations over a bottle of wine, we learned what cohousing entailed. We had planned to stay only six months, but it took 13 months before we found out what it really takes to co-develop, co-design, and co-inhabit this new type of neighborhood — and why it is so important.

We find cohousing communities immensely inspiring. Cohousing has a unique ability to create a positive and humane environment and meaningful and sustainable relationships. This is evident in the feelings of those who live there and our own observations and comparisons of cohousing developments with other, typically more traditional, housing schemes.

This finding is fortunate because it is clear that traditional forms of housing no longer address the needs of many older Americans. Dramatic demographic, economic, and technological changes in our society have created a population that lives longer, ages healthier, and is looking for alternatives to current housing situations as it ages. Successful housing solutions for these "young-old" seniors reflect seniors' desire to maintain comfort, control, and independence. Indeed, the booming growth of pre-planned, suburban-style "seniors-only" housing developments is testament to this trend. However, despite slick marketing campaigns to the contrary, these pre-planned "communities" simply do not meet the real long-term needs of today's seniors. They are speculative, for-profit development schemes, like any other of their type. It is not community. It's business.

Individuals often now live many miles and perhaps a world away from their extended families. Traditional forms of social and economic support that people once took for granted — family, community, and a sense of belonging — must now be actively sought out. As a result, many seniors are mis-housed, ill-housed, or even homeless simply because they lack, or feel they lack, appropriate housing options. But there are better options.

Intergenerational cohousing is a well-established form of housing in Europe and North America. Cohousing specifically designed and built for *seniors* is somewhat more recent. Pioneered in Denmark and successfully being adapted in other

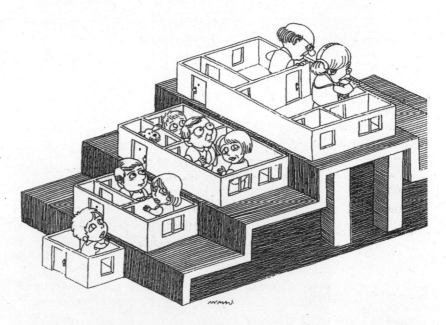

Southside cohousing courtyard, Sacramento, California.

countries (including the US), the senior cohousing concept re-establishes many of the advantages of traditional villages within the context of 21st-century life. It is community re-defined. This book is designed to provide seniors with the inspiration they need to be proactive in planning for their future living needs; to give them the knowledge and resources to examine whether senior cohousing is right for them; and to show them how to build such a community.

Portions of chapter 2 first appeared in *Cohousing: A Contemporary Approach to Housing Ourselves.* I hope that this new book will help put cohousing for seniors on the map in North America.

— Charles Durrett.

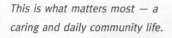

This is what matters most — a caring and daily community life.

Part One
Introducing Senior Cohousing

Imagine a living arrangement in which multiple, individually owned housing units (usually 20-30) are oriented around a common open area and a common house — a place where community is a way of life. Imagine residents who actively cooperate in planning the project with one goal in mind — to recreate an old-fashioned neighborhood that supports friendly cooperation, socialization, and mutual support. Imagine senior cohousing.

CHAPTER 1

Taking Charge of the Rest of Your Life

Some years ago I lost my husband and went through a difficult time. But I am glad that I lived here when it happened since it meant that I never felt unsafe. I was not together with other residents all the time, but I knew they were there for me if I needed them. And when I came home at night I could feel the warmth approach me as I drove up our driveway.

—Møllebjerg in Korsør, Denmark

So many American seniors live in places that do not accommodate their most basic needs. In the typical suburb, the automobile is a de facto extension of the single-family house. Driving is an absolute requirement for a person wanting to conduct business, shop, or participate in social activities. As we get older, as our bodies and minds age, the activities we once took for granted aren't so easy anymore: the house becomes too big to maintain; a visit to the grocery store or doctor's office becomes a major expedition; and the list goes on. Of course many, if not most, seniors recognize the need to take control of their own housing situation as they age. They dream

Conversation after dinner at Bellingham Cohousing, Bellingham, Washington.

The author and his mother, Rosemary.

of living in an affordable, safe, readily accessible neighborhood where people of all ages know and help each other. But then what? What safe, affordable, neighborhood-oriented, readily accessible housing choices actually exist?

The modern single-family detached home, which constitutes about 67 percent of the American housing stock, is designed for the mythical nuclear family consisting of a working father, a stay-at-home mother, and two point four children. Today, less than 25 percent of the American population lives in such households. Almost 25 percent of the population lives alone, and this percentage is increasing as the number of Americans over the age of 60 increases. At the same time, the surge in housing costs and the increasing mobility of the population combine to break down traditional

Meeting the Kristensens

When Katie and I were in Denmark in 1984-85 researching our first book about cohousing, we interviewed a couple who was planning one of the first senior cohousing communities there.

I met Mr. Kristensen, a 67-year-old retired high school principal, at a planning meeting for his new cohousing community, Abildgården. We discussed not only the common elements of Abildgården, the cozy common library, the bright and airy dining room they planned, but also the open floor plan of his own new house in the cohousing community, in which the kitchen, dining, and living areas were part of the same space but distinct at the same time. The "overlapping" would allow the smaller spaces to appear larger, and at the same time would create opportunities that larger, closed off spaces wouldn't.

After the meeting, we drove to his current house and parked out front. As we walked to the front door Mr. Kristensen mentioned that this 2,900-square-foot house was now too big for them.

In the house, I was impressed by the turn-of-the-century china cabinet, the stately dining table, the highboy, and the grandfather clock. They would never be able to get all this into their new 1,000 sq. ft. cohousing unit. "How can you leave all of this?" I gasped, involuntarily. "Sell it, give it to the kids," Mr. Kristensen exclaimed (he'd been asked this question before, I thought).

"We've made up our minds (without regrets), and there's no looking back," Mrs. Kristensen (65) interjected. We'll sell the house and most of the furniture that we've collected over the last 40 years, and our parents collected 40 years before that."

"We'll keep what's meaningful, but we'll sell the rest and one of our cars, and we'll travel around the world. Abildgården will be finished just in time for our return."

"Our life's role won't be reduced to being curators or caretakers of things until we can no longer do that," Mr. Kristensen continued. "We're going to be a part of something that's more interesting than this furniture. There, our house will be part of a neighborhood, and 'life's ☞

community ties. And, for the first time in the history of the US more women live without husbands than with.

Currently, seniors represent a record 12.4 percent of the American population, which, with the swell of post-WWII baby boomers entering seniorhood, will increase to 20 percent by the year 2030. Clearly, action must be taken, and quickly, to correct these household and community shortcomings. But what can be done, and by whom? How can we better house ourselves as we age?

I believe that the answer lies in senior cohousing communities. Having visited many of these communities, I'm now a firm believer that 20 seniors stranded on a desert island would do better at taking care of most of their basic needs than the same 20 left isolated or in an institution.

Typical senior housing. Expensive, but no one wants to be here.

maintenance' will be half the trouble — not by paying someone else to take care of us, but by cooperating with the neighbors. We'll have more time to live. After discussing every detail of the plans, we feel like Abildgården is ours; we built it, not brick by brick, but discussion by discussion. It will be worth more to us." Mrs. Kristensen continued, "Statistically, one of us will die in the next ten years. Then, statistically, the other will remain in this big house for another ten years, increasingly dependent on our children and the government. Then one day, the children will become impatient with having to be with one of us for our birthday, Christmas, Easter, Mother's Day, whatever, and they'll find a more institutional setting for us where we'll have 'company, support, and attention,' but it won't necessarily be what we want. And by that time, we'll be too weak and tired of burdening our children to object to whatever they come up with. And we'll live out our lives there, dependent and unhappy. Instead, we want to stay independent for as long as possible. And we want to be in control of our future and our lifestyle. We believe that by helping to create it now, we'll have the community we need to rely on for support, and not rely on institutional care."

Well, the Kristensens' project wasn't done when they returned — they never seem to be finished quite on time — but they have enjoyed what appears to be the independence with intradependence goal that they were seeking.

"Why would I want to live in senior cohousing — wouldn't it be better to live in mixed-age cohousing?" is a relevant question. Neither choice is better; it's a personal decision. But it's amazing how often young people are hanging around in senior cohousing. Kids visiting, grandkids visiting, neighbors visiting. And it's a more fun place to hang around for them than typical senior or assisted living facilities.

Searching for a Solution

When I was in Denmark a couple of years ago to further study senior cohousing, I was there, admittedly, for somewhat selfish reasons. The agonies of placing my own mother in an assisted-living facility were still fresh. Her story is, unfortunately, typically American: at 72 years old and determinedly, but detrimentally, living alone, she could no longer competently care for herself. Her children, doing their best, had reached the limits of their competency. Institutionalized assisted care, and eventually nursing care, were her only options.

Or were they?

With my mother needing immediate care, she moved into the most agreeable facility we could find and afford. In the meantime, we continued to search for institutional care for her that was not an institution. But what we found was a business system designed to care *for* people, not *with* people. The most agreeable senior living facilities can be so large and impersonal that even a well-meaning staff of caregivers cannot truly care about their clients; moreover, institutional, language, and cultural barriers often create a palpable distance between client and staff. Although they may be competent in their care-giving skills, staff are often young and speak English as a second language. Many seniors, for a wide variety of health and cultural reasons, have great difficulty communicating with them. This, of course, does not endear the staff to the clients; and the staff, in turn, can have little patience with this often-cranky elderly population.

Institutionalized American seniors also bear a heavy economic burden as they age. Skilled nursing and convalescent care costs much more than in-home care, and competent in-home care is expensive, starting at about $6,500 a month in California. That nest egg goes all too quickly.

Worse, before the disabled elderly can collect medical benefits, they must spend down all of their assets. The result is that the elderly who have the audacity to linger too long have little or no wealth to support themselves with or to leave behind.

After 20 years of designing, building, and living the cohousing life in the US, I was certain there had to be a better way for seniors, too.

A Danish Solution Again

In Denmark, people frustrated by the available housing options developed cohousing: a housing type that redefined the concept of neighborhood to fit contemporary lifestyles. Tired of the isolation and the impracticalities of traditional single-family houses and apartment units, they built housing that combines the autonomy of private dwellings with the advantages of community living. Each household has a private residence, but also shares extensive common facilities with the larger group, including kitchen and dining areas, workshops, laundry facilities, guest rooms, and more. Although individual dwellings are designed for self-sufficiency (each has its own kitchen), the common facilities are an important aspect of community life for both social and practical reasons — particularly for common dinners. The common house is there to compensate for

Silver Sage Senior Cohousing residents chatting in the common kitchen.

many of the things that the car used to provide: bridge, dinner out, friends, singing, music, etc.

So I found myself back in Denmark, confident in my understanding of cohousing yet intent to learn all I could from my Danish elders. And what I found was almost unexpected and utterly refreshing, and that was the extent to which they actually were living the better life in senior cohousing.

Imagine . . .

It's five o'clock in the evening and Karen is still going strong. After she

In cohousing, community is right outside your front door.

puts away the last of the gardening tools, she picks up a basket of vegetables and freshly cut flowers. She feels energized to finish the day as strongly as she began it. Her long-time neighbor and "shade tree mechanic" Andrew passes by to tell her that he successfully changed the wiper blades on her car. Grateful, Karen offers him a few of the choice flowers in her bunch. She knows his wife will love them. "All in a day's work," he smiles as he accepts.

Instead of rushing home to prepare a nutritious dinner for herself and her ailing husband Paul, Karen can relax, get cleaned up, spend some quality time with Paul, and then eat with him in the common house. Despite his recent health troubles, Paul wouldn't miss a common dinner

The Senior Predicament

"I'm getting old, and everything around me is getting old too," said Margo Smith, the 70-year-old, white-haired organizer of a Grey Panther meeting of six women and two men in Berkeley, California.

"I live in an older house, and just getting a leaky faucet fixed seems to take days of time — if I can find the money and someone to do it. I have to pay, pay, pay to have small things done. I am completely encumbered by my house and I'm not interested, or even willing, to encumber the lives of my children. They have their own families now, not to mention the careers I encouraged them to have."

"My next door neighbors are a young family on one side, and a single guy on the other. When I drive to see others my own age, people get behind me and honk — it might be my neighbors, for all I know. Just because my reactions have gotten slow, which is why I drive slowly, doesn't mean I shouldn't spend time with others I have something in common with. But I do wish I had a community based more on proximity."

Across the Atlantic, 71-year-old Else Skov lives in a large two-bedroom apartment in a senior cohousing community in Denmark. She moved into her home some 15 years ago with her husband, who died two years later. She is not lonely, largely due to the community's unique layout, which includes a common house where residents can meet with other residents after dinner to exchange stories and humor, or make plans to go to the opera together.

The difference between the two situations is cohousing. Senior cohousing offers a new approach to housing and, for many seniors, a new lease on life. Aside from a basic adherence to democratic principles, senior cohousing developments don't tout a specific ideology beyond a desire for a more practical, social home environment. Cohousing is not a commune, nor is it an intentional community; it is simply a functional neighborhood that works.

— it keeps his mind agile and makes him feel useful and wanted. It invigorates him on a daily basis.

Walking through the common house on the way home, Karen stops to chat with the evening's cooks, two of her neighbors, who are busy preparing broiled chicken in a mushroom sauce with new potatoes. The flowers and vegetables she brings to them couldn't be better looking, or better timed. Several other neighbors are setting the table. Outside on the patio, others are finishing a pot of tea in the late afternoon sun. Karen waves hello and continues down the lane to her own house, catching glimpses into the kitchens of the houses she passes — here, a neighbor's grandchild does homework at the kitchen table; next door, George completes his ritual after-work crossword.

As Karen enters her house, relaxed and ready to help her husband with his medications and other needs, she thinks they will have plenty of time to stroll through the birch trees behind the houses before dinner.

Karen and her husband, Paul, live in a housing development they helped design. Neither is an architect or builder. Karen considers herself a semi-retired schoolteacher; she volunteers in an afternoon reading program at a nearby elementary school. Paul is a retired lawyer. Ten years ago, recognizing the fact they were soon going to join the ranks of senior citizens, they joined a group of families who were looking for a realistic housing alternative to the usual offerings of retirement homes, assisted-living facilities, and institutional nursing care. At the time, they owned their own home, drove everywhere, and knew only a few of their neighbors. But they knew someday their house would become too difficult for them to maintain. They feared that one or both of them would lose the ability to drive. And if — forbid the thought — one of them unexpectedly passed away, how would the other manage? Would the survivor become a burden to their grown children? One day,

Common dinner in a senior cohousing community is prepared in turn, usually by one cook and one assitant. However, its significance goes far beyond sharing food and effort. Such dinners are the heart of cohousing, for they are the catalyst for many other social activities. Breaking bread together is a timeless community building experience.

Paul noticed a short announcement in the local paper:

> Most housing options available for seniors today isolate them and discourage neighborhood atmosphere. There is an alternative. If you are interested in:
>
> • Living in a large, social community in your own house.
>
> • Participating in the planning of your home.
>
> • Experiencing an alternative to institutionalized health care.
>
> Perhaps this is for you.
>
> We, a group of 20 families, all 55 years-of-age and older, are planning a housing development that addresses our needs for both community and private life. If this interests you, call about our next meeting.

Karen and Paul attended the meeting. They met other people who expressed similar concerns and fears about aging and their current housing situations and heard zeal about the possibilities that other options could afford. The group's goal was to build a housing development with a lively and

When the weather is right, common dinner is often held outside the common house.

positive social environment. They wanted a place where individuals would have a sense of belonging, where they would know people of all ages, and where they would grow old and continue to contribute productively.

In the months that followed, the group further defined their goals and began the process of turning their dream into reality. Some people dropped out and others joined. Two and a half years later, Karen and Paul moved into their new home — a community of clustered houses that share a large common house. By working together, these people had created the kind of neighborhood they wanted to live in. And in all probability they will live there for the rest of their lives.

Senior Housing as Community

Cohousing provides the community support missing in previous homes. It downsizes liabilities and upsizes quality of life. Cohousing is a grassroots movement that grows directly out of people's dissatisfaction with existing housing choices. Cohousing communities are unique in their extensive use of common facilities and — more importantly — in that they are organized, planned, and managed by the residents themselves. The great variety of cohousing community sizes, ownership structures, and designs illustrates the universality of

the concept. And where cohousing has gone, so goes senior cohousing — each community has its own needs, and only the residents themselves know what is truly best for them.

After all, a home is more than a roof over one's head or a financial investment. It affects the quality of a person's general well-being, one's confidence, relationships, and even one's health. It can provide a sense of security and comfort, or elicit feelings of frustration, loneliness, and fear. A woman who worries about when to shop for groceries and get dinner on the table while taking care of an ailing spouse is often unable to concentrate on a job or reserve time to spend with friends or other family members — let alone take time for herself. Not all aspects of housing can be measured by cost, rates of return, or other traditional

Senior cohousers seem to be consisitently upbeat with love and support from their community family.

Welcome home. The first household to move into Nevada City cohousing.

real estate assessments. While this book does discuss cohousing financing methods and market values, a more important concern for senior housing should be the people themselves, their emotional well-being, and the quality of their lives. Seniors are used to watching out for their future financial needs, especially when they see retirement on the horizon. "If I retire now, I'll have this amount of money per month," and so on.

Cohousing affords them the opportunity to look out for their emotional well-being when kids have moved, friends have died, and spouses are infirmed or non-existent. I came to realize that seniors moving into senior cohousing are the ultra-responsible ones — they're looking at all aspects of the horizon.

The men and women living in senior cohousing communities are perhaps the most honest and clear-eyed people I have ever encountered. They completely accept the fact that they are aging. They admit they can't do everything they once did. They know the slope is downhill. That's life. But acknowledging this basic truth does *not* mean they are fatalistic. Rather, they have taken charge of their remaining years with the expressed intent of achieving the highest-quality life possible — for as long as possible. For them, this means choosing to build their own community where they live among people with whom they share a common bond of generation, circumstance, and outlook. And they have a great time doing it.

"Hey, we're getting older, and we're going to make the most of it. We've had a lot of experiences, and now we're going to have some more."

Babyboomers — Danish and American alike — are not content with what institutions have to offer. They are used to taking charge of their own lives.

CHAPTER 2

Cohousing:

An Old Idea — A Contemporary Approach

Cohousers are simply consciously creating the community that used to occur naturally.
— Hans S. Anderson, cohousing organizer

In villages, people work together to build a schoolhouse, raise a barn, harvest the crops, celebrate the harvest, and more. Similarly, residents in cohousing enjoy the benefits of cooperation, whether by organizing common dinners, social activities, or caring for an elderly resident. Both communities build social relationships by working together to address practical needs. Cohousing offers the social and practical advantages of a closely-knit neighborhood consistent with the realities of 21st-century life.

In non-industrial communities, work is integrated with the rest of life. Small towns are not divided into residential, commercial, and

Retail streetside at FrogSong Cohousing.

17

FrogSong Cohousing, a mixed-use project that won Best in American Living Award as well as Best Smart Growth Award in 2004.

Hearthstone Community North Denver, Colorado.

industrial areas; rather, residences are built on top of shops, and cottage industries flourish in neighborhoods. Although cohousing developments are primarily residential, daily patterns develop that begin to weave work and home life together again. Most cohousing residents (if they are still working) go outside the community for their professional work, but there is also informal trading of skills within the community. One resident, a plumber, tends to a leaky faucet; another helps repair a neighbor's car. Several residents make wine together. A woman who makes pottery finds her best customers are fellow residents who buy her goods for gifts. These neighbors know each other's skills and feel comfortable asking for assistance, understanding they will be able to reciprocate later.

Technological advances make it increasingly common for people to work part-time or full-time at home. In most living situations today, working

at home can be very isolating (we know a computer programmer who could easily work from home, but chooses to drive 45 minutes to the office for companionship). The cohousing environment allows residents to enjoy the benefits of working at home without feeling isolated. As the trend toward working at home continues to grow, so cohousing responds; a recently completed cohousing community in Northern California included office space adjacent to its common facilities. In addition to office spaces, there is a coffee shop, a hair salon, and other commercial and retail establishments. With a tip of the hat toward traditional village life, some residential cohousing units are situated above the business spaces. Cohousing takes the loneliness out of being alone.

While incorporating many of the qualities of traditional communities, cohousing is distinctively contemporary in its approach, based on the values of choice and tolerance. Residents choose when and how often to participate in community activities and seek to live with a diverse group of people. Cohousing is a "best of all worlds" solution.

While cohousing is becoming popular in Europe, it remains a relatively new concept in the United States. The first American intergenerational cohousing projects were built here in 1991. Currently, there are more than 100 of these communities in the country, about 20 more are under construction, and there are another 120 to 150 or so in the planning stage. The trend is catching on. Before we look in detail at *senior* cohousing — what it is and what it can be — it is good to know something about what *intergenerational* cohousing communities are.

Six Components of Cohousing

Cohousing can be found in many forms — from urban factory loft conversions to suburban cities to small towns. Whatever the form, cohousing projects share the six components that are listed here and described more fully below:

1. Participatory Process: Residents help organize and participate in the planning and design process for the housing development, and they are responsible as a group for final decisions.

2. Deliberate Neighborhood Design: The physical design encourages a strong sense of community.

3. Extensive Common Facilities: Common areas are an integral part of the community, designed for daily use and to supplement private living areas.

4. Complete Resident Management: Residents manage the development, making decisions of

common concern at community meetings.

5. Non-Hierarchal Structure: There are not really leadership roles. The responsibilities for the decisions are shared by the community's adults.

6. Separate Income Sources: Residents have their own primary incomes; the community does not generate income.

1. Participatory Process

Active participation of residents, from the earliest planning stages through construction, is the first — and possibly the most important — component of cohousing. The desire to live in a cohousing community

Nevada City Cohousing, Nevada City, California.

Intergenerational cohousing is usually kid oriented.

These folks are laying out their houses and streets like no speculating developer ever could. A functional neighborhood starts with the street. Participatory site planning has played a key role in getting out of the box of default suburban site planning.

provides the driving force to get it built, and in some instances, the residents themselves initiate the project.

The number of residents who participate throughout the planning and development process varies from project to project. Often a core group of 6 to 12 families establishes a development program, finds the site, hires the architect, and then seeks other interested people. Typically, all of the houses are sold or rented before the project is finished. In some cases, the resident group collaborates with non-profit housing associations or a private developer, but even then, the residents play a key role.

The participatory process has both advantages and disadvantages, but no cohousing community has ever been

built any other way. Even with the proven success of cohousing, developers hesitate to build on their own, and probably couldn't do it successfully even if they wanted to. Experience shows that only people who seek new residential options for themselves will be motivated to push through the planning and design process without making serious compromises.

Future residents usually play a key role in getting the project approved, especially when citizens, planning commissions, and even city councils are prejudiced against multi-family housing. Neighbors fear that cohousing will attract "unconventional" people, adversely affect the neighborhood, and reduce property values. Such fears are completely unfounded and are dispelled once neighbors get to know the future cohousing residents. Cohousing residents tend to be conscientious, taxpaying citizens, active in school and other community activities; cohousing developments have helped to stabilize neighborhoods and make them more desirable.

Many resident groups have been able to push their projects through the labyrinth of barriers they've met with. When a city council denied approval of one cohousing project, the residents built models, went to meetings, and eventually convinced the council they were respectable citizens with worthy intentions. When banks questioned feasibility, residents risked their own assets to convince the bank to give them the construction loan. When cuts had to be made to build within a construction budget, residents insisted the architect cut the size of amenities of the individual units to preserve the common facilities. Few developers — for-profit or nonprofit — would ever take such measures or risks.

Organizing and planning a cohousing community requires time for group meetings, research, and decision-making. But anything worthwhile requires time and effort. People organize to build schools, town halls, fire stations, and churches, so why not a viable working neighborhood? Residents volunteer their time because of their commitment to the idea and their own desire for a more satisfying residential environment.

Environmental Advantages

In addition to its social advantages, cohousing offers numerous environmental benefits. Although there is room for more data, it appears that, depending on the design, cohousers on average drive about 60 percent less and use 50-75 percent less energy for heating and cooling than they did in their previous homes (for a family of three). In our Nevada City single-family house, where we lived before moving into the Nevada City cohousing community, our energy bill ran right at $150/month both in winter and summer. Living in Nevada City Cohousing, our bill for house heat and domestic hot water ran about $15/month. Air conditioning for this hot summer climate was zero because the building envelope was so energy efficient and because the passive cooling measures (cross ventilation, holding the night cooling, etc., were so effective. Every other new house built in the area and almost all old houses employ an air conditioner.

Cohousing residences are about 60 percent the size of average new American houses, and cohousing communities on average occupy less than 30 percent as much land as the average new subdivision for the same number of households and 50 percent as much as the same individuals did before moving into cohousing. And cohousing members drive about 60% less.

What impresses me most about working with cohousing communities is watching the best intentions of the group for living lighter on the planet percolate to the collective consciousness after being initiated by a few individuals. And as much as I'd like to take credit as the architect, my job is really little more than provoking the group a little, sharing a great deal of experience with them, and then as best I can, facilitating the co-education process of the participants (see Study Group II). But community is really the secret ingredient to living lighter on the planet. First and foremost, we need to know how to do it and learn how to cooperate. When people listen to their neighbors and prospective neighbors about saving energy, they seem to hear it better than by listening to an architect.

Some seniors prefer intergenerational cohousing. There are 21 seniors (and 37 kids) in Nevada City Cohousing. Other seniors prefer senior cohousing.

Nevada City Cohousing.

The most active members are likely to attend one to two meetings a month for one or two years. The process can be long, but those now living in cohousing communities universally agree it was not only well worth the effort, but one of the best things they ever did for themselves, their families, and the larger community.

A feeling of community emerges during the period when residents are working together to reach their common goal. Typically, few participants know each other before joining the group. During the planning and development phases, they must agree on many issues closely tied to their personal values. Despite the inevitable frustrations and disagreements, the intensity of the planning period forms bonds between residents that

greatly contribute to the community after they move in. Having fought and sacrificed together for the place where they will live builds a sense of pride and community that no outside developer can "build into a project."

2. Deliberate Neighborhood Design

A physical environment that encourages a strong neighborhood atmosphere is the second most important component of cohousing. People often talk about how enjoyable it would be if they could live somewhere where they knew their neighbors and felt secure. Yet, few residential developments include areas where neighbors can meet casually. Cohousing residents can build an environment that reflects their desire for community. Beginning with the initial development plan, residents emphasize design aspects that increase the possibilities for social contact. For example, placing parking at the edge of the site allows the majority of the development to be pedestrian-oriented and thus safe for seniors and grandchildren alike, which enhances the neighborhood atmosphere. Informal gathering places are created with benches and tables. The location of the common house determines how it will be used. If the residents pass by the common house on their way home, they are more likely to drop in. If the common house can be seen from many of the houses, it will be used more often.

Physical design is critically important in facilitating a social atmosphere. While the participatory development process establishes the initial sense of community, it is the physical design that sustains it over time. Whether the design succeeds depends largely on the architect's and organizing group's understanding of how design factors affect community life. Without thoughtful consideration, many opportunities are lost.

For senior cohousing, design must be tailored to seniors, but every possible interior safety feature does not have to be installed at the outset. It is critical that every possible measure should be taken to avoid an institutional look. Houses should be warm and inviting and well lit. The common house should be giving and community-sustaining — like a Parisian café. A flexible building design is also important, so that the units can be modified to suit owners who are aging or who are new owners. Every senior cohousing community I visited had remote parking. When asked, these especially conscious seniors said things like, "I used to simply drive directly into my garage. But it's more important for my long-term well-being to see, talk to, and hang out with my neighbors. While the community is built in the

planning phase, the design sustains the community once the honeymoon has worn off."

3. Common Facilities

While each private home is a complete house in and of itself, just like any traditional home, cohousing communities have common areas that supplement the private houses. Private houses in cohousing can be smaller than typical houses because features such as workshops, guest rooms, and laundry are located in the common house, and because large-scale entertainment can happen there. The common house is an extension of each private residence, based on what the group believes will make their lives easier and more economical, not to mention more fun and more interesting.

Common work days like this one at Bellingham Cohousing take care of outdoor maintenance. Commonly, people are obligated to 20 to 30 hours per year to maintain common real estate. Older residents often help shop, make snacks, or do related administration but never underestimate their work ethic.

One lawnmower for 30 households, for example, represents a huge savings over one lawnmower per household. Items like ice chests, camping equipment, bike repair equipment, as well as hundreds of other items stored in cohousing not only save money but also room.

According to the Census Bureau, the average size of new homes built in the US at the start of the 21st century was 2,324 sq. ft. The average private house in a cohousing community is 1,250 sq. ft. On the other hand, the average common house for a typical 30-unit cohousing community averages 4,000 sq. ft., including workshops and other buildings.

The common house, which supplements the individual dwellings and provides a place for community activities, is the heart of a cohousing community. It is a place for common dinners, afternoon tea, games on rainy days, a Friday night bar, crafts workshop, laundry facilities, and numerous other organized and informal activities. The common facilities often extend beyond the common house to include barns and animal sheds, greenhouses, a car repair garage, and in one case, a tennis court and swimming pool.

These facilities provide both practical and social benefits. For instance, the common workshop replaces the need for every family to have the space and tools to fix furniture and repair bicycles and cars. Expensive tools, such as a drill press or table saw, become much more affordable when several households share the cost. Not only do residents gain access to a wider range of tools through a common workshop, but they also enjoy the company of others using the shop or just passing by. They may also share and learn new techniques and skills along the way.

Residents do handywork and hang out in the common house of a senior cohousing community in Denmark.

Hanging out at the common house terrace. Every block should have a common place where people can walk and talk to neighbors.

The concept of a common space in clustered housing is not in itself unusual. Many condominium developments have a clubhouse or community room. However, a clubhouse significantly differs from a common house both in the way and to the extent the space is used. Typically, a clubhouse is rented out by individual residents for private parties, or used for owner association meetings or exercise classes. Moreover, the clubhouse is usually small, providing only just enough room to accommodate small-scale entertainment needs. The exception is "adult" complexes, which may incorporate a bar and a well-equipped gym into its common area. Regardless, there is no place set aside specifically for children, and most of the time the clubhouse is empty and locked. The clubhouse idea is a nice touch on paper but in reality such rooms are usually poorly utilized. In contrast, a cohousing common house is open all day and is considered an essential part of daily community and even private life.

As cohousing has evolved, the common house has increased in size and importance. Today, the size of private dwellings is often reduced in order to build more extensive common facilities. These changes were dictated by experience. For instance, many residents of early cohousing developments were reluctant to commit to common dinners, thinking they would be nice once or maybe twice a week, but not on a regular basis. Yet, when the common house is designed well, common dinners have proven overwhelmingly successful, and today most new cohousing groups plan for meals in the common house several times a week, with about half of the residents participating on any given evening. Substantial space is thus allocated in the common house for pleasant dining rooms and spacious kitchens. Children's play areas are often included, so that children can be children, and adults can sit and converse in an adult-oriented environment. The specific features of the common house depend on the interests and needs of the residents. Their use is likely to change over time in response to new community members and needs.

FrogSong Cohousing, Cotati, California. A place that encourages a sense of community and allows for casual interaction among residents is an important characteristic of cohousing.

In intergenerational cohousing, kids are the agenda. In senior cohousing, seniors are the agenda.

> "We have a lot of activities together that are not planned. Except for dinner, the unplanned activities are often more fun than the planned ones. But we need the planned ones in order to make sure that the unplanned ones happen."
> — cohousing resident

The community kitchen is designed for efficiency. Although meals for over fifty people can be prepared here, it still has a comfortable residential feeling.

By allowing residents to become acquainted, discover mutual interests, and share experiences, common facilities and activities contribute greatly to the formation of a tightly knit community. These friendships then carry over into other areas. As one resident said: "The common house is an essential element. Through the activities there, life is added to the streets. Without it, the sense of community would be hard to maintain."

The common house is also an asset for the surrounding neighborhood. It can be used for meetings, classes, neighborhood organizations, and cultural programs. One Danish cohousing group organized a film club that attracts participants from the entire town. As the community's primary meeting place, the common house has infinite uses both for the residents and their neighbors.

4. Resident Management

In keeping with the spirit in which cohousing is built, residents — owners and renters alike — are responsible for the community's ongoing management. Major decisions are made at common meetings, usually held once a month. These meetings provide a forum for residents to discuss issues and solve problems.

Responsibilities are typically divided among work groups in which all adults must participate. Duties like cooking common dinners and cleaning the common house are usually rotated. Under a system of resident management, problems cannot be blamed on outsiders. Residents must assume responsibility themselves. If the buildings are not well maintained, they will have to pay for repairs. If the common activities are disorganized, everyone loses.

Learning how to make decisions as a group is not easy. Most people grow up and work in hierarchical situations. Residents must learn to work together and find the best solution. They may adopt organizational formats developed by other groups, or create new methods for themselves. It is a process of learning by doing. Residents told us that over time they become more effective at working together and then were able to apply the lessons they learned at home to their work lives or to other organizations to which they belonged.

5. Non-Hierarchical Social Structure

Although residents state opinions about certain issues (for example, people who frequently use the workshop might propose the merits of investing more money on tools), the community shares responsibility. The community doesn't depend on one person for direction. A "burning soul" may get the community off the ground, another may pull together the financing, and another may arrange the venue for each meeting. This division of labor is based on what each person feels he or she can fairly contribute. No one person, however, dominates the decisions or the community-building process, and no one person should become excessively taxed by the process.

6. Separate Income Sources

The economics of most cohousing communities are more or less like a typical condominium project. There is no shared community effort to produce income. As the example of a typical commune model has shown, when the community provides residents with their primary income, the dynamics among neighbors change — and it adds another level of community beyond the scope of cohousing.

A Unique Combination with Diverse Applications

These six components have come to define cohousing. None of these components is unique, but the consistent combination of all six is. Each builds on the others and contributes to the success of the whole.

Although these components are consistently present, their applications have been diverse. Each community is different because each was developed by its residents to

address and realize their particular needs and desires.

The Architecture of Cohousing

A central path usually connects the individual homes. Often, a common terrace faces the houses and can seat everyone for dinner or other activities. There are gathering nodes along the walkway, such as a picnic table or sand box. Such nodes are associated with every five to nine houses. The houses have front porches at least seven feet deep and nine feet wide, so people will actually use the space.

The kitchen is oriented toward the common side of the house, with the sink facing the community, so residents cooking or washing dishes can see people coming and going. More private areas (such as living rooms and bedrooms) face the rear, or private side, of the house.

Strawberry Creek Cohousing in Berkeley, California won the Best in American Living Award in 1996.

What really matters in community are relationships, mutual concern, and a caring community life.

Optimally, residents can see the common house from most, if not all, of the houses and can see if others are using it. The common house generally contains a common dining room, a kitchen, a media room, a laundry room, a sitting room, and other activity rooms such as a workshop, craft room, music room, and others depending on the group's desires. In a senior cohousing community, the common house often has large guest rooms to accommodate an extended visit from family or for professional caregivers if residents need help.

Further Considerations

Building a viable cohousing community requires that the residents remain true to more than the spirit of the ideal. As such, the following issues greatly influence how a cohousing community develops, both in the short and long term.

Community Size

While the average cohousing development accommodates 15 to 30 households, some consist of as few as nine families. Living in a small community can be more demanding because residents depend more on each other. If one person temporarily needs extra time to concentrate on professional interests, thereby limiting community participation, the others feel the loss. However cohousing works best when everyone has five or six other people that they strongly relate to, so that on Friday after a hellish work week they can find someone to moan to. Sometimes a few individuals get lost in smaller communities because there isn't someone who they relate to. Having generated lots of empirical date, the Danes are clear: "Don't try to get consensus with more

Bellingham Cohousing common terrace is a great gathering place.

...and so are the front porches of Strawberry Creek Cohousing,

than 50 adults or 35 seniors. There are other problems with too many people. Decisions get delegated (Who cut down that tree?); people can't get what's important to them on to the agenda; and they don't have a chance to discuss agenda items with folks before the meeting."

The average size of a cohousing community, 40-100 people, allows residents to retain their autonomy and choose when — or when not — to participate in community activities. Many people are seeking a supportive environment, rather than a new family type. The freedom not to participate sometimes can help to create a living environment that accommodates people's changing needs over the years.

Location

Locations of cohousing developments are limited by two factors, the availability of affordable sites and finding enough people interested in living in cohousing there. The majority are situated just outside metropolitan areas where sites are affordable and yet within reasonable distance from work, schools, and other urban attractions. That said, there are no hard and fast rules about location. Some cohousing communities are located in the inner cities. By contrast, at least ten communities have been established in semi-rural settings, some of them using a refurbished old farmhouse for

FrogSong Cohousing from the air.

the common house. While these developments have a "rural atmosphere," most residents will commute to nearby cities for work. Bottom line: *cohousing residents decide for themselves which location will work best for their particular desires and needs.*

Design

Most cohousing communities have attached dwellings clustered around pedestrian streets or courtyards, although a few communities consist of detached single-family houses. Some communities mix attached dwellings with detached single-family structures. More recent complexes have dealt with their northern climate by covering a central pedestrian street with glass, thus allowing access between residences and the common house without needing to "go outside."

Sigrid says that cohousing works for her because at home she has as much privacy as she wants, and right out her front door she has as much community as she wants.

Cohousing is generally a new design enterprise because it is difficult to create the desired relationships between spaces in existing buildings. Nevertheless, several communities in Denmark adapted old factory buildings; and another adapted an old school building. In another case, residents renovated nine dilapidated row houses to create a charming community in the inner city.

While all of the newly constructed Danish developments are low-rise in scale, in both Denmark and Sweden high-rises and sections of huge housing projects have been converted to cohousing to overcome impersonal environments that encouraged vandalism and high occupant turnover.

Types of Financing and Ownership

Cohousing developments utilize a variety of financing mechanisms and ownership structures, either by choice or by local ordinances: privately owned condominiums, limited-equity cooperatives, rentals owned by non-profit organizations, and a combination of private ownership and nonprofit-owned rental units. In each case, residents initiate, plan, and manage the community, whether or not the units are owner-occupied or rented. In Denmark, 18 of the 20 developments built before 1982 were completely privately financed and owned, similar to American condominiums. Then, for a period, most projects took advantage of new government-sponsored, index-linked loans that structured the developments as limited-equity cooperatives. More recently much government funding of nonprofit schemes has been withdrawn, including financial support for cohousing. Some cohousing projects have resulted from collaborations between nonprofit organizations and resident groups to build rental units. (See Appendix C for more on the economics of cohousing.)

Other than sometimes determining who can afford to live in the development, financing makes little difference in the actual functioning of a cohousing community. Thus, cohousing differs from other housing categories, such as cooperatives and condominiums, which are defined solely by their type of ownership. Cohousing refers to an idea about how people can live together, rather than any particular financing or ownership scheme.

Priorities

The priorities of cohousing groups are as varied as the residents themselves. In addition to seeking a sense of community, some groups emphasize ecological concerns, such as solar and wind energy, recycling, and organic community gardens. In other developments, residents place less priority on community projects and spend more time on individual interests such as local theatre groups, classes, or political organizations. And, of course, others are devoted to seniors.

Why Cohousing just for seniors?

Why would someone want to create a cohousing community dedicated to seniors? There is no simple answer, since housing is an individual choice. Mixed-generational cohousing is an option for seniors who are enticed by the hustle and bustle of children and the energy for life they generate. But regular cohousing communities typically focus their energies in places where seniors have already been — building careers, raising families, and the like. As well, concerns of younger

> ### The Intergenerational Argument
>
> Since senior cohousing came onto the scene in 1985, people often debate which is "better" for seniors: intergenerational cohousing or senior cohousing. I have long ago chosen to stay out of this argument. My suggestion: go with what feels right for you! That's the beauty of having options. Some seniors love intergenerational cohousing, others swear by senior cohousing. Only you know which is right for you, and I believe that it's inappropriate to pass judgment on which is better. It's an individual choice.

cohousers do not usually hinge on health issues. While some seniors find the youthful vigor of a regular cohousing community to be refreshing, others feel like they've "been there, done that." They value living in a senior community that has been designed around their unique needs and aspirations for company, for quiet, etc. They appreciate an environment in which they feel supported in their activities, health needs, and in possible contemplative practices.

So what alternatives are there? For too many Americans who find themselves either widowed and lonely or otherwise unable to effectively care for themselves and their homes as they once did, a planned retirement "community" or assisted-care institution beckons. It's an odd predicament: most seniors have been capable, reliable people throughout their adult lives. They raised families, owned

People meeting on their way to and from their destination is one thing that maintains community in cohousing.

Economic Advantages

Senior cohousing makes sense for a variety of economic reasons. Residents purchase smaller, custom-tailored, low energy-use, well designed houses. The unit size alone means a low relative cost, both to build and also to furnish and maintain. Seniors typically pare down their possessions to join the community, and many welcome the task knowing they will be able to share common items. As well, fewer personal items and fewer rooms mean less to take care of individually. Seniors offset the smaller unit size with a large common house and its extensive array of common amenities. Moreover, by cooperating on upkeep and by pooling their resources, cohousers reduce some of their cost-of-living expenses, including those involved in hiring and housing outside caregivers.

FrogSong Cohousing Community.

themselves alone, and now locked down behind the walls of a gated compound. As for the seniors in assisted-living care, they become, in effect, patients within an institution, where hired staff dictates the choice of food, the people with whom they can socialize, and the types of activities offered. At best, activities might be modified with residents' input, but essentially the residents have given up control of their lives. And there's no going back.

By contrast, in senior cohousing the residents themselves make their own decisions. They are not alone, nor are they lonely. They collectively decide who will cook, what to cook, when to eat, and so on. After dinner, they go to a show or play a card game. They set up quilting racks, make music, and plan the next workday.

Since relationships are paramount in a cohousing community, residents live next door to their friends and, over time, their previous best friends (from life before senior cohousing) move in. These seniors live among people with whom they share a common bond of age, experience, and community — a community they themselves built to specifically meet their own needs. These relationships provide purpose and direction in their lives and are as meaningful as any they have ever had. This is why cohousing is perfect for seniors.

property, worked in various jobs, and/or ran their own businesses. They were active members of a larger community. But those seniors who choose the planned retirement community route too often find

Senior Cohousing:

A Proven Approach — A New Application

We all helped paint the bike shed and the fence by the parking lot. And those who could not manage to paint took care of the food and drinks for the rest of us. Maybe we were not very efficient in a work-related sense, but we were very efficient from a social point of view, and we had a lot of fun while painting.

— Resident of Rynkebakken in Lejre

Senior cohousing takes the concepts of cohousing and modifies them according to the specific needs of seniors. The result is a cozy little village that invites involvement, cooperation, and friendship — a re-creation of earlier times when community participation was viewed as an essential part of social, mental, and physical health.

The people who first envisioned senior cohousing are ordinary citizens who, passionate about their ideas, simply made their personal dreams a reality for many. Along the way, they learned many invaluable lessons for creating, building, and living in a seniors-only cohousing community. In a nutshell, senior cohousing is similar to the mixed-generational cohousing model, with the following modifications:

- Careful agreements among residents about co-care and its limits.

Silver Sage Senior Cohousing, Boulder, Colorado.

- Design considerations appropriate for seniors.
- Size limitations (a maximum of 30 living units, usually 15-25).
- Senior-specific methods for creating the community, for example, Study Group I (see Chapter 7).

But before we discuss the specifics of these modifications, a bit of background is in order. After all, we can't know where we're going until we know where we've been.

History of Senior Cohousing in Denmark

The Danes first addressed housing for low-income seniors in 1900 when they converted an old monastery into housing for the elderly. There, many people slept in small cubicles in dormitories, a primitive arrangement more suited to monks or schoolboys than to the elderly. However, the residents bonded with one another and developed a mutual support system that worked very well. Many of the residents refused to move when later offered more physically substantial housing.

In 1933, legislation was passed that allowed old workhouses to be converted into senior homes. Unfortunately, these facilities were very substandard. After World War II, private nursing homes were built, mainly for the chronically ill, and all seniors were granted a small pension.

Beginning in the late 1950s, programs to help seniors remain in their own homes were established, programs similar to American programs like Meals on Wheels and Nurses on the Go. But these programs didn't solve the problem of loneliness and isolation. As a result, in 1964 a group that called itself "Boligtrivsel i Centrum" or "Quality of Living in Focus" was founded to address a broad range of social ecology issues for seniors. But its work was only very slowly recognized and it wasn't until 1983 that this group received several grants.

In the meantime, the Danes reformed their social security system. In 1976, they put nursing homes and senior housing under one agency. What was a good idea on paper went horribly wrong in practice: seniors who moved into state-supported residences lost their pension and were granted only a small monthly allowance; moreover, they lived with little or no privacy and virtually no independence — they lived in an institution. The Danes described this housing as "the gate to hell," and the elderly clung to their own homes as long as possible. (An unspoken advantage to this avoidance of public housing was that it saved the government money.)

Residents from the first Danish senior cohousing group, Midgarden, Copenhagen.

The entire system needed an overhaul, and in 1979, the government formed an advisor group, the National Senior Committee, to improve the country's overall approach to senior issues. They succeeded in raising awareness about senior issues. To counter the view that seniors are merely old, frail people who are mostly a burden to the state, this group advocated that seniors are productive, valuable members of society and helped imagine and devise ways to keep them productive and connected.

Senior Councils sprang up spontaneously in some cities, and they advised local officials about senior matters. The groundswell soon became policy, and in 1997, the national government mandated such

Glacier Circle, Davis, California.

councils. Additionally, a private national organization with similar objectives, called DaneAge (similar to the American Association of Retired People, AARP), was founded and became a popular force.

The Cohousing Model

In 1982, two Danish women, Tove Duvå and Lissy Lund Hansen, started to campaign for independence-oriented housing for seniors. They touted a successful model that was already in place: cohousing. But they ran into many roadblocks. A critical issue was whether the government would sponsor nonprofit cohousing. Potential residents wanted it because nonprofit status would offer apartments for rent at reasonable prices. Politicians, of course, were wary: How difficult would it be to rent these apartments to newcomers who might — or might not — be interested in a cooperative community?

State-Supported Care, Danish Style

In Denmark, there is government support for individuals to stay in their private house as they age. The government delivers medicine (but doesn't pay for it all anymore) and some food, and it provides personal care and basic housecleaning services. So when people move into a senior cohousing community they are in effect complementing their government services with those that will be provided by their neighbors.

These Danes know that government officials and workers won't sit and play cards with them, or share a pot of tea and chat. And these official caregivers certainly won't pull the weeds from their garden, come by for a birthday surprise, or invite them over for a snack and a movie. The Danish healthcare system, as good as it is, doesn't provide emotional support, and, obviously, can't do everything. This is why, even in Denmark, people are choosing to live in senior cohousing versus staying in their single-family houses. In-house care is on the wane in Denmark, yet another reason why senior cohousing is becoming more and more popular there.

Finally, the women succeeded in finding a developer, Lejerbo, a non-profit housing developer, who was willing to attempt the project; and in 1987 the first Danish senior cohousing complex, Midgården, came to be. The public response to this new development was overwhelmingly positive. Hundreds attended forums sponsored by the nonprofit Quality of Living in Focus (closed in 2001). Now private for-profit consultants (similar to the Cohousing Company in the US) have taken over this job to help seniors realize their projects.

Henry Nielsen's Model

In 1995, another significant event in the history of senior cohousing occurred. Henry Nielsen, working with Quality of Living in Focus, developed a comprehensive model for the creation of senior cohousing communities that recognized the specific needs of seniors. It was a break-through. At last, here was a model — a blueprint, if you will — to help these groups successfully navigate through an otherwise uncertain process.

Nielsen's model is based on the participatory process, and it neatly incorporates issues of co-care, design considerations, community size, and the group formation processes, among many other things. Once Danes began to use Nielsen's method, the quantity and quality of senior cohousing communities increased significantly.

Wolf Creek Lodge group meeting, Grass Valley, California.

Realities of Government-Provided Co-Care

Some people think that since the Danes have lots of government care they don't need as much co-care as we here in the US do. In fact, the illusion of government care slowed the Danes down because they thought, "Why bother finding alternatives, since the government will come to my house with food, medicine, and even take my blood pressure?" But then people found the type of care provided to be at the whim of government funding and lacking in social regards with its changing personnel (some of whom couldn't speak Danish). Also, since 1991, the Danish government has been backing out of care for elders and everyone else. In 2001, the three Danish right-wing parties came into power and their platform advocated senior cohousing as a cost-effective method of housing the elderly. However, once in power they completely withdrew government funding for senior cohousing (many other nonprofit programs were also dismantled). Today, implementation of senior cohousing in Denmark is completely privatized but still going strong.

The vision of Denmark being the welfare utopia is quite dated. Since most Americans have never had such illusions, in some ways, it's easier for us to see the need for creating our own solutions.

The Tale of Two Communities

For a variety of reasons Midgården was built in two segments. The first segment was built by, and for, a committed cohousing group. These people had bonded into a group as they struggled together through the various phases of planning, design, and construction. It remains a vibrant success story.

The second segment, by contrast, was offered to people through official announcements and newspaper ads — not unlike any other contractor-initiated condominium project. The individuals who answered these ads were less ready for the cooperative aspects of cohousing, and, having had no common bonding experience, found it more difficult to make the community work as envisioned. (Even today, this second segment has far fewer social activities than the first group.)

These side-by-side examples illustrate that resident participation in the planning and development process is essential to the success of a senior cohousing community.

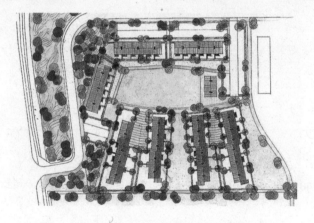

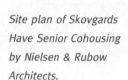

Site plan of Skovgards Have Senior Cohousing by Nielsen & Rubow Architects.

Henry Nielsen recognized that groups wishing to create a senior cohousing community needed a comprehensive model for realizing their goals. Nielsen's aim was ambitious and multi-faceted. He sought a model that would:

+ Make senior cohousing an option for everybody (not only the strong-willed).

+ Identify and solve key problems that all seniors encounter during the process.
+ Enhance the social aspects of the process, which, in turn, foster strong and durable communities.
+ Make it easier and more satisfactory for developers and municipalities to start or support new senior cohousing projects.
+ Guide the process from start to finish — and beyond.

The Nielsen model has several critical elements, each of which will be discussed in more detail later in this and subsequent chapters:

+ **A qualified advisor.**
+ **Feasibility and Informational phases.**
+ **A first study group (Study Group I): Consciousness raising.**

Resident Turnover

Do not be alarmed if (or more accurately, *when*, you face turnover. It is simply an inescapable part of the participatory process. Some families are pressured to find other housing before the project is completed; people may move for job opportunities; and others, for whatever reason, decide they are not ready for cohousing. In one project with a long planning period, turnover left only four households that had participated from start to completion. However, the number of residents who participate in the entire process is not critical to the success of a project once it is completed. The backbone of the project is a combination of the success of the process and the subculture of the people who intend to live there. When members leave, they pass the baton on to the new organizer/resident. In general, we find that it is best to start the design process with a minimum of six households and to avoid dipping below six if possible.

- ◆ A second study group (Study Group II): Participatory design.
- ◆ A third study group (Study Group III): Policy.

Nielsen's model can work just as well in the US as in Denmark.

Nielsen and the Participatory Process

Though Nielsen's model introduces a level of certainty to an uncertain process, it is not meant to be an absolute procedural doctrine. The participatory development process, by its very nature, requires flexibility and compromise. As such, every situation presents issues differently, determined by the participants, the development strategy, attitudes of local officials, and many other factors.

While Nielsen's model outlines timelines for each phase and the timing of key decisions, it is important early in the planning process for each group to set its own realistic timelines. The group should make every effort to adhere to their timelines, even though it is difficult, if not impossible, to control outside influences. If the decisions required of residents are made as scheduled, the process will keep moving forward, and there will be less resident turnover during the development process.

Bellingham Cohousing, Bellingham, Washington.

Musical activities in the common house.

Dinner in the common house at Nevada City Cohousing.

The cohousing development process can be trying at times, requiring residents and consultants alike to take on unaccustomed roles. Residents must assume greater responsibility (and risk) than they might expect. Consultants need non-traditional skills, such as the ability to facilitate decisions, to communicate development concepts to laypersons, and to foresee the consequences of different choices. Participation is what makes senior cohousing work, but it is Nielsen's model that provides a senior-specific and efficient structure for creating it.

Who is Involved: Roles and Responsibilities

The Nielsen model identifies the different groups, or parties, that are involved in creating a senior cohousing community and describes the roles that each should play. Before discussing each of the phases in detail, let's look at the roles and responsibilities of each participating group.

The Senior Residents. The most important task of the senior group is to create their community. Regardless of how much support they get from outside the group, it is the residents themselves who decide what sort of community they want and how to go about making it happen. Creating a vibrant community requires that individuals work to find the highest common denominator.

The Advisor and Project Manager. Many distinct groups of people are involved in creating each and every senior cohousing community: residents, government officials, contractors, neighbors, and others. Therefore, to best facilitate the different groups, Nielsen recommends a highly qualified third-party advisor, a champion who works as a counselor and a coordinator among all the actors, who will follow the project all the way from the initial idea to a well-functioning senior cohousing community. In reality, this role may be one or two people. The advisor helps organize the group; a project manager may come in later to move the project forward with the bureaucrats; and sometimes it's the same person.

During the initial discovery meetings, the advisor functions as an educator and facilitator for the residents and prepares them for the process, and, to some extent, their future life in the cohousing community. In the planning and construction phase the advisor helps the seniors solve questions ranging from budget concerns to how to best organize meetings. In addition, the advisor must ensure that the residents participate fully at appropriate points in the process.

When it's the appropriate time to bring the local municipality into the process, the advisor will inform and educate the local politicians and officials about the special issues and advantages connected with cohousing.

Pleasant Hill Cohousing, Pleasant Hill, California.

The Project Manager

A couple of years ago I did an all-day seminar in Washington, DC with 150 Native Americans representing 88 tribes from states ranging from Alaska to Florida. The topic was getting new housing and schools built on reservation land. Unfortunately the government's default design at the time was tract-like single-family houses on one-acre sites spread equidistant across the landscape. Everyone complained that this land-use approach was compromising important relationships (such as between grandmothers and granddaughters who used to be able to walk to each other's house when they lived in a trailer court), but the spokespersons for each tribe had not been successful in realizing anything better than the government solution. Isn't it ironic that a California architect was reintroducing village life to the Native Americans via the concept of cohousing? But apparently this new level of participation is what is needed to keep these reservations from simply mimicking American suburbs. At the end of the day, I asked the participants, "What do you think prevented you from making your project happen?" The majority answered that it was the lack of somebody who only had one thought when they woke up in the morning: "What do I do to move this project forward?" These were folks who had the land and the money. But they didn't have a good project manager.

Hanging out between the houses at Doyle Street Cohousing, Emeryville, California.

Common house at FrogSong, Cohousing.

The advisor can also educate the municipality on how it can help find new residents for the cohousing project, should the municipality wish to be involved in that way.

Since the advisor has to balance the wishes of the different actors, he or she sometimes will have to defend the wishes of the seniors, sometimes the local officials' side of things. All the while, the advisor's goal is the same as that of the senior group — to see a strong and vibrant senior cohousing community emerge.

Bottom line: Until the project is well off the ground (under construction), the advisor or project manager is the person who needs to wake up in the morning and ask, "What do I have to do today to move this project forward?" If the project manager is not successful in constantly moving the project forward, the resident group needs to replace him or her. A lot of people think that they can do this job, but most cannot.

The Municipality. Be it within a city's limits or in unincorporated land, once a senior cohousing group identifies a potential site for their community, it's time to get local officials involved. The local municipality plays an important role early on in the process in terms of accommodating for zoning regulations, public service availability, cost feasibility considerations, and more. Misconceptions about cohousing persist; people often think that "cohousing" is another name for "hippie commune," straight out of the 1970s. It is important that the municipality gets a realistic picture of what senior cohousing actually is. If you can get a slate of key local officials "sold" on the idea of the project early on, both already committed and potential residents will feel more secure going forward. It is a comfort to know that local officials won't hold up, pick apart, drive the costs up, or block a project before it really even starts.

While it is extremely useful to have all the bureaucrats on board, it is not absolutely essential. Too often they are the last people to "get" it. Luckily, in our private enterprise system, one can propose anything, and — with enough tenacity and public support — champion it through. It's not unusual to be voted down 2-3 at the first hearing or two, only to win 5-0 by the third hearing. It has happened many times that dissenting bureaucrats have come up to me *after* a cohousing project is built to say, "I can't believe I didn't support this wonderful neighborhood from the very beginning." In any case, after the project is officially approved and supported, the municipality's role diminishes. But sometimes a small group of officials will follow the project or even assist in the group's quest for potential residents.

The Senior Associations. Every town has associations of one kind or another dedicated to the enhancement of quality of life for seniors. Most towns have many such resources: legal councils, medical support organizations, discussion groups, lobbyists, educators, etc. Once they see that you are improving the quality of life for many seniors, that the community is about more than rhetoric, and that you will be a great asset to seniors citywide, they can become key allies in your venture.

The resident group doesn't have to shoulder the full burden of educating and advocating senior cohousing

FrogSong Cohousing.

to the municipality and the local community at large. They can enlist various associations to recommend the cohousing project to the municipality or help plan and host the initial public meetings and seminars, among

Pleasant Hill Cohousing common house, Pleasant Hill, California.

Design that Facilitates

When it comes to senior cohousing, a really good architect is a choreographer of activities and behavior. Not so much a creator, but an enabler. If the seniors wish for a quiet and harmonious lifestyle where both long conversations and vibrant activities are the norm, a good architect will design an interlocking set of common indoor and outdoor spaces to facilitate this way of life. A well-designed community encourages otherwise incidental and insignificant interactions to become meaningful events that foster deep, life-long relationships.

A simple porch creates a soft edge between the public and the private space.

Southside Cohousing, Sacramento, California.

other things. Although not all associations will be useful, the resident group should keep in contact with the helpful associations as the project progresses — their connections within the community can be invaluable.

The Architect. For a senior cohousing project, an architect does more than just deliver blueprints. Balancing both the technical needs of the developer and the inspiration of the senior group, he or she must have the willingness and ability to participate in the collective process where a large group of people has to work

together and create the new project. If this is a new way of working for the architect, he or she may be surprised at how different this kind of work is; it's a real challenge to ensure that everyone gets heard, dead-locked issues are overcome, and that the community design is both livable and on budget.

The architect's most important job, however, is to teach the senior group about the realities of planning. The seniors have to make very important design decisions — decisions that will directly affect how much they will spend, how long the project will take to build, and how they will live there once it's built.

The Developer. The developer's role is large and complex. In some cases, the developer is, in reality, co-developer with the group, and perhaps even co-developer with the project manager. In some cases these professionals may take on risk and not be paid until later in the project. The developer not only manages the development and finance process, but also works with the residents and architect, and often takes on the risk associated with the housing development itself.

Developers of speculative residential housing usually work on a risk-for-profit basis; generally, 10-25 percent of the total selling price is targeted for developer and investor profit. This profit is simply included in the price of a given property; the buyer really has no way of knowing what corners may have been cut in order to ensure the developer's profit.

In a cohousing development, by contrast, since the residents plan their own community they will have far greater access to, and control over, the financial details. The seniors will know what they are getting right from the start and will participate in making decisions.

In the case of nonprofit developers, the developer will be the actual owner of the completed project. However, most of the decisions about what to build, and where to build it, are made by the architect in cooperation with the seniors. The nonprofit developer is, however, always responsible for the project's construction and the financing; and as such, he or she has the right and the duty to intervene if he strongly disagrees with decisions made by the group.

After the seniors move in, the nonprofit developer role changes to that of a regular administrator. The maintenance work is ideally shared between the cohousing group and the nonprofit administration, where the nonprofit entity takes responsibility for bigger projects and the seniors are responsible for basic day-to-day maintenance. If the resident group is active in the maintenance, their sense

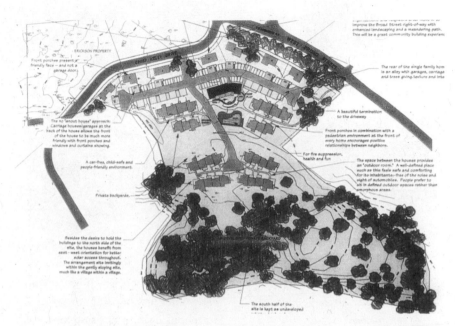

Nevada City Cohousing site plan.

Sketch of Hearthstone Cohousing Community, North Denver, Colorado.

Sketch of "elder rich" (mostly seniors) Fresno Cohousing which is currently under construction.

Clustering the homes creates a village environment and preserves open space. Nevada City Cohousing, Nevada City, California.

of ownership increases. The development is not just housing for seniors (warehousing) but housing for *people*.

Nielsen's Five Phases Explained

Each phase presents its own set of challenges and rewards. My explanations here are supported by more than twenty years of experience in creating successful cohousing communities, using Nielsen's model in the second decade. Each of these phases is explored in more detail in Part Three.

Feasibility Phase:
Do We Have a Project?

The Feasibility Phase is a critical phase — the point at which the viability of a project is carefully analyzed and the basic questions are asked: Is there interest in the community for a senior cohousing community? Is

there land close enough to local amenities (preferably within walking distance) and other support services for seniors? What sort of funding is available from potential residents, traditional banks, the government, or investors? What financial tools and safeguards are available to best utilize and protect the assets of the residents? Will the local government be willing to provide land subsidies?

Three main events occur during the Feasibility Phase:

+ A core group forms.
+ A site is identified.
+ Financing options are found.

At this stage, the group will have a general overview of the project in terms of:

+ Viability
+ Ownership
+ Site
+ Entitlements
+ Zoning
+ Funding
+ Budgets

The group will also be able to:

+ Assess the support of its allies.
+ Assess the support of the municipality.
+ Assess the support of other professionals.

Can one or two people do all of this? You bet. You don't have to be a Tove Duvå or a Lissy Lund Hansen to get a project up and running. You just have to believe that life will be easier, more fun, more interesting, more economical, and of better quality if you live in cooperation with your neighbors; and then decide to make it happen. And, unlike Duvå and Hansen, you also don't have to trial-and-error your way through — Nielsen's method and a seasoned advisor can really help here.

Information Phase: *Spreading the Word; Development Strategies*

Once the various aspects of the Feasibility Phase are met, it's time to broaden the scope and bring other interested seniors into the picture. This phase begins with a well-publicized, one-day public meeting where local seniors get an overview of all aspects of senior cohousing. Not only do they learn about cohousing as a concept, but also the dynamics of the specific project at hand.

Interested seniors begin to learn the process required to move from envisioning a new community to getting a community built. In addition to community-building in the social sense, which enables the group to work well together, they will need to gain an understanding of the design and development process in order to participate fully in creating the built environment. This learning process includes considering development strategies, financing options, and legal agreements. Often groups will attend a Getting-It-Built weekend workshop (offered by experienced cohousing developers) that gives a full overview of the cohousing development process and will get their group up and running.

Study Group I: *Aging Successfully/Aging in Place* (3 months)

Study Group I is a workshop where participants explore the issues of aging in place, define what aging successfully means to them, and begin walking down a deliberate path toward their vision of success.

The purpose of this phase is to create a general knowledge about alternatives. Just as important, though less tangible, future residents clarify their hopes and dreams while learning how to work cooperatively with each other. Study Group I typically

Wolf Creek Commons group planning meeting.

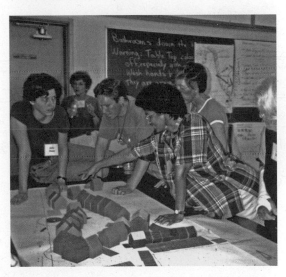

Cohousing is helping to plan your own neighborhood.

Having fun in the common house at Doyle Street Cohousing in Emeryville, California.

Hearthstone Cohousing, Denver, Colorado.

meets weekly for ten sessions, usually over three months. Often groups will have an outside facilitator conduct the sessions, using the Cohousing Group's Study Group Workbook to guide their sessions.

Some of the topics covered in the workshop include:

+ What is your aging scenario?
+ Aging in place pros and cons for various housing types.
+ Group process: Working together.
+ Co-care and outside care.
+ Co-healing: Staying healthy through community.
+ The economics of getting older.
+ Philosophy, spirituality and mortality.
+ Cohousing communities and various cohousing designs: How to build community and create ownership (usually includes a fieldtrip).

This is an important phase for anyone considering senior cohousing. This is also the phase in which long-lasting bonds are often made between future residents. Working through tough issues about aging, facing them together, and coming up with creative solutions is an important bonding experience.

Study Group II: *The Participatory Design and Development Process* (3-5 months)

This study group is meant for those who will actually move into the completed community of 15-25 units. In it, the senior cohousing group will realize its community. The seniors and their architect will design the cohousing community in a series of workshops. They will develop and finalize the architectural design criteria, design the site plan, common house and living units, and then secure the financing and hire a contractor.

Study Group III: *Policy*

In this phase, residents prepare for life in a senior cohousing community. They discuss and decide how to make agreements and establish policies regarding the details of issues such as common meals, pets, who takes care of whom, etc. Residents, the developer, and the project advisor decide on a process for taking in new residents in the future, and methods for turning over vacancies. They also identify ongoing maintenance needs.

Each of these phases will be explained in detail in Part Three, *Creating a Senior Cohousing Community.* But before that, let's take a look at how the process worked in a few actual communities in Denmark.

Part Two
Senior Cohousing in Denmark:
An Inside Look

We have had enough general discussions. Let's take a closer look at some real places and the people who live in them. The following case studies give a small sampling of the variety of senior cohousing applications. We begin with a close look at one community's planning process and how they were able to design a community with strong roots in fertile soil.

CHAPTER 4

Munksøgård:

Strong Roots in Fertile Soil

Munksøgård [munk-so-gore]
Roskilde, Denmark
20 Units
Architects: Mangor & Nagel
Programming, schematic design,
and design development: Nielsen &
Rubow
Completed: 2000

I t's early on the evening of the summer solstice. The weather is warm
and the sun won't go down. The air
smells of hay and flowers. In the
common garden, a lamb from the
community's own flock is being
roasted. Outside the common house,
a group of four is preparing a salad
for the evening's outdoor potluck
party. Some children are working on

the traditional witch-puppet, while
others are playing soccer on the adjacent field. Other people are setting
the tables in the garden.

The entrance to Munksøgård
Senior Cohousing.

51

The Munksøgård senior "village."

At 6 o'clock all of the residents from the five adjacent cohousing groups start pouring in and get seated. This yearly solstice party goes on all night. The bonfire is lit and people gather around it, singing traditional midsummer songs. Munksøgård's trailblazing seniors revel in this lifestyle, one they dreamed about when they joined the project a decade ago. Their separate cohousing community shares a site and some common facilities with four adjacent mixed-generation cohousing communities.

In July 1995, about a dozen young environmentalists from Copenhagen got together to create a new cohousing project with a senior component. They envisioned a community with significant diversity in the ages and backgrounds of the residents: older and younger, high and low-income, quiet and gregarious, and big families as well as singles. There would be a broad variety of common facilities and activities that would draw people together in their daily lives and establish the sense of community that characterizes a village. In short, it would become a modern version of the traditional village, one that pointed toward the future and could inspire others. Additionally, these people wanted to create a building project to sustain both environmental and social ecologies.

When the environmentalists arranged a public meeting in Copenhagen to present their ideas, 200-300 people showed up. Without a site, developer or architect, the project

The front of the common house is where people meet. In 1980, when I first lived in Denmark, I walked past single family homes, apartments, condiminiums, more single family houses and nothing special — not much life, and pretty much like the US. Then I walked by this one project, where people lived between the houses, not just in the houses. And you saw neighbors stop and chat, and commune like an old-fashioned village. That's cohousing.

still seemed very vague, and in the following months many people dropped out. The remaining group of about 100 people sat down and wrote a very idealistic proposal. The new project would consist of five different cohousing communities, each laid out as a courtyard complex: one community of 20 units for young first-time settlers under 31 years of age; a second community of 20 units for families and singles; a third community of 20 units for seniors over 50 years of age; a fourth community of 20 co-operative units; and a fifth community of 20 owner-occupied units. One main goal was to make the houses as ecologically sustainable as possible without sacrificing basic comfort. Grey water from the kitchens and bathrooms would be cleaned by a biological filter and then discharged into the small river that bounds the site. Composting toilets would be installed so that the project wouldn't have to be attached to the city sewer system. The goal was to achieve a 20 percent decrease in water consumption and to make the cohousing community essentially non-polluting.

Over a period of about a year, the project was discussed and revised at bi-weekly meetings. After the group had agreed on their program, they connected with Copenhagen architects Nielsen & Rubow, a firm well experienced with cohousing. The

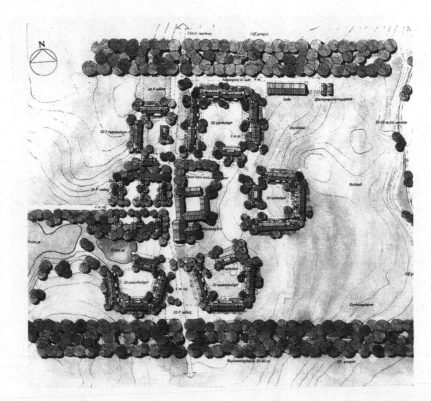

Munksøgård site plan with the five cohousing communities encircling the old farm.

group found a large rural site outside of the university town of Roskilde, near a station on the commuter train line to Copenhagen. Nielsen & Rubow developed an initial feasibility plan in which houses were laid out in a circle around an existing farm on the site with a central courtyard. The farm, Munksøgård (the monk's garden), was to serve as a common building for all the residents. A large part of the site was to remain undeveloped, partly as a recreational area and partly as a vegetable garden.

The group then found a nonprofit developer, the local Roskilde

Seniors prepare common dinners out in the sun where others can see them and stop by to say hello — and also chop some carrots. Food is one of the major reasons people give for choosing cohousing. Compare this food preparation with how it's done in typical assisted living facilities, where it is unlikely residents can or will get satisfactory meals. Equally important, residents miss out on planning and preparation — a good way to feel involvement and a sense of achievement.

"Cooking is a responsibility I embrace," said Ingrid, "partially because I only have to do it every five weeks and partially because my other neighbors have been doing it for me for the last five weeks. I owe them a good meal, don't you think?"

Cooperative Housing Society. The project was put out to private bid to five contractors. Throughout this process, some ecological features were compromised, either to save money or improve accessibility standards. Among other things, the composting toilets were replaced with low water use toilets with two separate flush choices.

The group agreed on the importance of quality and diversity in their common meals and confirmed that car parking would be relegated to the periphery. For economic reasons, the seniors built two-story houses. At the meeting where they came to decide who would get which apartment, 18 out of the 20 seniors got the apartment they wanted. The stairs were not considered a problem in Munksøgård. Although cost-cutting required that the originally planned internal staircases be replaced by external ones, the seniors felt that walking up and down the stairs daily help them to stay fit. The senior group also insisted on wheelchair access to the ground floor units, skid-free bathroom floors, and roll-in showers. The three residential buildings contain:

+ (8) 1-bedroom units
+ (8) 1-plus-bedroom units
+ (4) 2-bedroom units

The confidence that the nonprofit housing developer had in the senior group was so great that the elderly members weren't required to make a large down payment before they moved in. The down payment for others was $3,200 to $4,400/unit — equal to two percent of the purchase price. This is slightly more than the cost of regular housing; however, when access to a variety of common facilities and the shared lifestyle opportunities are factored in, this is not a particularly expensive proposition.

In 2000, after five years of planning and construction, the seniors moved in. As of this writing, none of them has yet moved out, and 80 people are on the waiting list to move in. Despite initial disagreements about sustainability issues, Munksøgård senior cohousing has become a great success.

Cars are not permitted beyond the parking lot, except at move-in and for extenuating circumstances, but there are plenty of wheelbarrows standing around for people to carry their groceries from their cars to their home.

In addition, the seniors enjoy a variety of common activities, such as playing bridge, singing in a choir, and picnicking. The most important activity they share is their common dinners in the common house, five nights a week. Cohousing groups often invent new common activities. The group at Munksøgård has a "let's see what happens" philosophy as they continue to explore different activities. In reality, people seem to most enjoy the many spontaneous activities that develop naturally.

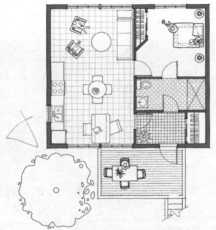

Munksøgård private house plan.

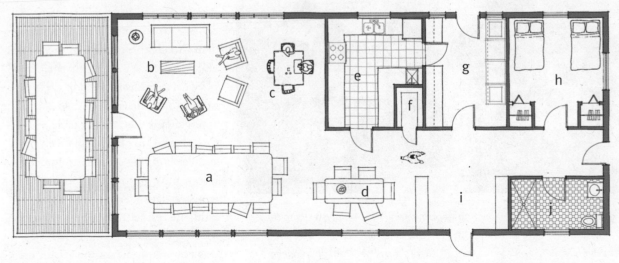

Munksøgård *common house plan: a. dining; b. sitting; c. cards; d. crafts; e. kitchen; f. storage ; g. laundry ; h. guest ; i. entry ; j. bathroom. The workshop, another reading room, barn, storage, and mechanical room are elsewhere.*

When the front of the common house is situated where most people can see it from their houses, then in classic cohousing fashion, activity attracts activity. People see a few people having tea, and before you know it, there's a tea party!

Common dinners open conversations and opportunities. "What are you doing this weekend?" "Maybe work in the garden. Why?" "Lars and I are going to take the motor boat out on the bay. Why don't you join us?" There's a real sense of spontaneity and enjoying sport events, going to movies and the theater are common activities cohousers like to share.

The Munksøgård senior group wanted to live near a community with children, and the concept has worked. "Everything would be so tidy around here and life would be so boring," one resident said. The seniors still prefer to eat the common meals separate from the other groups; but parties for two or three — or even all five — of the communities are popular. Despite their proximity, the seniors are adequately self-contained and don't rely much on the neighboring communities. Senior cohousing has also had a profound influence on the personal interaction that

residents share. The senior residents' own children and grandchildren come visiting more often than before, and frequently stay a little longer. Some of their adult children complain that since their parents moved into Munksøgård, the seniors rarely phone them anymore.

Healthcare vs. Co-Care Agreement

A common concern for people moving into senior cohousing is what will happen to them when they get older and have problems taking care of themselves. This has caused experts and laypersons alike to argue for written agreements about the expectations of co-care and mutual favors within a given senior cohousing community. The Munksøgård seniors, by contrast, have chosen to have very few written co-care agreements; instead, the residents decide these limits for themselves along the way — currently three people with cars have agreed to drive others to the hospital in case of an emergency. Emergencies aside, though co-care often only involves simple shopping errands and minor favors, most of the residents don't like to be too dependent on their neighbors. Said one resident: "I came here for the social contacts. Helping each other was not an important motive for me — it was more knowing that you are there for each other, if needed."

Sweat Equity as Cost Savings

The Munksøgård residents made their own clothes-drying shed. In many ways this is a perfect post-move-in project. Put the sticks together, brace it up, and put some clear corrugated panels on top of that. Voilà! A practical (and ecologically sound) place for drying clothes when the weather is bad.

Projects completely independent of the regular construction are a great use of time, money, and effort.

Obviously, not every group will want a clothes-drying shed. But that's beside the point. What gets built after move-in has everything to do with the personalities involved. This group did quite a few projects like this because they had the inclination, skills, and building know-how. It was also less expensive for them to do the work themselves rather than hire outside contractors.

Another resident echoed this sentiment: "We're not going to become an assisted-living arrangement," said Olaf Dejgaard. He continued, "It's so easy to do someone's laundry, if needed. We do some shopping, lots of small errands. But all the intimate stuff — dressing, bathing — we leave to professionals. This means that what we will do can remain loosely defined."

In general, Munksøgård seniors rely on the Danish health care system for their healthcare and in-home help. Though the Danish healthcare system is free at point of delivery, in-home care doesn't provide someone to live and laugh with. Moreover, the Danish state-sponsored healthcare is on shaky ground politically and financially, meaning Danish seniors increasingly feel like they have to figure out how to best take care of themselves.

Concluded Dejgaard, "We look after each other. We eat together, talk together, and are interested in each other."

Hedda Lundh, another Munksøgård senior said: "You get hooked into having all these people living around you. If you're ill, they bring up food, and you're constantly asked if there's anything they can do for you." The last time Hedda came back from a vacation, someone had turned the heat on in her apartment just before she got home and put a basket of homemade rolls on her kitchen table.

Mutually Beneficial Partnerships

The common vegetable garden provides residents with organic

Residents implement lots of work projects like building a new greenhouse.

...but mostly it's an excuse to have a party and a beer.

"Chip in and do what you can," that's the prevailing attitude at Munksøgård. The seniors here did all the painting themselves. Those who could not paint made lunch or watched the grandchildren of those who were busy with ladders and paintbrushes.

produce, and the livestock from their fields even provides some organic meat. Jens Asger Hansen, who is a member of the farming and gardening group, said: "I'm happy to live here and I think it has all happened in a harmonious way. My wife and I are social people who like the fact that the people we most enjoy spending time with live next door. But there is a very precise and defined balance between open doors and private life here."

The average age of these seniors is now 67 years. Olaf feels that this is too

A Summer's Day at Munksøgård

One summer morning, a couple is leaving their flat at 6:30. They go for a walk every day at this time, come rain, shine, snow, or darkness, to "keep in shape" as they like to put it. When they get back they let the eight hens and the rooster out into the run that the seniors built recently. A little later, the man, whose turn it is to see to the hens, cleans out their coop and feeds them some corn, scrap vegetables, and water. Now more of the cohousers are up and about, and there is a constant flow of people to the mailboxes that hang at the gable end of the common house, picking up letters and the daily paper. Some of them enter the common house to see what the day's cook is serving for dinner that evening. There is a list hanging on the notice board where you can mark down whether you are coming to the 6 o'clock dinner. Depending on how many people are going to eat, one or two helpers join in with the kitchen tasks. One woman brings her washing to the laundry in the common house. The laundry is rotated on a first come, first serve basis. The machines are always running so we only need two for the 20 households. And we built a drying shed so we can have a chat while we hang up and take down the drying.

At 10 o'clock, one of the cohousers has made a pot of coffee and placed it on the table at the benches by the south wall of the common house. Others gather around, and the talk is lively. The day's plans are being discussed, amongst other things. Just now we're building a greenhouse so that we can grow our own healthy cucumbers and tomatoes. Each of the common activities has a "boss" in charge, and this job is rather complicated. Some of the residents who are involved are getting ready to start working on it. The kitchen garden is almost 13,000 square feet, and it needs a lot of work from the seniors who enjoy that responsibility. We have a four-way rotation of the crops, and in the spring and fall more helping hands are needed. The potatoes look good, and the beans are ☞

high, because there is a considerable amount of common work to be done. The Munksøgård group is now trying to attract more people in their 50s. The seniors do most of the work themselves without hiring outside help; this includes snow clearing, house maintenance, landscaping, tree planting, and work in the vegetable gardens. The senior group even painted the outsides of the houses themselves. While the younger seniors painted the houses (with considerable Tom Sawyer-like assistance from neighbors and their own children), the older residents cooked and made coffee for the group. Since moving in they have

For Munksøgård seniors, community living means turning a mundane domestic chore into something more — a social event.

ready to be harvested. Two of us decide to do it today and put them into the freezer. About half of our vegetables come from our own garden.

Nearly everyone has a bicycle. Two of the cohousers get their bikes out of the storage shed that we also built ourselves, and cycle about three miles to the nearest shops. We could use our own cars or take the bus, but most of us prefer to get some exercise and go by bicycle.

Other things to do include mowing the lawns, tending the flowerbeds, trimming the hedges or working in one of the five smaller gardens, but today it's hot, and everyone's too busy enjoying the sunshine. Five of the "girls" take advantage of living relatively close to the beach, and set off on their bikes to go for a swim.

Later in the afternoon, someone has made another pot of coffee and found some nice cookies, and some of the cohousers gather together under the sunshades to enjoy them.

Lovely smells waft out through the kitchen windows where dinner is being prepared. Our common dinners are made mostly with beef, lamb, eggs, and chicken from our smallholding, and vegetables from our garden. It's a lovely evening, so we decide to have dinner on the common house terrace, overlooking the pond. Everyone lends a hand setting up the chairs and tables, and putting up the sunshades.

After dinner, once the tables have been cleared away, we form two teams and play petanque for an hour or so. A couple of us are pretty good at it, and there's some gentle teasing going on.

As the day draws to a close, I go across to the hen house and close it up for the night. A few of the cohousers go into the common house to share a bottle of red wine; the others head back to their own flats to relax with the late news after a pleasant day. ▪

— Olaf Dejgaard, 2005,
a 72-yr-old resident at Munksøgård

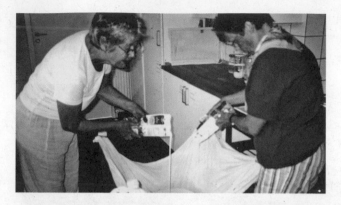

Making cheese. Traditional activities are life affirming and culture sustaining (no pun intended).

Gardens are usually a major design component in senior cohousing.

Senior cohousing creates a timeless sense of place with a cozy little village that invites involvement, cooperation, and friendship.

also built a workshop, a storage shed, a greenhouse, a clothes-drying shed, and a hen house.

The senior community garden is the best kept of the five gardens. There is a general agreement that the older seniors work less than the younger ones, or that they do less physically demanding work. These duties help keep people active and are of great importance to the social life in the community. It is interesting that the buildings in the senior cohousing area are in better condition than the buildings in the mixed-age cohousing. It turns out that five people who have time can do infinitely more than 50 who, with young families to raise and careers to pursue, have no time at all.

The Danes, like Americans, value the ideals of individualism and self-sufficiency. These notions are defining aspects of their society. In this regard, Munksøgård is profoundly Danish: the residents aren't so much living in a mutually dependent relationship as they are engaged in mutually beneficial partnerships. But it's more than that. These seniors have created a community where friendships run as deep as family. A world where each individual's social, physical, and emotional well-being is sustained one dinner, one project at a time, every day and in the company of others.

CHAPTER 5

Other Danish Senior Cohousing Communities
Otium, Gimle, Mariendalsvej, Korvetten

The organic. The hurried. The cautionary tale. The ideal. Four Danish senior cohousing communities. Four different processes for creating the communities. Four different outcomes. Since its inception in the mid-1980s, the senior cohousing movement has spread rapidly throughout Denmark and is showing no signs of slowing. Demand for this type of housing has been enormous from day one. It is evident that this is exactly the type of housing Danish seniors truly yearn for.

Remarkably, the senior cohousing movement was started by proactive, enterprising seniors themselves — not by the government, by investors, or by other professionals.

Today more than 200 Danish senior cohousing communities have been established in a country of five million people, and a series of new projects is on its way. Due to its self-grown

Else Skov in her kitchen in Otium Senior Cohousing.

character, the movement has given birth to a variety of types of senior cohousing communities — some more successful than others. The following four Danish examples show how different the conception, the planning process, and the result of a senior cohousing project can be. Valuable lessons can be learned from these hard-earned experiences of the Danes.

Else Skov after dinner in the Common House.

Otium: The Organic
Birkerød, Denmark
16 units
Architects: Tegnestuen 6B
Built: 1988
Tenure: Cooperative

Inventing the Wheel

In the fall of 1984, a group of middle-aged people in the town of Birkerød got together and started debating the need for better housing arrangements for seniors. Worried about the prospects of spending their retirement in institutional homes, they

Living in Otium

Else Skov moved into a large two-bedroom apartment in the Otium senior cohousing community when it was built. She lost her husband some years later. Else is in great shape for her 71 years. She and I walk over to the common house. Along the way she describes the community's layout and its social life: how the peripheral parking gets people out of their cars, and how the centrally located common house helps people to mix. Indeed, people run into each other and chat everywhere we go. Else stops and greets some seven people on the way — a smile, a hello, a plan for later that night, one for later that week.

When Else and her husband were in their mid-50s they started to reconsider their housing situation. At the time, they were living in a big house and wanted something smaller. They talked about the option of senior cohousing (then newly invented) but had their doubts. Wasn't it a bit early to consider senior housing at all, more than ten years before they planned to retire? Eventually, they decided to go for it and joined the local group that was designing Otium. Else had her doubts early on; however, she loved it once she moved in — and it was essential once her husband died. (Usually it's 🖙

were looking for alternatives. They wanted to grow older wisely.

After a while, they decided that they would like to build their own housing community, but they weren't sure about how to do it. Their vision was to create senior housing as a community with lots of common activities, but also with a great deal of respect for each other's privacy. Birkerød had several vibrant intergenerational cohousing communities to lend inspiration, but at the time no one had attempted cohousing solely for seniors. The group had its questions and doubts about whether it was possible. How would it work? Who would take care of them? Would they know how to deal with serious illness and death? And most important, did they have the energy

and resources to carry out such a big project?

Problems and worries aside, the group was very eager to make it happen. The approach they chose was to

Otium site plan.

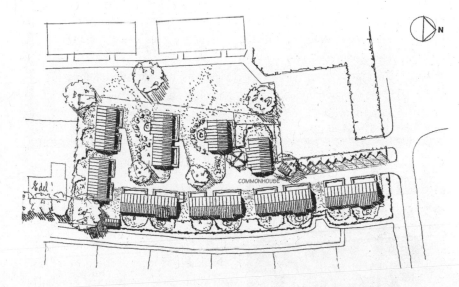

the other way around. The husband's not sure; then about three weeks after move-in, with his feet up on the coffee table, he brags about what a good idea he had.)

When Else's husband passed away, living in senior cohousing was a great relief for her. During that difficult time she received a lot of support from the other residents, and, because she was living in a tight-knit community, she didn't feel alone and abandoned, as she probably would have if she had been living on her own.

Afterward, she was happy that she had made the move from the large suburban house to the more moderate

unit in Otium before she became a widow. The fact that she had done it when she still had the energy gave her enormous freedom later. As Else said: "What do you need a big house for in your senior years? After all, you can't eat brick! Living here makes it possible for me to do everything I want. My living costs here are half of what they were when we had the house. Now I have more money to spend, and I can travel more easily. All I need is here. I get much more out of my money. It's such a pleasant way to live."

A Common Economy

The common economy at Otium is a straightforward affair.

1. A guest at Otium pays $6.75 per night to rent the common house bedroom.

2. Using the laundry machine costs $1.50, and each resident pays a laundry fee every third month. The money goes into a common maintenance account.

3. Community costs such as taxes, electricity, heating, and water are in the common budget that the community agrees on once a year. An attorney in Copenhagen administers the legalities.

Common dinner in Otium.

start an incredibly careful programming and design process. With great energy and lots of ideas and vision, they met once a month for the next three years to thoroughly debate all thinkable aspects of their future senior cohousing community. In reality (and without knowing it), they were using a very protracted version of Henry Nielsen's three study group senior cohousing design model — before it was even created. Had they had his model, their process of course would have gone much faster. Nonetheless, they did exactly the right thing by addressing all issues as early as possible, before they turned into conflicts. Luckily, the group had good leadership and great discipline. They could discuss all matters freely, and reach consensus on all major decisions. Everybody got what he or she wanted from the beginning — and in

the end, everyone was happy about the result. The many common experiences from the process made the group bond and create a strong community long before the project was actually built. They were able to purchase a site from the county and financed the design process themselves.

After three and a half years of programming, designing, and construction, the residents finally moved in to their new homes in the spring of 1988. They decided to name their community Otium, which is a romantic Danish term for retirement. Their patience was rewarded.

When I visited, Otium reminded me of living in campus dormitories at college. After dinner, people got up and went to pre-planned activities; others joined in, and still others dreamed up other activities and went off to do them. Some residents, having been out the night before, hung out at the common house, drinking coffee and chatting.

Community Design

In Otium, the private houses are laid out along a pedestrian street to give the project a village-like feel. (Advice from the local police confirmed the seniors' belief that the closer their houses were placed to each other, the less crime there would be.) There are three sizes of one-story private houses at Otium: 748 sq. ft., 840 sq.

The Guest Rooms

Guest rooms in senior common houses are usually larger than guest rooms in intergenerational cohousing. They are designed to allow for a family to have an extended stay, or even for caregivers to live in. They are more like suites, with their own bathroom and, with full use of the common kitchen, sitting room, laundry, and other amenities, they can feel like luxurious accommodations.

Sometimes common houses have several guest units, some for guests and others for caregivers. Caregivers might move in to assist a resident in a typical caregiver capacity (dressing, showers, etc.) for, say, ten hours per week at first. Meanwhile, they might have a full-time or part-time job elsewhere, or they might be a student who needs the part-time employment and inexpensive housing.

Sometimes the caregiver is a professional who works at a more typical assisted-care facility nearby. And later, when more folks need care in the community, the same caregiver might become full-time help there. The best part of this scenario is that caregivers grow to be much more than hired help; they become part of the community.

ft., and 1,078 sq. ft. The houses themselves have zones with varying degrees of privacy. The kitchens and front gardens face the common area, while the living rooms face private gardens in the back of the houses. The private houses are wheelchair accessible and easy to keep clean; simple, low-maintenance architecture was a programming priority. The size and facilities of the common house compensate for the moderate size of the private houses. The common house has a large living room, a kitchen, and a laundry room, and there is a guest room in a separate building.

This Is a Life . . .

A functional neighborhood, like a functional family, meets and discusses issues, comes to commonly agreeable solutions, works together, and plays together. Obviously the issues involved are different, but the sensibilities are the same. A dysfunctional neighborhood, like a dysfunctional family, is non-communicative and estranged.

In Otium it is clearly apparent that the residents work with and know each other very well. There is a familiarity, a laugh, a cajole, a whisper, an encouragement, that is quite unlike the perfunctory politeness and tense humor of a typical group of suburban neighbors at the yearly block party.

The residents of Otium are individuals who had real responsibilities before moving in. And once they became members of Otium, they in no way shied away from any responsibilities. However, once in Otium,

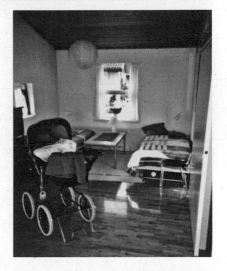

The guest room at Munksøgård.

surrounded by a group of their peers, they offset these responsibilities by having a good time. They spontaneously jumped in the car and drove to the beach, went bird watching, took off to the movies, the theater, and much more. For them, Otium is more than a community, it is an exit strategy where they plan for and get the most out of their remaining 20-25 years — without being a burden on their children, without having to completely rely on "assistance," without compromising their own potential for happiness and independence.

The residents of Otium planned their course of action as carefully and deliberately as most people plan their own financial security, except that they added a plan for their actual lives. By planning early on to be part of a vibrant community, they knew that they wouldn't have to plan for it later. Their happiness is not a function of week-by-week planned functions; instead, their happiness is a natural extension of their overall vision.

"This is a life," as the Danes would say, "with goods in it."

Gimle: The Hurried
Birkerød, Denmark
12 Units
Architects: Frederiksen & Knudsen
Completed: 1993
Tenure: Cooperative

In ancient Nordic mythology, Gimle was a house in heaven. Here warriors rested after their battles in the company of gods. In 1993, when this senior cohousing group settled on a name, they chose Gimle.

Gimle was initiated by the local branch of DaneAge (a senior advocacy group similar to AARP) in a Copenhagen suburb. In the early 1990s, a group in the county's chapter of DaneAge was debating senior housing issues; another group was looking for a site for a new senior housing project. The two groups eventually got together and decided to make a senior cohousing community.

Square Footage

Keep it warm, keep it elegant, keep it cozy, and keep it within budget. Smaller houses in senior cohousing optimize affordability in more than just the obvious way. Size also directly affects lifestyle, in that the smaller a house or a unit is, the easier it is to keep up. Moreover, smaller size usually means better materials can be used — and the better the materials, the more comfortable the house and the less to fix later on. Smaller personal units also mean more money for the common house, which enhances the private life.

Typically 600-1,000 sq. ft., these one-bedroom homes are quite livable, with the kitchen, dining, and living room all in one; the bedroom, bathroom and "plus room" (office or hobby room) is off to the side. The 3,000 sq. ft. common house supplements every house, so in a sense, every individual unit is a 3,600 to 4,000 sq. ft. house.

They quickly finished their version of Study Group I (see Chapter 7), and, with help from the municipality, they found a site and a developer and finished their feasibility work. A couple of state grants helped fund the project. And they were off to the planning and development phase (their version of Study Group II).

Getting It Off the Ground

In order to get its grants, the group had to work very quickly. The potential shortcoming of such a tight

---

Life in Otium

Interviewer: Charles Durrett

A number of Otium residents sat down and talked with me about their community. Included in the conversation were: Else, a 71-year-old retired secretary; Anders, a 75-year-old retired headmaster; Leif Behrend, a 69-year-old retired factory owner, and other cohousing residents who happened to pass by during the discussion.

Charles: In Denmark, you are able to retire at the age of 60, and that means that you probably have more than 20 years left of your life. You have to ask yourself the question: "Do you want your golden years to be on your own terms or in the terms of others?"

Anders: Well, you can't just sit and wait for the government to help you.

Else: One of my reasons for joining this new cohousing group about fifteen years ago was that I wanted to create a life in my old age that motivated and inspired me to be active. I wanted to make my own decisions and I wanted an easier life here than I had when I had to take care of a big house and garden and all of that. I didn't want to feel dependent on my children. It would give me peace to show them that I could take care of myself and it would release them from that burden.

Charles: A lot of people say: Why not just build the cohousing community, and then later, find people to live there?

Leif: Yes, they say that. I'm proud to tell you that we have been involved in the process from the beginning, and because we participated in the planning of our new home, the project became an exact answer to our needs — not another bureaucratic or businessman's estimation of our needs. The trick was to let the professionals do their jobs, but be clear about what we wanted.

Anders: From September '84 to spring '88 we met once a month to discuss the ideas that we had about living together in a community. Most of us knew each other from the beginning, because we came from the same town in Denmark, but during the meetings, we got to know each other better and better. One could say that we actually built the social community even before moving in.

Leif: Those who simply wanted separate houses left, and those who wanted to live in a shared house left too. But those of us who decided to go on with the process came to the conclusion that community was what was important to us. We wished to live in a ☞

friendly connection with others, but we all had a healthy respect for each other's privacy.

Charles: You could say this is in the middle between a lot of support and no support in your life.

Else: Yes, each resident maintains her independence and chooses how much she wants to participate. You can see that the houses are situated like that on the site. We have a small garden on the other side of the house where you can choose to be by yourself and where the other residents visit only if they are invited. There are backyards I hardly have been in, in these 15 years in this cohousing community.

Charles: It's obvious that with senior cohousing in Denmark there are not as many cooperative activities as with mixed cohousing, such as in Trudeslund, where they have common dinners seven days a week.

Else: Our cohousing is only for retired people. Only seniors live here. In Trudeslund, most of the residents are young people with jobs and children to take care of. They need a lot of support and they have a lot of support. Their cooperation is used to make everyone's life easier. People there have young children and have careers where both parents work. Here we have the luxury of spending a couple of hours deciding if we'll have an additional dinner this week or not. In mixed cohousing, where people have jobs, kids, and belong to the PTA and 15 other organizations, they just want to figure it out once and not talk about it again for 20 years. In mixed cohousing, half of the common activities are planned. In senior cohousing, maybe only 20 percent are fixed. Most things that we do together we figure out day to day.

Charles: Many seniors feel that their lives are changing, and the surroundings don't fit their needs anymore. Was the idea of becoming really close neighbors with each other designed to address your real needs?

Another Otium resident: Yes, it's a good feeling to know that my neighbors in cohousing care about me. It's very important for us to feel safe in our homes and our surroundings.

Anders: And in the cohousing community, there's always someone nearby in the daytime and at night. I lived alone in a house before I moved to Otium. When the children were small, it was easy for me to get in touch with the neighbors, because we had the children in common. But in my older years I was all alone in the house, and all the other houses on the street, with all the young people and new families, were empty in the daytime. Here, there is great importance attached to social contact. The fact that people are always home makes us feel secure and (laugh) we simply can't help meeting each other when we step out of the front door.

Leif: We also feel safe taking a trip, because we know that there will always be someone to keep an eye on our house while we are gone. We haven't had any crime here at all in the 13 years I have lived here.

Charles: Does living in a cohousing community make it a more pleasant, less expensive, or easier way to live?

Anders: I pay 6000kr ($1000) in rent per month, which is a little higher than my rent before cohousing.

Else: Yes, but I think because of the shared facilities there is the feeling of getting more for your money. I spend half as much in costs, outside of rent, as I used to. But I think we all agree on the fact that it isn't ☞

because of any economic interest that we live at Otium. And although it's obvious that our costs are lower, we live here for dozens of other more important reasons, such as emotional support, rather than just to save money.

Anders: Frankly, we bring people together like this to live in a cooperative community where our emotional well-being is as important as our physical well-being and, most importantly, without treating each other in a self-conscious kind of way where people say: "Now, how are we today?"

Leif: Compared to the time when I lived in my own house, I now feel that my responsibilities are reduced. But, even though it is easier to cope with life at Otium, we still have the responsibility to make the community work. Once a month we meet and have a special dinner together, and then we have the opportunity to discuss problems and make democratic solutions and agreements.

Anders: In this way, problems don't get out of control. It's very important that some people take leadership roles in the group, because that ensures that everything is taken care of. Besides all the rules we have worked out together, we don't really have many committees here because we simply expect people to use their common sense.

Else: One could say we have unwritten rules about having the discipline and responsibility and the will and the strength to cooperate with other people in a community.

Charles: It is indeed life affirming to hear you talk because you sound so vigorous together. You want to take your future into your own hands and make your own decisions. You have dreams that you want to realize and

it really sounds as if you take life as a gift, not as a burden . . . Sometimes you get the impression that aged people practice the negative in the fact that they are getting old. They lose their strength, feel depressed and lonely, and then they become an economic and social burden to society.

Else: People get in-home nursing care from the government if they want it, but we don't need as much help from outside as we would if we lived alone. It comes naturally for us to take care of each other here. In some settings, taking care of each other is a burden. Here it becomes more of a privilege.

Anders: The town has an economic interest in supporting our cohousing community and has profited from the several senior cohousing communities being built here. It seems to help the economy of the town when elderly people move out of their big houses. Back in the 50s Birkerød was a village in the countryside and there was a farm here where the cohousing community is now situated. Then in the 50s and 60s Birkerød suddenly grew very fast, which meant the prices for houses were rising. The people who moved into the houses that we left are people with a good incomes and that has been great for the local economy.

Yet Another Otium Resident: That's what it all is about. The newcomers have double income — and are therefore double-good taxpayers (laugh).

Leif: We influence the culture in our society; we are the visitors who have the time. That's good for the town, too. ▪

Smaller houses in senior cohousing are designed to improve lifestyle. This sketch illustrates a small unit in Fresno Cohousing.

schedule was offset by using architects who were very well versed with senior cohousing and who had encountered similar criteria many times before. The architects designed Gimle with houses along a street, resembling a small village. The down payment per unit was about $33,000 (200,000Dkr), resulting in a monthly payment of $830 (5,000Dkr). At the time, these houses were relatively affordable. In 1993, the project was finished and the seniors moved in.

Despite having started out as a group, the new residents didn't really feel like they knew each other by move-in. There had been too few discussions about how the social life should be in Gimle. The residents eventually started common dinners, aerobics classes, bridge, and other activities in the common house, but they wished that they had taken Study Group III a lot more seriously. It would have saved considerable time and frustration.

Overall, Gimle is a fairly well functioning cohousing community. As a testament to its success, more than 40 people are on Gimle's waiting list. There is no doubt however, that the community would have been fundamentally different (and better) if the residents had been given a little more time to go through a thorough programming and design process.

More than most senior cohousing communities, this has become a community for individualists. Nothing seems to appeal to the entire community, but the diversity of the activities means that there is something for everybody; classical concerts, university lectures, trips to art exhibitions, sailing, long-distance bike trips, bowling, or just games of petanque on the community street. As Eigil Niclaysen, 72, put it: "You hear about what other people are doing and that often gives you the inspiration to try it too." Eigil does yoga and goes bowling with some of the other residents, and he is sure that if it had not been for them, he

Gloria at her home in Nevada City Cohousing.

Two Gimle Residents

In 1993, Rita Svendsen, 72, was among the first residents to move into Gimle. She used to run a shop selling homemade chocolates in Birkerød, but had retired ten years previously. After her husband died she lived alone for some years, but she grew increasingly tired of taking care of a big house on her own. When she first heard of Gimle, she contacted DaneAge and got an apartment there. Rita is visually impaired, and after she was treated for a tumor on the pituitary gland she became very sensitive to fevers. If her temperature exceeds 101°F, she falls unconscious. The other residents at Gimle are very aware of her condition, and each morning they make sure that she is up and doing well. This gives her an enormous sense of security.

Dan Nielsen, 69, is a retired engineer. He tells how his children visit more often since he moved into Gimle. "It's also a great relief for them to know that we're happy here; that we have someone to talk to." The grandchildren also come more often now. They think Gimle is a fun place.

probably never would have dared to do those things. The residents also arrange common trips to the supermarket, since only half of them have cars.

Time Banking

So many outside activities leave little time for residents to do their required community work — planting, repairs, and the like. Getting all this community work done can, at times, be a problem. To ensure that the maintenance work actually gets done, the residents of Gimle have developed a system of "time banking" (it was developed after they moved in). All residents have to participate in common work tasks for a certain number of hours each year. Residents who work more than they are supposed to, get their extra hours saved in the time bank. For those who work less, they accumulate a deficit. The hours can then be bought or residents can pay them back by working more hours the next year. This system allows people to save up hours for their senior years while they still have the reserves of energy. Or it can simply allow people to pay the community for their absence when they don't have the time to participate in the common work.

Time for a chat in one of Otium's small units.

Two happy Otium residents on their way to a common potluck dinner.

Overall, the system of time banking has been successful, so much so that other senior cohousing groups have created interesting variations on it that are wholly germane to the sensibilities of their own community. For example, in another senior cohousing community, residents start out with a requirement to perform 20 hours per month of common work (including common dinners). This amount then decreases to zero hours per month after 20 years of residency. In yet another senior cohousing community, if you perform charity work out in the community-at-large, those hours are counted, or partially counted, toward your cohousing community work responsibility.

These Danish senior cohousing time-banking systems work because residents who move in, stay (there is a considerable wait-list to get into each community). Moreover, like any other small village, older seniors are expected to do less; they did their share, and younger residents respect that. New residents therefore come in with the expectation of doing a little more than the older, more tenured residents.

In truth, however, most residents work more community hours than required for as long as they can. They

Residents of Gimle Senior Cohousing.

The semi-private area in front of the house creates a soft edge between the private and the public space. Perfect for sitting, seeing neighbors, and storing your later-in-life crisis toys.

simply enjoy contributing to their community in a meaningful way.

Mariendalsvej: A Cautionary Tale

Copenhagen, Denmark
22 Units
Architect: Box 25 Arkitekter
Completed: 1992
Tenure: Rental
Common House: 4,735 sq. ft. (440 m²)

It rarely happens that a cohousing community misfires. Usually disputes within a cohousing community are minor and can be solved without jeopardizing the community itself. It is very rare that a cohousing community fails. Nonetheless, this is what happened in Mariendalsvej.

Inspired by the success at Midgården, the first Danish senior cohousing community, the Danish nonprofit organization Lawyers' and Economists' Pension Fund initiated the Mariendalsvej cohousing project. Their vision was to enhance the life of seniors by creating a rich community life. They would achieve this by creating a housing development that featured individual apartments and various daily functions and activities that would make the lives of the residents easier, more fun, and more engaged — the very qualities that distinguish senior cohousing from typical institutional senior housing. A

rich community life would therefore emerge, and the institutional character of too many senior facilities would be avoided. A noble plan, to be sure.

Best Intentions

A group of consultants and architects were commissioned to develop the project and its 22 units. The architecture was meant to combine three elements: urban life, community, and sustainability. A small senior group was actively involved in the design development process — monthly meetings, field trips, and the construction of multiple models (even 1:1 mockups of parts of the interiors). The

A private balcony in Gimle.

Visionary design doesn't do it alone. Mariendalsvej Senior Cohousing was meant to be the ideal new type of senior housing but it did not live up to its expectations.

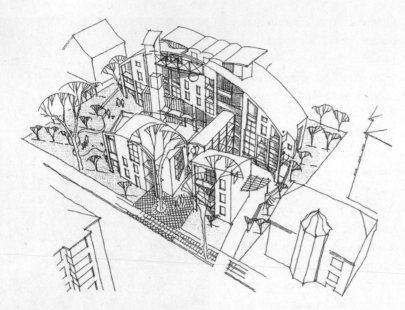

Perspective sketch of Mariendalsvej Senior Cohousing.

Ole, the last resident from the original Mariendalsvej cohousing group.

would include a large common room with an open fireplace, an indoor swimming pool, a large room on the top floor, guest rooms, and a garden. This design was approved and construction began.

From the beginning, the bold appearance of the new building in its late 19th-century surroundings drew a lot of attention to the project. Significant media attention prompted paradigm-changing speculation. Was this the new way of housing seniors; was this an all-new way of looking at seniors and their needs? But despite all of the support and the best intentions of the participants, one crucial factor was overlooked: the Fund hadn't signed up and involved enough tenants to fill all of the available units. This resident shortcoming was partially because the Fund let the project get too expensive, and partially because they tried to limit purchase to members of the Pension Fund itself.

The Fateful Sellout

Despite the massive public interest in the project, it proved difficult for the Fund to find tenants within its own membership rolls. Within the Fund itself, general interest among high-income prospects was low — these individuals had very particular demands and expectations and found the apartments to be too small.

Lawyers' and Economists' Pension Fund supported them financially, in conjunction with the Danish Ministry of Social Affairs and Energy Authority (a department of the Ministry of Economic Affairs). The resident group found a site in the Copenhagen district of Frederiksberg and the Fund then financed both the purchase of the site and the construction of the project.

At Box 25 Architects, the two architects commissioned to do the design came up with a rather non-traditional scheme — a four-story brick-clad building with a gigantic curved roof. The building would contain 14 one-bedroom apartments (840-960 sq. ft.) and eight two-bedroom apartments (1,020-1,100 sq. ft.). The extensive common facilities

Moreover, the Fund found it difficult to convince them about the advantages of cohousing. Despite protests from the existing core group, the Fund, running out of options, decided to sell the remaining 16 of the 22 apartments to anyone interested — not just those interested in senior cohousing. The Fund vigorously marketed to people who first and foremost wanted to buy a house in the area, arguing that the "community" could be built with the new residents, after move in. For these open-market sales, the concept of cohousing was tacked on as an afterthought. This was a devastating turn of events for the future of the cohousing community.

When Cohousing Isn't Cohousing

The new buyers liked the location and could afford the increased prices. However, none of the new buyers bought into the cohousing concept. Once the project was sold out and completed, the six original households tried their very best to generate interest among the new households in cohousing-style living, starting with common dinners (they'd built state-of-the-art common facilities after all). However, they found that no one was interested in the basic cohousing principles of common decision-making, cooperation, compromise, and consensus. Some residents even openly obstructed it. They refused to see the

virtues of living as a member of a diverse community, or the benefit of cooperating with their neighbors on anything. This doomed the cohousing effort. In effect, even before the community had been created it ceased to exist.

The original resident group (six households) was passionate in their wish to create a community together. But as the members of this group grew more and more disillusioned with the direction of their failing community, they moved out until, as of this writing, one last originating household remains. They don't try to organize anything any longer. They also are considering moving out.

Mariendalsvej Today

Today, Mariendalsvej functions like a better-than-average condominium project — they do indeed have nice common facilities — and residents gather together as a group usually once a year for a holiday party. But the residents otherwise have little or no social interaction with each other. The common rooms are rarely used. This particular project, that seemed so promising a decade ago, has become noteworthy for what it failed to become.

Lessons Learned

The reasons for this particular group's failure to create a viable cohousing

Mariendalsvej has state of the art common facilities but they are rarely used.

Private balcony at Mariendalsvej.

community are obvious in hindsight, and this example offers some lessons that all prospective cohousing groups need to consider.

Perhaps the most important lessons learned from Mariendalsvej are those having to do with a resident group's formation processes and its leadership roles. Involved professionals likewise must understand the cohousing concept well. Problems in the partnership between the resident group and the professionals become manifest in many interlocking ways:

1. Costs go out of control.
    Without a strong core resident group to hold the line in terms of budget, there is real danger that costs will creep up beyond the reach of potential residents who are interested in the cohousing concept (already a limited pool of potential buyers). For a developer, increased building costs simply mean the final selling price will be proportionally higher, usually not a problem when a property is sold on the open market (with a bigger pool of potential buyers). As for Mariendalsvej, the costs problems were made worse because the architect (the lowest bidder) had no cohousing experience and no sense of cost control. Costs didn't creep up, they escalated. This priced potential cohousing buyers out of the market, which increased the developer's risk beyond what it thought reasonable. In a panic, the developer put the remaining unsold units on the open market, thus dooming the cohousing community.

2. Original intent is lost.
    Without the leadership of a strong resident group, the developer may not fully support, or perhaps even understand, the cohousing concept enough to see the project through with its original intent intact — that of creating a *community*. In Mariendalsvej, as costs escalated, the Fund (the developer) lost track of the project's mission and sold out the cohousing concept in favor of selling units. Instead, the developers should have asked themselves: "How do we serve these future residents who went out and secured the funding grants, who helped get the project approved? How do we fulfill this model of housing that we set out to create?"

3. Feasibility Phase is skipped.
    Without a strong group process in which a group of people embark on the common task of developing the project, committing themselves, and taking responsibility, the opportunity for group formation

and bonding is utterly lost, and the community itself might fail. In the case of Mariendalsvej, the group (through lack of cohesiveness and will) allowed a developer to start the project too quickly; that is, before they knew that they had enough people. And the developer, failing to appreciate or understand the cohousing concept, failed to perform basic cohousing feasibility studies and market research. Because the developer failed to match 22 households with the project's 22 units prior to construction, it was impossible for them to determine if their market had 22 households that could both afford the units and would buy into the cohousing concept. A strong resident group would naturally address questions like: What should the unit prices be for cohousing in our market? What can each household in the resident group afford? A developer might not address these basic questions. A "you can add the community after move-in" philosophy simply does not create cohousing. Prospective buyers cannot be forced to buy into the cohousing concept itself. An individual or family is either predisposed to cooperating with neighbors or is not — no one is going to be "talked into it."

4. Recruitment and marketing are ineffective.

In an ideal world, the number of potential residents matches the number of units from inception to move-in. However, in the real world, potential residents enter and leave the group at different times for any number of reasons. That's life. But when households leave the group, the group itself is not in peril. A committed core group can (and does) fill vacancies through recruiting and marketing efforts, typically done at key times during the development process. However, if basic feasibility work hasn't been done appropriately, the task of filling the community will be all but

A successful senior cohousing community is primarily a function of individuals who come to the table planning to give cooperation the benefit of the doubt.

impossible, as the experience in Mariendalsvej testifies. A cluster of condos is not cohousing. All the window dressing in the world will not make up for a weak foundation.

Otium, Gimle, and Mariendalsvej are three organic models from the infancy of Danish senior cohousing. These faltering attempts made it clear that the random method of making senior cohousing wasn't good enough. Obviously, there was a need for a less organic, highly deliberate method. In 1995, Henry Nielsen, an employee of the non-profit group Quality of Living in Focus, gathered the experiences of ten years of senior cohousing projects in Denmark and created his five-phase model of how to make successful senior cohousing. The model has made the process easier and more satisfactory for everybody involved: seniors, officials, developers, and architects. Before, potential residents might have had good reason to be reluctant to embark on the process, but they could do it with confidence using Nielsen's model. Behold Korvetten.

Korvetten: The Ideal
Munkebo, Denmark
16 units
Architects: Clausen & Weber
Tenure: Rental
Completed: 1988

Since 1995, many senior cohousing communities have been built using Nielsen's method and its five phases: Feasibility Phase, Information Phase, Study Group I, Study Group II, and Study Group III. Because it is a process that delivers results, it should come as little surprise that 20 of the last 25 cohousing projects built in Denmark have been senior cohousing. While there is not significantly more demand for senior cohousing than for regular cohousing (there are plenty of young families), the senior groups are more organized. To see the result of the five-phase study group method you have to study the Danish senior cohousing projects built after 1995, and look at the method itself.

Korvetten senior cohousing was initiated in 1996 by the municipality of the city of Munkebo (population, 5,740). In the 1960s, steel workers from all over Denmark moved to the town to work at the expanding local shipyard. This generation bulge was reaching retirement age, and the need for more adequate senior housing was imminent. The municipality contacted Quality of Living in Focus, and together with Henry Nielsen, they arranged a public information meeting to find out if there was any interest in creating senior cohousing in Munkebo. Sixty people showed up, a number that exceeded the expectations of the facilitators. Forty-seven

Hanging out in the common yard.

seniors then attended two seminars following the meeting, and eventually 42 decided to start a Study Group I facilitated by Henry Nielsen. This was considered to be too many individuals for one cohousing community, so the group was divided in two, with the aim of creating two senior cohousing communities.

The city council found two sites and voted unanimously to support the projects. The advantages for the municipality were obvious. The seniors would get great housing, existing rental housing would be made available for others, and most likely the seniors would have a better quality of life and need less home care.

The first resident group had 22 members between the ages of 52 and 78. Their Study Group I turned out unexpectedly successful. Somehow the group members built up such a great confidence in each other that they could discuss almost everything — even private matters that they wouldn't usually have shared with strangers. Maybe it was the many common experiences from the shipyard (where a lot of the residents had worked) that made them bond so strongly at an early stage in the process. They soon started getting together outside the Study Group program for parties, trips, and folk high school stays. They also started having an annual summer solstice

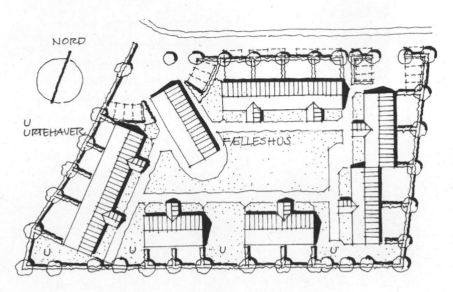

Site plan of Korvetten.

party — long before move-in. Some of the shyer residents even felt that their experience with the group changed their personality in a positive way. It made them more self-confident and extroverted, and it significantly enhanced their general social life.

Encouraged by the initial success, the city let the group choose the architect and developer themselves, and together they made the mandatory local area development plan for the site — a highly unusual procedure. Three city officials were appointed to help the group and to smooth out the planning submittal process. The developer, without much interference, then let the group make design decisions with the architect and the project advisor. Their building site was beautifully situated on the Kertinge Bay, and it was even close to a supermarket, a doctor's office, and public transportation.

The seniors and the architect designed the project as five one-story buildings, with private houses and a common house surrounding a large common yard. The residents envisioned that the yard would be used for a variety of common activities: barbeques, parties, games, or just hanging out together on a bench in the shade.

The twelve private houses were designed in three sizes: 625 sq. ft., 825 sq. ft., and 900 sq. ft., all with a full or partial view of the bay. All front doors face the central yard and, from the large bay windows in the private kitchens, residents can follow what is happening outside. The common house was designed with a kitchen, a large dining/living room, a laundry room, a guest room, and a storage space. Moreover, the common house was placed near the parking lot to serve as an entrance to the community. Unfortunately, the first proposal went 30 percent over the budget, but the developer made a list of potential cost-cuts, and then let the residents decide which of them they wanted. In June 1998 the seniors moved in with an air of optimism. The residents named their new senior cohousing community Korvetten after an old type of sailing ship.

In general they were very satisfied with the community-creating process. All agreed that the study-group method was the key to their success. Their experienced project advisor was especially valuable because he already knew answers to many of the seniors' many questions.

Today Korvetten is a well functioning senior cohousing community. The fact that the resident group is so tight-knit, as the residents are wont to point out, is that they run the community with practically no interference from the developer or the city. Problems like neighbor complaints are solved within the group. The residents themselves also manage the waiting list of future residents.

All involved admit that Korvetten would not have been built, at least not so successfully, without the study-group method and the deliberate community-building processes it produces. One of the most encouraging aspects of the more deliberate process is that it worked well for blue collar folks who are not used to a lot of meetings and would have been averse to figuring out systems from scratch.

Part Three
Creating a Senior Cohousing Community

In the early days, a cohousing community could take as many as five to seven years to go from the first meetings to move-in. However, since cohousing is now better known and much more clearly defined, that full-cycle development process can now take as little as two to three years. Today, groups in the planning process of their community can visit existing cohousing developments. They can take for granted issues such as common dining, smaller individual residences, peripheral parking, community bylaws and covenants, not to mention the community-building process itself.

In the same way that the American experience in building mixed-generational cohousing closely corresponds to its Danish precursor, the Danish experiences for building senior cohousing are directly applicable to developing senior cohousing in the United States. Although some elements are regionally specific, such as site identification, methods for land acquisition, and financing options, most of what is involved is quite universal. When Kate and I worked with a new group in Auckland, New Zealand or Calgary, Alberta for example, the zoning issues were remarkably similar to what we face everyday in the United States. The politics also were identical. Everyone wanted to know: "How will it affect *my* neighborhood?"

Based on Nielsen's model (in this book, we slightly modify Nielsen's model in order to adapt it to the US) and the decades of Danish experience in creating senior cohousing, what follows is a system specifically designed to build a senior cohousing community from the ground up. Divided into five distinct but interlocking parts — Feasibility Phase, Information Phase, Study Group I (group formation), Study Group II (participatory design process), and Study Group III (policy) — this approach is a proven and practical process that builds not only the physical neighborhood, but weaves the social fabric of the community itself.

I grow very weary of Americans who say, "Oh yeah, the Danes can do that. It's a small country, with a homogeneous population." Baloney! Cohousing gets created in Denmark exactly like it does in the United States. A couple of people get off their butts and say, "Hey — let's do this," then they go out and find the people to help them do it, and often do large portions of the organization and recruitment themselves.

CHAPTER 6

Feasibility:

Do We Have a Project?

Getting Started:
The Core Group

In the US, as in Denmark, a cohousing community typically begins when a small group of people, a single family, a group of friends, or even an individual, decides that cohousing might just be for them. Maybe they know somebody who lives in a cohousing community. Maybe a friend waxed eloquently about it over dinner. Maybe they read a book like this one. Or, as is increasingly the case, experienced developers like Cohousing Partners and Wonderland Hill Development will initiate the process and provide the means for interested households to create a core group.

Feasibility Basics

In terms of senior cohousing, feasibility is simply taking the time up front to consider the big-picture items as well as the critical details. These details create a long list that requires close attention and a sharp pencil. But with the help of someone who knows what he or she is looking for (this is where the advisor is really helpful), it's not a daunting task, and finding the answers can sometimes be done quite quickly. As necessary as this Feasibility Phase is, it is too often under-considered.

A complete and exhaustive overview of a potential project in a given area is the first job. Some of the points to consider are:

+ If we build here, here, or here, what will be the development costs?

‐+ What is the town's experience with planned unit developments? Variances?

+ Where are the multi-family zoned sites?

+ What sites can be rezoned to multi-family? (Most of our sites are rezoned.)

+ What are the zoning limitations?

+ Where are the services, neighbor-hoods, and public transportation facilities that we want to be near?

+ If we build here, here, or here, what are the houses likely to cost?

+ How are comparably sized houses priced?

+ Who are the best land brokers in town?

+ How can we find sites not on the market; who do we have to contact?

+ If the realtor is not working fast enough, who else will we get to work for us?

+ Are toxins present on the site, and if so, what will it cost to remove them?

+ Who does the best soil evaluation in town?

+ What are the costs of earth and infrastructure work for the site?

Nevada City Cohousing resident group in one of the preliminary meetings.

- What are potential off-site infrastructure costs?
- What are people particularly sensitive to these days? Cutting down
  trees? Noise, light, or traffic?
- Are there wetlands, artifacts,
  archeological remnants, natural
  amenities, bird habitat, etc., that
  will need to be protected?
- Budgets, budgets, budgets.

Bellingham Cohousing resident group.

Optimal Size

Deciding on the right size and number of households seems to be one of
the big challenges facing Americans
contemplating senior cohousing.
Senior cohousing communities in
Europe have shown over and again
that the optimum size is not too big
— and not too small. Create a community that is too big, and an
institutional feel and sensibility will
result. Create a community that is too
small, and the community will become
more like a large family and not a
neighborhood of actively engaged
households.

In Denmark, a senior cohousing
community usually features from 15 to
25 households. And while 20 households is widely considered to be the
optimum number, sometimes economics dictate that a community will need
as many as 30. Beyond 30 households,
it is best to split the development into
two or more separate but parallel

projects (or perhaps to spin off a couple of single-family homes). Regardless
of the number of households in a given
senior cohousing community, there
consistently seems to be about 1.3
people per household, per community.

Do not underestimate the importance of finding the right size for your
community. It bears directly on the
success of community building.
Americans tend to give inadequate
consideration to the social side of
cohousing developments. Size is subjective, and therefore malleable, right?
Not really. At any given scale of community size, the social patterns within
each are, in fact, very predictable and
getting these right has a profound
impact on the community created.

Creating a Cohesive Organization

In this challenging Feasibility Phase,
groups often have difficulty maintaining their focus. Identifying (though

Silver Sage Senior Cohousing.

not yet acquiring) a good building site often serves to rally the group because it lends direction and momentum to what can otherwise be a rather abstract project.

The Quest for a Site

Many groups, no matter how organized, unified, and focused, have been frustrated by the search for a site. It is usually best to get professional help here (it's hard enough for them to do it); experienced professionals who know what they are doing can work and act more quickly and get better results.

In urban and suburban areas, sites are often expensive and hard to find, and competition for appropriate sites can be fierce. Core groups consisting of just a few households have to compete with experienced developers; and developers who are familiar with the steps involved in securing land can act quickly to make decisions and put up option money. In rural areas, zoning, septic system requirements, and the cost of off-site infrastructure improvements can rule out many otherwise ideal sites. All these challenges make finding and securing a site a watershed moment in the cohousing development process. Because a small core group of households may not have enough capital to move quickly on a potential site, the actual acquisition of the site may have to wait until the community achieves a critical mass of households. If this is the situation, then local Study Group I sessions are the best way to build up membership.

With the site identified (or decided upon), and an advisor on board, a group can begin to focus the project and create group cohesion. A group can choose to start the Study Group I process; it can assess and even finish the Feasibility and Information Phases of the project prior to starting Study Group I; or it can conduct Study Group I and feasibility assessments at about the same time.

At this point, a group will likely be quite anxious. With so much work already done and perhaps even palpable pressure coming from elsewhere (maybe a group must put down option money for a site soon or lose the option), a group typically wants to get their project built. Right now. As a result, they may feel a need to put off the community-building aspects of the project for later. Just keep in mind that while a site is a great motivator and seriously coalesces a project, it is only one component of the project.

In order for the core group to proceed efficiently once a site is identified, it first must take the time to develop an effective working structure, explore shared values, and sharpen its group process skills as it forges a development strategy. The more cohesive the core group, and the more clearly defined its goals, the more feasible the project will be. It is best to complete Study Group I before optioning a site. We recommend that a core group (no matter how small) identify a site before proceeding into any further development, as a site gives tangible focus and purpose to a group's efforts.

Information Phase: Understanding Cohousing Development Strategies

Building a cohousing community can be a daunting undertaking. The sheer number of details alone can cause some groups to stumble. However, it is not necessary for any group to reinvent

Nevada City Cohousing.

this wheel or go it alone, especially in these early discovery phases. The Cohousing Company and others provide a "Getting-It-Built" workshop that is designed to get a group up and running in short order. This two-day workshop is invaluable for clarifying the development and group processes for cohousing; it covers the basics of the development process and various possible development scenarios, the financial and legal aspects of cohousing, project management, participatory design, and group process.

Development Strategy

Sometimes the initial core group decides the development strategy without exploring all possible alternatives. While groups in the early stages need to be careful not to discuss so many possibilities that they never move forward, they also need to carefully consider what the most appropriate strategy for their particular situation is. How many households will their community ideally contain? Will the resident group act as developer? Should they joint venture with an experienced developer? How can the group best accommodate the concerns of local officials?

Questions such as these should be asked early on. If, for instance, local officials and neighborhood organizations are concerned about preserving open space, a design that addresses that concern is more likely to gain support. Conversely, there have been many cases where officials have overloaded projects with requirements in order to address citizens' feelings about limiting growth. Insightful officials are often keen to champion projects because cohousing usually presents so many pluses: affordable housing, sustainable design, infill housing, strong communities and neighborhoods, support for seniors, and green development. Once municipalities see how cohousing can meet and even exceed the stated goals of their own general plan, they will often support a project.

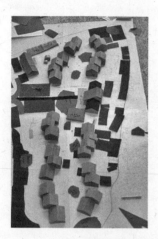

Muir Commons house blocks layout from design workshop, Davis, California.

Why Would Developers Get Interested in Senior Cohousing?

1. Marketing — it seems that most developers are always second guessing "what the market wants." It amazes me how many millions of dollars goes into trying to answer this question and yet only 70 percent of the answer is right. Why not ask the market directly? Why not build communities in which future residents actually tell the developer what they want?

2. Buyers — pre-qualified buyers means less risk.

3. Powerful allies — there's nothing like a group of motivated seniors to help get a project approved (even a larger project that they are a part of).

Organized, voting seniors are extremely effective in getting elected officials to listen and act.

4. Gratification — there's nothing more gratifying for a builder than meeting a group of people who want a village, building it for them, and then seeing a real neighborhood with life between the buildings.

5. Success breeds success — cohousing communities anchor the success of a new neighborhood. A recent case in point is Elitch Gardens in Denver, Colorado, where a new 32-unit cohousing community successfully energized the social and marketing efforts of a much larger development of many hundreds of units.

Once a resident group is ready to move toward site acquisition, they must begin thinking less as home-buyers and more like developers who are willing to take the initial risks required to get a project off the ground. Before a resident group (regardless of its size) can know what is possible for a site — even how many units can be built at what cost — money must be invested (unsecured and completely at risk) to answer other feasibility questions, such as soils and toxins analyses, design viability, and legal investigations.

Throughout the Feasibility and Information-gathering Phases, these resident-developers must constantly assess the obstacles that might threaten the project, and they must face difficult questions along the way: Can planning approvals for the number of units necessary to make the project financially feasible be obtained? Will the soil give the necessary percolation for a septic system? How much will financing cost?

So what is a core group consisting of just a few households to do? They have a potential site, and have to move fast on it to get an option, but don't have all of the finances necessary to both get the site and conduct all of the feasibility studies. In this case, it might be best for the core group to take a step back and partner with a developer and/or get an architect.

Working with a Developer

In our experience, when a core group of residents partners with a developer, their project moves faster, more efficiently, and is less costly (especially if the developer knows how to work

Sonora Cohousing site plan. Tuscon, Arizona.

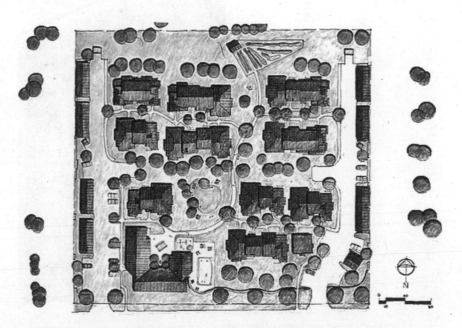

Financing

One of the principal hurdles to determining the feasibility of a cohousing development can be in getting a construction loan. On the whole, banks do not understand the cohousing concept, and what they do not understand, they are reluctant to finance. But now that cohousing has a viable track record, this is becoming less of a problem. Committed buyers, who have already invested time and money in the project, and a developer with a good track record, are usually readily financed.

with a cohousing group). Core resident groups that partner with an experienced development team — project manager, developer, architect, lawyer, and other key consultants — reap huge benefits in terms of actually moving a project forward. The ideal development team is experienced in residential real estate development and also understands the specific needs of the cohousing process.

Common laundry facilities foster community and sustainability. This resident takes it one step further by deciding to air dry.

This partnership is especially valuable for core groups who wish to create their community in urban areas where few developable sites remain, and where land as well as pre-development costs are exorbitant. In these places, the high costs of development leave little room for mistakes during the complex process of getting a project through the planning approvals, financing, and construction. The developer not only manages this process, working with the architect and other consultants, but also reduces the risk associated with housing development. But the group must adequately vet the developer. The most important question to ask: "Is this developer experienced and successful in cohousing development?" There are no licensed cohousing developers, but there are people who have done it before.

In cohousing, the developer cannot solely bear the project's financial risk should the project fall through or units remain unsold. The group has to share in this liability, or even take it on. The reason is simple and

Two Methods

In Denmark, there are two principal methods of building senior cohousing. Both rely on an organization to facilitate the process. One method employs a nonprofit development firm; the other uses a for-profit professional design and project management firm. In both methods, the process begins with a group of people who either know each other already (sometimes referred to as the core group), or who sign up on a list of interested parties. The professional facilitators sometimes are responsible for bringing a group together; more often they enter the picture only after a core group has formed.

important: if the developer assumes the risk, then he has license to make many non-cohousing, unilateral decisions — like selling units to buyers who are not interested in cohousing. Developers who build cohousing must exercise impeccable integrity and understand and share in the cohousing spirit with the resident group.

A regular developer most often works on a risk-for-profit basis, budgeting 10 to 25 percent of the total selling price as developer and investor profit. A conventional house buyer cannot know what compromises may have been made to meet that budget. Certainly, many developers are conscientious in their building practices, but in speculative housing development, countertops and floor coverings are what sell houses to prospective buyers, rather than less visible features such as quality wall construction and excellent insulation. In cohousing, with the residents involved in the process of planning their community, development is more a service-for-a-fee than a risk-based undertaking.

In cohousing development, the developer and other professionals feel more accountable, and the quality of the work itself is a higher priority. Residents may initially question the percentage of profit that a developer stands to receive, until they come to understand just what they are getting for their money.

I believe that cohousing (and specific projects) are better served when

Sonora Cohousing.

The Role of the Developer

The developer's job can encompass some or all of the following roles:

* Targeting properties and assessing the feasibility of each.
* Coordinating pre-development work such as toxins assessment and soils testing on the site.
* Working with design professionals.
* Facilitating the acquisition of planning approvals and permits.
* Financing some or all of the pre-development costs.
* Securing outside investors to provide required equity.
* Arranging for construction financing.
* "Signing on the bottom line," to assume the risk for the construction loan.
* Hiring contractors and consultants.
* Overseeing the construction on a day-to-day basis.
* Absorbing some of the risk (i.e. cost) of unsold units.
* Assuming responsibility for blame for delays and frustrations and taking steps to overcome them.
* Budgets, budgets, budgets.

Sonora Cohousing.

the developer's role is to provide a specific service rather than a product. That way everybody is on board to create the most value for the least cost to residents. If costs go up, then the house prices go up too, unless cost overruns are offset. Ultimately, it is at least partially out of the developer's profit that unexpected delays or cost overruns are taken. It is part of the developer's expertise to be able to predict budgets and time lines with enough accuracy to maintain the prices that buyers are expecting to pay, and still earn a living. The last thing you want for cohousing in America (and therefore model neighborhoods with a broad and positive legacy) is for residents to make $100,000 selling their house, while the developers lose money.

Balance of Risk and Control

There are many possible relationships between a developer and a cohousing group, reflecting varying degrees of risk (and therefore control) assumed by the residents. In the end, whoever has the most money at risk makes the final decisions. Certainly, it is not always easy for a group to work with a developer, no matter how sympathetic that developer might be to the cohousing concept, but knowing and separating the two roles makes it a much less stressful experience for all involved. Developers are generally no more accustomed to working with groups than groups are accustomed to working with developers. But working together, projects get built. And it can be a very rewarding experience for everyone if the project stays deliberate.

At one extreme, a cohousing group might see a distinct advantage in building a project without an outside developer, meaning that the resident group takes on the full risk of their project themselves. Taking all the risk means they are able to make all of the decisions. Empirically, in the US, this scenario has led to projects taking longer and costing more, or sometimes not happening at all. It has also led to wonderful finished projects, but it is a much more difficult route, without question.

At the other extreme, a cohousing group could concede all risk to a developer. The developer then pushes the project through the inevitable

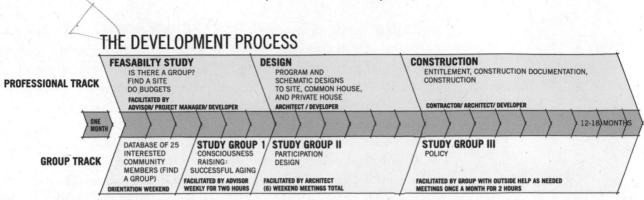

THE DEVELOPMENT PROCESS

PROFESSIONAL TRACK

FEASABILTY STUDY
IS THERE A GROUP?
FIND A SITE
DO BUDGETS
FACILITATED BY
ADVISOR/ PROJECT MANAGER/ DEVELOPER

DESIGN
PROGRAM AND
SCHEMATIC DESIGNS
TO SITE, COMMON HOUSE,
AND PRIVATE HOUSE
ARCHITECT / DEVELOPER

CONSTRUCTION
ENTITLEMENT, CONSTRUCTION DOCUMENTATION,
CONSTRUCTION

CONTRACTOR/ ARCHITECT/ DEVELOPER

ONE MONTH

12-18 MONTHS

GROUP TRACK

**DATABASE OF 25
INTERESTED
COMMUNITY
MEMBERS (FIND
A GROUP)**
ORIENTATION WEEKEND

STUDY GROUP 1
CONSCIOUSNESS
RAISING:
SUCCESSFUL AGING
FACILITATED BY ADVISOR
WEEKLY FOR TWO HOURS

STUDY GROUP II
PARTICIPATION
DESIGN
FACILITATED BY ARCHITECT
(6) WEEKEND MEETINGS TOTAL

STUDY GROUP III
POLICY

FACILITATED BY GROUP WITH OUTSIDE HELP AS NEEDED
MEETINGS ONCE A MONTH FOR 2 HOURS

---

financial and political obstacles. Be careful, though. If the developer has too much say, the common house might be tiny, or the site plan compromised because the developer didn't have anyone to help argue his or her case at City Hall. The houses might each end up including one of everything (washer/dryer, storage shed, guest room), undermining the usefulness of the common house. Garages might be attached to each house, guaranteeing a short circuit in the long-term success of the community. In all those cases, community would be compromised because residents will not need — or be able — to cooperate as much.

These extremes are not just theoretical. Real cohousing projects have emerged from each extreme but were frustrating for all involved. In general, a more middle-ground approach in which the roles are clear and a developer works in true partnership with the resident group produces a rewarding cohousing process and a great place to live.

Other Considerations in Working with a Developer

It is vital that a developer allow a group access to business and background information that will affect the project. Before taking a developer onto the project, the core group should not hesitate to check the track record and financial background of anyone they are considering. Likewise, a developer should be up front about his or her financial position, since a strong financial statement is essential to getting a project built. Groups have to be wary: developers may have good intentions but may not actually have the wherewithal to pull off a complex project like cohousing.

Beyond providing information, the developer needs to be thoroughly acquainted with the hard realities of budget and time constraints in order to advise the residents about the consequences of their decisions, while still allowing them to weigh the possibilities for themselves. The developer's role is by no means easy, but as cohousing groups across the country are discovering, it's easier to work with developers than to do the job themselves, and it always seems to be less costly.

One successful way to work with a developer is to agree that if decisions are not made within a certain time, then the developer will make a default decision. When a developer is

Temescal Cohousing, Oakland, California. Cohousing architects have had to learn to build economically and sustainably.

too flexible, he or she is not doing any favors for the resident group. Changes and delays mean increased costs. More on this important issue in a bit.

Consultants

Enlisting the assistance of consultants — advisors, facilitators, architects, lawyers, and financial planners — who are supportive of the group's goals significantly expedites the development process and supports meeting a budget. The more experience they have had with cohousing, usually the better.

Consultants who are familiar with land and development costs, financing possibilities, and ownership options can assist in defining the realistic financial expectations early in the process. Consultants who are themselves committed to the cohousing concept are more likely to provide the nontraditional services required by the participatory process, such as extra meetings, field trips, explanations of options, or facilitation of group decisions. At the same time, consultants must not dictate decisions for the group. And just because their hearts are in the right place does not mean that they can get the job done.

When selecting a consultant, keep this saying in mind: "By the time you know the tricks of the trade, you have the attitude of the trade." Watch out for consultants who get flustered

Support for Seniors

There's a world of help out there for seniors who need help in getting the word out to others interested in creating their own senior cohousing community. For example, the cohousing community we are currently building is in Grass Valley, California, population 10,922. Some 22 percent of the population is over the age of 65, meaning that there are about 2,400 seniors in the area. Those seniors have access to a fairly impressive range of services, given the city's size and its location in rural Nevada County. What follows is just a partial list:

+ Nevada County Department of Community Action.
+ Nevada County Adult and Family Services Department, a part of the Human Services Agency.
+ Nevada County Senior Center, which provides a drop-in center as well as a centralized source for information.
+ Senior Net, an educational service teaching seniors how to use computers.
+ High Noon Senior Nutrition Program, for both congregate nutrition and home-delivered meals.
+ Legal Services of California, providing paralegal assistance to elders.

+ Area 4 Agency on Aging Friendly Visitors Program, matching volunteers to homebound seniors.
+ RSVP of Nevada County, a program helping retirees and seniors to volunteer their spare time.
+ Paratransit services, offering door-to-door transport for local trips.
+ Senior Outreach, registered nurses assisting seniors in obtaining in-home services to prevent premature or unwanted institutionalization.

There are similar associations and organizations available in most towns. All are there to promote the interests of seniors, from putting the word out to recruit potential members, to providing meeting space, to sponsoring study groups, to supporting your project during the city planning meetings, to providing services once you live there. This kind of support is worth knowing about in Study Group I, and worth understanding in detail in Study Group III. And at the end of Study Group II, these folks can be great assets in the political process of getting your project approved. The best way to proceed is to go meet with them and see what they do.

---

when novices question their expertise. A good consultant is able to listen very carefully to what people are trying to say, stays patient, is never patronizing, and never feels threatened.

Sometimes, professionals within the resident group are able to provide some consultant services. While this may ostensibly reduce costs, it can also create conflicts between the personal and professional interests of the resident/consultant, so think carefully before following this route. Whether or not a group member should act as a consultant depends, of course, on who that person is. I've been the architect of both communities that I've lived in the United States.

The first time was fine; the second time, it was more challenging.

Chris Miller, mechanical engineer and resident of the Nevada City Cohousing Community, is one of those people who never had any difficulties in combining these two roles, for two reasons: First, there was never any question that he was always looking out for the interests of the group,

BiC's Nonprofit Approach

Over the years the Danish organization Quality of Living in Focus (Boligtrivsel i Centrum, or BiC) has established a method for creating a new senior cohousing group that is strikingly efficient. It augments the system created by Henry Nielsen. As soon as 25 names are registered in the national database for senior cohousing in any given city, the organization initiates the process of getting a project organized there.

Meanwhile, one or two "project coordinators" from the organization go through the phone book for that city (particularly government and nonprofit sections that deal with senior concerns) and set up meetings with the directors of three or four different agencies that provide services for seniors.

At the same time, they meet with nonprofit and for-profit housing developers. They say, "Look, you're in the business of making housing and you sometimes do senior housing. We have 25 households that need and want housing, and a few who can afford larger houses to help offset the costs of the smaller units. We've been talking to city officials and we think that there is the potential for real cooperation here. In addition, because this is cohousing, future residents can help bring pre-development funding to the project and to the entitlement process."

The project coordinators meet with the local for-profit developers who specialize in building clustered-family housing projects. After a town slide show, the project manager also sets the Study Group I process in motion (see Chapter 7).

Like most Danes, most Americans are not familiar with housing developers. Some current developments are attractive enough, but their basic structure does not support the goals and needs of a senior cohousing community. However, with input from cohousing groups and dedicated design professionals, there's no reason why a nonprofit or a for-profit organization can't build excellent senior cohousing communities in the United States. Since 2002 BiC's funding has been sharply reduced, and a number of private consultants have taken over. Their intention is just the same. As soon as 25 people in any given area are motivated to move into senior cohousing, it's their job to help them achieve that goal. They will:

+ Find local resources
+ Find sites or find a way to find a site
+ Carry out site feasibility studies
+ Help find a developer
+ Help find the group a venue to hold Study Group I
+ Help find facilitators for Study Group I
+ Help facilitate Study Group I, if necessary
+ Help find an experienced architect for Study Group II

and second, although Chris was firm with his professional opinion, he did not try to control every aspect of every thing that came to his attention. For this group, he was the right man for the jobs he did.

A group member who is considering a turn as a professional consultant (for his or her own group) needs to do a gut check before starting to make sure he or she is really ready for what may come. The group also needs to be ready. If a consultant is not performing to the standard a group requires, it may be best to get rid of that consultant as soon as possible. But when that consultant is also a group member, this impulse can short circuit — it is painful to fire a group member. Hiring a replacement consultant can be awkward and carry an added expense.

In our experience working with many cohousing groups, we have seen both successes and difficulties in having a group-member/consultant. In the best case, he or she will work extra diligently to achieve the desired outcome. In a village, "conflict of interest" can work to everyone's advantage because it enhances everyone's accountability — you're really *on* — you really have to do a good job.

In considering how best to use consultants, residents must decide how involved they want to be in various aspects of the process. Whereas issues of ultimate livability need to be decided by the resident group, countless technical decisions can be delegated to the developer and to outside consultants. Everyone plays a role. Communities developed in recent years have felt it less important to be involved in every aspect of development and have been giving more responsibility to the architect and other consultants than did their predecessors. This is partly due to increasing economic pressures to keep to a strict timeline; it's clear that cohousing groups that establish clear criteria — and then get out of the way — control costs best. In addition, many European and, increasingly, American architects today have a firm understanding of how to design for the needs of prospective senior cohousing residents. Typically, residents play a very active role during the initial planning stages, and then delegate greater control to the architect and other consultants as the project moves forward.

I've noticed that since Danish architects are held in such high regard in their society (for good reason — they really do actively and visibly contribute to the viability of their society), residents rarely tend to second-guess them. However, not all architects should be treated equally: In Denmark, architects who have designed 15 or more senior cohousing

Strawberry Creek Cohousing, Berkely, California.

communities understandably do not seem to get second-guessed at all. Those who have designed only one or two need more resident involvement — they just don't know what they are doing yet.

Final Preparations

Once the core group has determined that their project is feasible, and they have a good start on the development process, it's time to build a larger community. A larger group of prospective cohousing residents meeting for Study Group I will engage in honest, straightforward, and realistic discussions about what senior cohousing is and what it isn't — and together they will learn what it means to manage ordinary and extraordinary tasks as a group, to age in place, and to build a community of their own from the ground up.

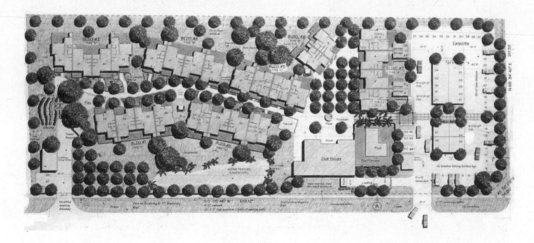

Site plan of Synergy Cohousing, Delray Beach, Florida.

CHAPTER 7

Study Group I:
Aging Successfully/Aging in Place

The purpose of Study Group I is to make vivid the opportunities, challenges, and difficulties of "aging in place" and the advantages that aging in community offers in comparison to the alternatives. This chapter is the most important in the book. The rest is hypothetical if you're still in denial about your own future and the realities of aging. The first vital task in aging in place is to find the *right* place. To do that, the Danes have embraced an "Aging Successfully" seminar approach so that people will do enough self-discovery to discover the right place for them.

Historically, "aging in place" meant that grandparents lived and died in their own home with extended family members there to care for them. Today, it may mean that, or it may mean aging and dying alone in the big suburban house where you raised your children. Those who begin with simply "aging in place" miss the key point: what is the right place?

This chapter is about how to consider — and then reconsider — your own life. Seniors who take the time and effort to take stock of their situation and develop a more self-deterministic scenario are likely to have a more successful and happy elderhood. Many seniors get their financial ducks lined up: their trust, their will, etc., but to look clearly at one's emotional well-being for the future is another story. Study Group

I is when people see their projection clearly and in focus, when people take stock of their lives and determine what they're going to do. Some move back to the town they grew up in. Some move next door to the kids. Some move to a shared house with other seniors. About 40% of those who finish Study Group I join an effort to get a senior cohousing project built or buy a home in an existing one, if one is available nearby.

Aging in Place: Aging Successfully

This seemingly straightforward issue is, in fact, far-reaching. What is aging in place? On the surface, aging in place is merely about living in one location, as well as possible, for as long as possible. But what about the real question: *How does one age in place successfully?*

As one ages, how does one effectively meet a host of changing logistic, social, and emotional needs? First and foremost, the individuals in the group must take a step back and decide what aging in place means to them and what they themselves want to experience. Only then can they plan for it.

Stepping back and taking a good look inward and then ahead into the future is exactly what happens in the Study Group I workshop. Participants discuss the issues of aging in place with their peers, they learn about their choices, and they create a personal vision of what aging successfully entails. Through the course of the workshop, they gain skills and tools that can help them plan to age successfully. Upon completion, participants will know if cohousing is for them. Some participants will choose senior cohousing; but all participants will begin to plan for successful aging, or at least to be conscious of what it means. Says one Study Group I participant and senior cohousing resident:

We did not all come to the same conclusion (about what would allow us to age successfully). Some chose to create this senior cohousing community; others decided to move closer to their kids. However, one thing is sure: we did all become more aware of what it was we wanted, and it seems that we all did something.

Study Group I: Then and Today

The first Study Group I meetings were organized by a group of teachers in Denmark who wanted to help elders age in place successfully. They saw their senior citizens fading away into isolation, or living in fear of being warehoused. They realized that the isolation of seniors does more than propagate a poor quality of life for

the elders of our society. It affects the entire society, and on multiple levels: as taxpayers, we pay for unsustainable and inefficient services; as children of aging seniors, we bear emotional and financial stress; as future seniors and grandparents, we face being pushed aside, but would rather continue to grow and contribute to society. Indeed, the interlaced web of our society suffers when our elders suffer. There was an evident need to use a holistic approach in reaching out to the aging. Study Group I meetings began with the goal of creating a space for seniors to talk about the issues of aging in place. The teachers simply facilitated the brainstorming

of how and where seniors could age most successfully.

The Study Group I meetings were a great success. Seniors finally had an opportunity to face the challenges and opportunities of aging with their peers. Once strangers, the Study Group I participants began to work together to address the issues presented at each meeting. As seniors supported and inspired each other through the process, they became empowered in their new social roles, and they developed relationships that created a strong foundation for continued growth in community. The discussions helped participants confront the realities of living and aging,

Session ten of Study Group I visits an up and running senior cohousing community.

Today, there is a group of Study Group I facilitators in the US who are trained to help seniors plan for successful aging using the Study Group I workshops. If you are interested in exploring the possibility of organizing a group of peers, contact McCamant & Durrett Architects and we will help you find a facilitator in your area.

and prompted them to plan for a possible future together by identifying the issues important to them. Says one cohousing resident, "Those Study Group I meetings created an openness between us as we learned each other's strong and weak sides. Without those meetings, I would not have the same relationship I have with the others."

Today, Study Group I is a key step for new groups who have already decided they would like to live in senior cohousing as well as those who are just exploring the idea. A community-building experience gives participants the skills and tools needed to set some basic community boundaries. Then, once everyone is in agreement, the group (or maybe just part of the group) is ready to consult with an architect and initiate the participatory design process (Study Group II). They will also be ready to start working with a developer. The more technical discussions — discussions about social agreements, co-care limits, legal agreements, and preparation for move-in — do not occur until Study Group III. Ask any architect, developer, or especially any group that has completed Study Group I, and they will tell you that the latter stages of community building came with greater ease thanks to the strong group formation that occurred in Study Group I.

Getting Started

Study Group I usually begins when an advisor, core group of elders, or developer publicizes an introductory, informational meeting. At the end of this initial meeting, interested participants sign up for Study Group I, and it's time to really start the conversation. Typically held as a series of ten classes (say, every Wednesday evening for two hours) at a community college, adult education school, community center, senior support office conference room, or somewhere similarly accessible, Study Group I classes cover a wide range of topics meant to expand the awareness around aging. These topics include:

1. **Aging in place and aging in community:** Assessing the implications of our current quality of life and beginning to define what we want; getting out of denial and into self-determination.

2. **Group process:** How to work together; learning new communication and decision-making skills. You can do anything if you know how to work together.

3. **Realities of getting older:** Physical, mental, and psychological; raising awareness and planning for successful aging.

4. **Co-care and outside care:** Understanding our choices in receiving, sharing, and giving care;

discussing the implications and setting guidelines for caring in community; how to accommodate nurses, other caregivers, and family.

5. **Co-healing:** The role of others in keeping us healthy and happy.

6. **The economics of getting older:** The finances of various seniors living arrangements.

7. **Philosophy, spirituality, and mortality:** Nurturing continued growth and strengthening bonds by exploring issues of the spirit and soul.

8. **Saging:** What we have to offer the world; growing into elderhood.

9. **Embracing risk:** The risk of staying where you are; moving back to a small town, moving in with the daughter; moving into cohousing.

10. **Case studies:** Senior cohousing neighborhoods; visit a cohousing community.

Right from the start, seniors openly discuss and digress into any specific issues that are dear to them. Sometimes groups even have camping trips where they discuss their hopes and aspirations around the campfire. Whatever the activities, members get to know each other and learn to trust each other. Sure, there is a lot of ground to cover. As such, Study Group I classes are typically held once a week and participants are asked to reflect on homework at home. Doing the homework is critical. It's the time that participants reflect on the realities of their life — not just the story they have been telling themselves (and therefore telling others). Whether done on a long walk, in the shower, or sipping a cup of coffee at the café and gazing out the window, the point of the homework is to get to the bottom of the real deal. As the classes progress, the issues become more complicated, the discussions more intimate, the revelations more profound. Sometimes trips are organized, such as boat outings, bicycle rides, or country walks. Eventually, most issues get covered in this honest process of discussion and discovery. Each meeting is an opportunity for growth. Now let's take a closer look into what each of the ten sessions has to offer.

Session 1:
Aging in Place/ Aging in Community

What is your aging scenario? Aging-in-place issues are best discussed in a group of about 15 to 25 people,

When older, it's wonderful to have neighbors who can easily come by, and to be able to just look outside to see what's going on.

for two hours at a time. Most people who have not been through it believe that's a lot of time. Everyone who has been through it says, "Wow — we just touched the tip of the iceberg." The goal is to give enough time for each individual to get to the deep and meaningful place where, by discussing issues together, participants can best address individual and collective life issues, needs, and circumstances. Everyone will get to a place they had not imagined before, and consider possibilities they hadn't previously contemplated.

At the first meeting, participants explore what aging in place has meant historically, and what it means today. At first, these types of explorations are done on a more philosophical, somewhat removed level. To help these

Hanging out in front of the strawbale common house of Sonora Cohousing.

initial meetings remain as objective as possible, group members should bring their favorite facts, figures, and statistics about getting older. I say this because people like to put the statistics out there — but what matter are real-life experiences and adjustments.

The facilitator can get the ball rolling by simply asking, "What does aging in place mean to you?" People will usually answer with their worst-case physical scenarios. A common refrain is, "When one of my neighbors hurt herself, she had to move in with her daughter or have someone move in with her. In either case it seemed like a decrease in her quality of life." In fact, having to move five times in the last ten years of your life to accommodate your needs is terribly destabilizing. Most people say that they want to die in their homes ("They'll take me out feet first"). This requires a plan for aging in place — in the right place.

Having to move out of one's home is a real concern, but it is only a small component of a bigger picture. At this stage, a group should try to avoid the obvious pitfall of discussing too many similarly grim scenarios, as this type of discourse too often digresses into discussions of how housing can best accommodate physical disabilities Solving accessibility design issues (Universal Design is covered later) sometimes feels like the answer to aging-in-place questions, but physical handicap accessibility is not the only issue, nor is it the cure-all solution. Spending time and money retrofitting houses for elders, only for them to move into assisted care soon after, is pointless. There are many other issues at work; they are just not as obvious or as tangible.

Let the call for handicap accessibility be raised (as it will be), but then let it go for the time being. With these worst-case physical scenarios set aside, a group can then focus its attention on how community, senior cohousing, single-family homes, or other scenarios holistically address the emotional, social, and logistical issues of aging in place. People start to see the big picture with these discussions; they see that it turns out that relationships with neighbors are also important, not just grab bars.

A good way to begin exploring the relationship between community and a high quality of life is by allowing participants to examine the effect that proximity to friends and services has on *their* lives. *How much do I drive for social purposes? How many times a year do I fly to see a friend?* These sorts of questions begin a reflection process in which participants go through a list of activities (such as cooking, watching TV, eating alone, eating with someone, relaxing with friends, etc.) and observe how much time they currently spend doing these activities, and how much time would be ideal for their happiness.

The key is figuring out how important company and community are in your life. When you go through a list of activities, it becomes clear what makes you happier. When the group is asked how a close-knit community could benefit them personally, thoughtful responses start to surface:

- "We'll get to know each other better."
- "I'll have neighbors I can depend on."
- "If I can depend on my neighbors, I can leave Henry for a week and go down the coast with my girl-friends."

Temescal Cohousing courtyard, Oakland, California.

• "I don't have to be home to feed the dog if I want to go away for a day or two."

• "I'll have people living next door who I can go to the movies with, have a glass of wine with, travel with, go to the opera with, talk with, be with, and all the other things that I didn't get to do when I had kids."

• "I won't have to worry about who lives next door. I'll know them, and I won't need to be afraid."

• "In fact, my neighbors can be my greatest amenity. If I fall down at night and they don't see me in the morning, they will come find me right away."

• "I'm so tired of the high turnover in the neighborhood where I live now. I can imagine it will be much more stable in cohousing since we've all put so much into it and planned it to be just what we want."

When real feelings get expressed, participants will see how various living arrangements will affect their own quality of life. Not only do their own aspirations become tangible, but new possibilities that they hadn't otherwise considered will emerge. It can be a huge revelation. For the first time, participants will see how their future is framed by privacy or how their next-door neighbors are their greatest

Care for the Elderly in Asia

Kala is a woman who I had the good fortune to sit next to on a recent flight I took to Chicago. As I spoke with her and her mother, I was amazed at the difference between the ways that people care for their elders in India vs. here in the United States. In most of Asia, the extended family, particularly the children, take care of the elderly. If the children have moved away, to the US for example, they can afford to hire help back home to take care of Mom and Dad. Labor is still relatively cheap in Asia, and there is extensive professional training in care for the elderly. In addition, in Asian cultures a great emphasis is placed on intergenerational socializing. Kala said:

"I made my children from age two spend a minimum of one hour conversing with their grandparents at each visit each weekend. They had no choice in the matter. I wanted them to get into the habit of sitting down with them and talking, and it worked. Now my 30-year-old daughter, who is a busy physician, comes over and talks with my mother once every weekend, for at least one hour."

Professional care supplemented with family interaction is great, but while Americans and Europeans may have more than covered the professional side, the family side is often lacking. Senior cohousing as a lifestyle is designed specifically to make up for this Western culture's social deficiency. After all, few of us have a Hindu mother to guide us and make certain we will be properly cared for in our old age.

amenity — even better than a golf course.

Session 2:
Group Process:
Working Together

To paraphrase author Ayn Rand, "In the end, each of us looks out for Number One." Stoic and strong words indeed, but somewhat off the mark. Only by cooperating with others, whether in cohousing or the rest of

Cooking community dinner at FrogSong Cohousing.

Why Western Children Spend Less Time Caring for Aging Parents

1. Raising a family in an increasingly complicated world is more and more time consuming. (Kids aren't just kids, they're highly cultivated and nurtured children who need to be driven to piano practice, and soccer games and more.)

2. There are fewer children per family to care for their parents, and it's less likely there will be one who can do it.

3. Children live farther away. With a global economy, children move to where the opportunities are. Their children then grow up outside the context of an extended family.

4. Most women work outside of the home and are less available than in previous generations (when they provided most of the care).

5. Children in Western societies are culturally less inclined to care for their parents.

Some have argued that our young adult population is more self-centered, more selfish. The days of hanging out on the front porch with an older person, the days of just being there hour after hour, having a cup of tea, breaking bread together, listening to stories, are over. We have to recognize this reality. Most older folks, of course, don't blame their children. They see their children as a product of their culture, something no one can ignore or fight, at least not without extraordinary vigor. After all, these grown kids are pursuing the careers that the parents themselves encouraged them to pursue.

While researching this book, one of the most common reasons people gave me for wanting to move into senior cohousing can be summed up with, "I don't want to be a burden to my children." A noble desire.

Other Topics Covered in Session 1:
Aging in Place/Aging in Community

These topics are covered in discussion and in homework:

1. How often do you get together with your neighbors now?

2. List the day-to-day activities that you pursue now. How much time does it take and what would you prefer?

3. How much time do you spend cooking? Do you more often eat alone than with company? Would you rather eat alone or with company?

4. How much time do you spend housecleaning?

5. How much time do you spend running errands? How many times a day do you drive?

6. Would you rather relax outside, alone, or with company? Do you like to go for walks?

7. How often do you have phone conversations with distant friends and family? Do you like to have long phone conversations?

8. Is watching TV a norm in your life? How often do you watch TV? Would you rather watch TV with friends or by yourself?

9. Do you enjoy watching movies? How often do you watch movies? Would you rather watch movies with friends or by yourself?

10. How often do you have guests in your home? Do you enjoy hosting friends or family? Would you rather visit a friend in their house?

11. Would you rather go out to eat or cook for yourself? Do you like to go out to eat with friends or by yourself?

12. Are you involved in any community clubs, groups, or organizations?

13. How often do you visit friends who are in walking distance?

14. Have you participated in much (or any) neighborly cooperation in your neighborhood?

15. Do you ever have dinner with your neighbors? Do you do any sort of activities with them? Would you rather drive across town to hang out with a closer friend?

16. How often do you bump into a friend and end up spending a pleasant afternoon?

17. How often do you socialize with your peers and discuss matters that are deeply important to you, spiritual or religious matters, or just the issues of the day (especially spontaneously)?

18. Do you ever have political dialogue with your friends or family? Are national, state, or municipal politics of importance in your life?

19. Do you have any hobbies? Do you like to create crafts? Do you like to create art? Do you like to make music? What medium do you like to work in?

20. Do you enjoy gardening? Are you interested in it more for the aspect of growing your own food, or for the enjoyment of growing things? Do you like to garden with a friend?

21. Are pets a part of your life? Are you a cat or a dog person? Do you mind having cats or dogs around even if they are not yours?

the world, can each of us truly look out for Number One, though this takes a little while to figure out.

Looking out for Number One, in the context of senior cohousing, a small town, or a family, means learning how to live in a cooperative social context — especially when you are somewhat dependent on others. It's a skill that can be learned. In cohousing, it *has* to be learned or people won't want to put up with you and you won't want to stay.

The Participatory Process

Listening to each other and getting along with others is key, whether in a resident group that forms with the intention of developing a specific site, such as with cohousing, or if you're just trying to get along with your neighbors or family. Many great activities require a group.

Of course, some groups work together better than others. How well a group works together is not so much defined by the individuals of the group itself, but by the skills those people have learned. Over the years I have seen some truisms emerge: Groups that institute thorough and deliberate group processes have fewer, shorter, and less-frustrating meetings. They experience better results through every phase of the building process. They enjoy a life that most closely matches their ideals after they actually

move in. Finally, and most importantly, they enjoy the process more.

A healthy process shows participants new ways to see the world, and above all, it sharpens their listening skills. Cohousing is a great opportunity to learn how to be more patient, tolerant, educated, and thoughtful. Conversely, when individuals are badly informed — or uninformed — about the particulars of tried-and-true successful group participation process, projects will invariably experience many unexpected problems.

Group Process

The single most important feature in the creation of a cohousing community is a coherent, fair, thoughtful group process. More important than money or land, a capable group process

Community landscaping project at Nevada City Cohousing.

Psychological Preparation

By Olaf Dejgaard,
resident of Munksøgård Senior Cohousing

As part of our journey toward living in our own cohousing community, we decided that a little psychological preparation might be useful. The change from living alone to becoming one of a group of 24 (in 20 houses) looked like a real challenge. So we attended a psychology course. I still remember the "catchphrases":

- Express yourself.
- Don't hide your feelings.
- Make yourself easy to read.
- When a conflict seems impossible to solve, imagine that your counterpart may be just 5 percent right, and try to identify the main problems with his/her point of view.

In December of 2000, shortly before moving in, we decided to formulate our own course, concentrating particularly on the handling of conflicts. We decided that everybody should attend. We hired a psychologist with experience in conflict studies, and the course ran three consecutive Sundays for five hours each.

Types of conflicts:

- Instrumental conflicts about goals, means, and methods.
- Conflicts about resources.
- Conflicts about values.
- Personal conflicts.

Solutions to conflicts:

- Avoidance, fleeing, giving in, sarcasm, making excuses.
- Use of aggression, attacking, threatening, use of violence.
- Meeting and discussing openly, accepting disagreement, examining the issue, being clear. 🖅

The courtyard of Doyle Street Cohousing.

can solve any problem or issue. Not having a good process is like a carpenter trying to build a house without tools — he has the raw materials but can't do much of anything with them.

Study Group I, the process of discussing issues at length before site acquisition and design, provides the best opportunity for a group to refine its methods of working together. It is a real "boot camp" for group process, and prepares a resident group for Study Groups II and III, where group decisions are made in rapid fire, and are consequential. The listening and discussion in Study Group I (especially the discussion about non-violent communication) translate into good discussion and decision-making skills for the later study groups.

How exactly the members of a given group determine their group process is up to them. Meeting formats and styles vary, but in the most successful groups, everyone has an opportunity for input. Without this, a few people can easily dominate the discussions, thus negating the community-building

The language of conflicts:

- Being conscious of the words you use, using relaxing, instead of escalating, language.
- Using "I" language instead of "you" language.
- Listening right to the end, instead of interrupting.
- Using open-questions instead of leading ones.
- Focusing on the problem rather than on the person.

Escalation of conflicts (disagreement):

- Saying it's "the other person's fault".
- Other problems come up.
- Dialogue is abandoned.
- Personal hatred, not just disagreement.
- Other people become involved.
- The protagonists end up having to avoid one another, "this town isn't big enough for the two of us."

Perhaps the most important part of the course was the many different points of view and opinions that were presented, which gave us a richer picture of those we were going to live with.

Having lived in Munksøgård for eight years now, I think we have succeeded in developing a viable, and a valuable decision-making culture. We have avoided making decisions that would be detrimental to any one member of the community. We have taken the time needed, sometimes letting a problem lie until a better proposal came up. We discuss proposals and work toward the solution until there is almost no resistance. For example, when we built a 550 sq. ft. shed, we had around 40 sketches of location, size, and shape before everyone was happy.

spirit that the participatory group process is designed to create. For some topics, small group discussions work best; for others, "round-table" discussions ensure that each person has an opportunity to comment on a topic. The job of facilitating meetings is usually rotated within the coordinating group or within the entire membership. Meetings can also be facilitated by an outside advisor. Some communities have found that small groups that meet between common meetings allow for more informal, hence less intimidating, discussions. A "meeting outside of a meeting" can allow people

Painting preperation at Munksøgård.

Hearthstone Cohousing common house.

the chance to gain a better understanding of the issues and of others' opinions. Such meetings often decrease the need for long discussions during common meetings. The end result is that the big group decisions are made more efficiently.

Most cohousing groups try to use consensus as much as possible, but fall back on a majority or two-thirds vote when time pressures require a prompt decision, consensus has been attempted, and a decision must be made. Some decisions may be delegated to committees.

Community Values

There are community values, and then there's community value — the value of community to an individual versus the cost of maintaining that community. At this stage in Study Group I, monetary cost is not at issue. Time is the issue. Specifically, time spent in meetings for the group to come to consensus over any given issue.

Since community consensus is a cornerstone of the cohousing concept (and is often a new concept to all involved), it is no surprise that the number one concern about cohousing has to do with meeting time. This is perfectly understandable. People, from their own experience, know that achieving consensus is difficult enough in a single household. But a community of 20 households who are just getting to know each other? How is that even possible?

First and foremost, each household or individual must understand that when meetings take too long, the value of the community diminishes. Each must learn not to make a mountain out of a molehill, and to trust others to do things without requiring the involvement of the entire group.

In cohousing, community problems, large and small, are most effectively solved when the big group brainstorms a solution, discusses it, and then delegates the job of a proposal to a committee. In this way, the community's values are intact and the value of the community is not diminished. Getting along in groups is not unique to cohousing. As a result of Study Group I, many people choose to move to a small town or to get more involved in their neighborhood. Listening, staying calm, or cofacilitating a discussion all make for more successful coexistence and, therefore, happiness.

Ultimately, a group's goal should be to create a fair and democratic policy — there is no better way to create trust. With relationships based on trust, people can achieve and accomplish much more as a group than as individuals. Groups will further develop their own group process after Study Group I. The immediate purpose is non-violent communication — (in the SG I discussions) and for everyone to recognize that community is only possible by learning to work together.

Accommodating Conflict

Community is about open communication. If a given individual or group is unable to discuss sensitive, delicate topics, it's better to discover the extent of those limitations early on in the process. But how do groups

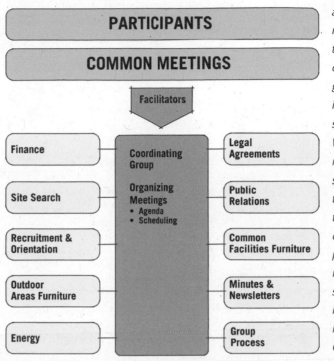

Committees ebb and flow as required. If something needs to be done, a few people get together and do it and call themselves a committee. When no longer needed, they dissolve. Some form of this is engaged throughout the development process on into residence. This structure for forming committees is introduced in Study Group I and refined in Study Group III.

Consensus

Fundamental to all cohousing is the concept that everyone who wishes to participate in making a decision can do so. In other words, everyone has a say in the business at hand, if they so desire. Thus, a clear decision-making process, based on consensus, is the first step in ensuring the complete involvement of all. When everyone is involved, people get to know each other quite well, and this fosters community. (Later, key items for the group to agree on include everything from when to meet, how often and when to eat together, etc.) The reason that

Session 2 is so early in Study Group I is so people will learn and listen and be respectful through the rest of the ten-week process. Not everyone "needs it" but then, no one needs all of the ten sessions. But those who shine during one particular session can be a model for others. For instance, people sometimes ask me why doctors would want to sit in on Session 3 when they already know about the physiology of growing older. People contribute differently to different sessions, and the doctor may in fact gain the most.

Other Topics Covered in Session 2: Group Process

Since not every tool devised for enhancing communication works with every group — it's beneficial to have plenty of options in order to bring out the best methods for each group. Below are some thoughts to keep in mind as well as methods that are highlighted in the Study Group I Workbook:

1. Valuable tools of group process are compassionate communication and cooperative decision making. These tools help to develop tolerance and healthy communication.

2. Group process in senior cohousing is egalitarian. It is a process where two individuals are able to attain, honor, and embrace a third opinion. The third opinion is what they have developed together through adjusting the opinions that they originally brought to the table. Two opinions adding up to a third one (the solution) is basic cohousing math.

$$1 + 1 = 3$$

3. Cohousing communities make decisions using consensus. In order to test the waters of consensus with your group, discuss a few personal as well as group goals.

4. Practicing compassionate communication in group discussions fosters the following attitudes, behaviors, and practices: accountability, assertiveness, clarity, compassion, consistency, directness, firmness, flexibility, friendliness, honesty, humor, ☞

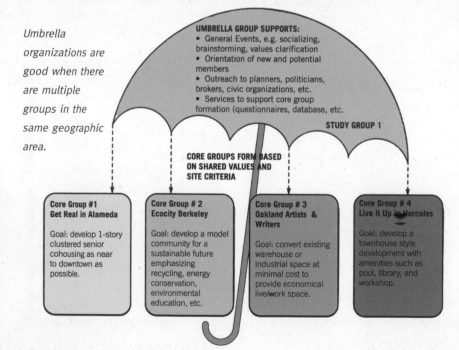

Umbrella organizations are good when there are multiple groups in the same geographic area.

UMBRELLA GROUP SUPPORTS:
• General Events, e.g. socializing, brainstorming, values clarification
• Orientation of new and potential members
• Outreach to planners, politicians, brokers, civic organizations, etc.
• Services to support core group formation (questionnaires, database, etc.)

STUDY GROUP 1

CORE GROUPS FORM BASED ON SHARED VALUES AND SITE CRITERIA

Core Group #1
Get Real in Alameda

Goal: develop 1-story clustered senior cohousing as near to downtown as possible.

Core Group # 2
Ecocity Berkeley

Goal: develop a model community for a sustainable future emphasizing recycling, energy conservation, environmental education, etc.

Core Group # 3
Oakland Artists & Writers

Goal: convert existing warehouse or industrial space at minimal cost to provide economical live/work space.

Core Group # 4
Live it Up in Hercules

Goal: develop a townhouse style development with amenities such as pool, library, and workshop.

discover and (hopefully) mitigate those limitations?

Seniors (like everyone else) should be formally introduced to the art of speaking with others in a way that best assures appreciation for what they have to say. Probably everyone knows at least one "crotchety old man" — someone with a bad attitude who doesn't endear himself to his neighbors. An impatient, unyielding know-it-all can be just as lovable as anyone, but first the layers of angst and anger need to be peeled away. Only then will that person be ready to receive the love and appreciation he deserves. I have seen many angry kindness, awareness, receptiveness, respectfulness, responsibility, responsiveness, self-motivation, sincerity, and thoroughness.

5. Disagreement within the discussion should not mean the end to the discussion but should be the beginning of a more meaningful and deeper discussion.

6. Be aware of character components that are constructive as well as destructive to the group's communication and decision-making process.

7. At of the end of the early meetings (and meetings when the group gets off-track), ask for ideas for what might have made the meeting more productive. More pleasant? More effective?

8. If you have all the ideas on the table, you have all the good ideas on the table.

9. Open communication allows for each person to hear the reasons behind someone else's opinion.

10. The group needs to value a functional group process. The better their group process works, the more the group will be able to accomplish.

11. It is only through this participatory process that cohousing communities have actually been built. Learning the process gives seniors the confidence to believe that if they choose to build a community with someone else, they have a good chance of being successful. ▨

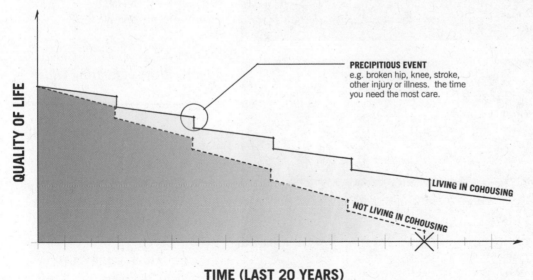

QUALITY OF LIFE

PRECIPITIOUS EVENT
e.g. broken hip, knee, stroke, other injury or illness. the time you need the most care.

LIVING IN COHOUSING

NOT LIVING IN COHOUSING

TIME (LAST 20 YEARS)

There are lots of ways to do surveys — but after interviewing hundreds of seniors, my favorite method was to simply ask — does this sum up your life before cohousing? (yes 100%), does this sum up your life after cohousing? (yes 100%). That was good enough for me.

seniors (the "I'm never going to get that novel written"; "I didn't spend enough time with my kids when I had the chance," sort of anger), who, in the course of planning a cohousing community, become lovable again.

For the sake of building a viable community that enhances the quality of life for everyone involved, individuals need to be able to listen, reason, and find common cooperative ground. Said one Danish senior cohousing resident:

> Some people in our group were very good at processing information and at the same time keeping the stress level low. Others were not. But because people are here for new life experiences, even at 70, they are motivated to learn to communicate in an open, honest, and diplomatic way. It's never too late to learn good manners.

> Very talented effective communication teachers can be found everywhere in the US, and they can really help a group to learn how to communicate effectively.

Session 3.
The Realities of Getting Older

Greeting card companies make millions creating birthday cards focused on the angst of aging — jokes about wrinkles, sagging bodies, and the loss of memory. The companies apparently fulfill a need for the aging population to get a brief, if sardonic laugh at themselves and others in their "plight" of getting old, as if it were some inevitable disease. Of

Coming home after work at Nevada City Cohousing.

Southside Cohousing courtyard, Sacramento, California.

course it's not — aging is a process, not a disease. We began "getting old" at age 28, our physiological peak.

The purpose of Session 3 is to contrast the previous ten years (physiologically) with the next ten years and the ten years after that. How are the knees, the eyes, the back, the brain, the hands, the feet, the skin, the ears, and the heart? You might not want to clear brush and cut firewood to the end of your life. Not doing these things will present other opportunities like hanging out with others, or cutting firewood with others — making it less boring.

The awareness of aging brings with it the concrete evidence of dying — everyone must die. There's no other option, so the fact must be accepted. But even when truly accepted, many people still have "angst" about *how* they are going to age. How does one "age gracefully," taking care of aches and pains and limitations — physical, financial, mental, and social — while maintaining quality of life?

Compounding the issue is the advance of technology in medicine, the increased awareness of healthy lifestyles, and the tremendous impact from the largest and most influential demographic group in history: the baby boomers, who are aging together with the same values, spunk, and determination that led them to change our society since their youth.

A Walk in the Woods

I was walking through the woods with a good friend of mine this summer. At one point I mentioned that my eyes have failed precipitously these last three years. He pointed out that since 45 is the maximum age that most hominids lived for nearly six million years, I am living on entirely borrowed time. In other words, my systems have started shutting down and I need to find other means to compensate. He finished by pointing out that at 52 I was lucky to be alive at all.

Most research about aging focuses on the new-found limitations of an aging populace. The research that needs to be done is on the phenomena of new-found capacities — the capacities for vitality that I personally can barely imagine outside of cohousing. Sometimes you hear seniors say: "I have a doctor's appointment today that will take up the whole day." What? We have so much more capacity than that. The trick is to format life so that going to the doctor is just one of a dozen things that get done today along with going to the beach with a neighbor to see the sun rise.

What we have from the Danes are models of entirely new systems that have successfully created supportive communities that work beyond our imagination in helping seniors live a high-quality life beyond physiological limitations.

Nevada City Cohousing.

These 60-year-olds join an already growing field in which two-thirds of all men and women who have ever lived past 65 in the entire history of the world are alive today. The fastest growing segment is centenarians — people over 100 years of age, 85 percent of whom are women.

As people advance through their 50s, 60s, 70s and beyond, they need to get real about the aging process. There are limitations that come with the changes. The ability to get around (mobility) and other abilities may decrease, as psychological, physical, and emotional changes occur.

Other Topics Covered in Session 3: The Realities of Getting Older

One of the most gratifying processes of the entire Study Group I session is looking inside of yourself and discovering that successful aging comes from a conscious commitment to continue one's self-education as well as developing a new set of life-enhancing strategies. Study Group I Session 3 addresses many thought-provoking questions and ideas:

1. Reflect back on the last ten years of your life. Now look forward to how you would like to see the next ten years of your life play out. Now look at ten years after that.

2. Make your dream your own. Not everyone has the same dream or desire for their future. What is your dream? Especially physically.

3. How many times a week does someone knock on your door just to see how you are doing? Is it too much? Is in not enough? How would you like to change that? What could you do together?

4. Is spontaneous socializing something you are missing in your life? If not — fine! If it is, how could you change that?

5. How are you getting your social needs met?

6. The homework in this session is specifically geared toward examining different types of change: mechanical and mobility changes; psychological and mental changes; physiological and health changes; emotional changes; and social changes. Delineate these in the context of both the last ten years and the next ten years.

We are social animals, and as we age and take note of our physical, mental, and/or emotional changes, it behooves us to find ways to connect, to "grow old together." People who grow grumpy are often bored. Boredom can lead to frustration and anger — and a lonely life of despair. A continuing, healthy involvement with others allows us to be more human — to embrace our humanity — including aging — with others who share in the process. This is what is known as aging in place successfully. So how does one go about doing that, and where?

Session 4.
Co-care and Outside Care

Why think about it now?

People come up with lots of different solutions to assure their physical well-being in their waning years: marry someone with health insurance; marry an ex-nurse who is younger than you (this happens); or move to a place with professional care. And then there is always the daughter — or is there? One of the things that people forget is that people do tire of caring for an older person — then it's off to the institution. Bill Thomas (who contributed the introduction of this book) describes a nursing home as a marriage between a hospital and a prison. Although nursing homes have figured out the "care" part, what people hate most about being older is boredom, lack of purpose, and helplessness. None of that is addressed in a nursing home "care" scenario. Moreover, nursing homes provide what Thomas calls the "three-trillion dollar dilemma"; institutions can't possibly care for all of those who require care, even at the paltry level of care that they do provide. And then, of course, it begs the question, would we want to be "cared" for at that level, anyway?

The topic of co-care is brought up early in SG I because at nearly every slideshow and presentation I do, someone asks, "What if everyone gets sick at once?" (by which most people mean, "What if I don't want to take care of others, but I want them to take care of me?"). People's fears over this topic are usually so blown out of proportion that they need to be addressed, and addressed as early as possible. The purpose of Session 4 is to contrast care at home, care in an institution, and possible care within a community.

Age of Residents

Broadly speaking, senior cohousing groups look for people over 50 who enjoy good health. Sometimes a group will set an upper limit of 65 or 69 at move-in. But the range can be 50-75. Physical health and chronological age often do not correlate, and

FrogSong Cohousing enterance from common house. Cotati, California.

there are exceptions to every rule. (One community I visited had a 74-year-old former movie star resident with a 36-year-old live-in boyfriend.) One recent senior cohousing project had an age breakdown of just over one-half aged between 50 and 60 years, a quarter aged between 60 and 70 years, and just under a quarter more than 70 years of age.

All the groups I interviewed agreed that it is best to stagger the ages of residents, erring toward younger people in the early days of the community when there is a lot of work to do. They also stated that all subsequent "move-ins" should be younger (never older than 69), again to keep the ages as staggered as possible. The most consistent age range was 55-69. A senior cohousing community in Denmark (in this case, they did not want to disclose the

name) just explained to me in length that after eight years, they now have their first less than fully capacitated resident. She has increasing dementia. Since there are 23 other adults to help her cope, it is not a burden, it's an honor. It's better to act on probability, not hope and not fear.

Age Range in Cohousing

After considerable discussion on the topic, and in order to come to a true consensus on the matter without acrimony, some groups cast secret ballots about what age ranges they think should be admitted to their community in future recruitment efforts. Some of the established senior cohousing communities in Denmark require that new applicants be no older than their early 60s and leave it at that. But everyone needs care at different rates as they grow older. We could review a long dissertation on the subject of ideal senior cohousing co-care agreements for acute disability, but three Danish senior cohousing residents sum it up well:

"We had a couple of elderly ladies living here without any family nearby or friends to take care of them when they got very ill. So a couple of us took care of them in the last part of their lives. We didn't do a lot. We were just there for them. The people from the city took care of all the nursing, and you could say that we took care of the

Neighbors socializing at Pleasant Hill Cohousing.

social aspect. We visited them, talked to them. Things like that," said one.

Another reports, "We even visited one of the ladies at night, because she kept getting out of bed. But in the end we could not take care of her anymore. Sometimes she didn't even know where she was. We couldn't handle that. We had to let her kids know it was probably time. She needed more care than we could give her. She had to move to a retirement home and we went to visit her there. In the end she was hardly ever present. We

What Neighbors Do

People who enter into a senior cohousing community plan to bond with their neighbors in some fashion. However, what compels a person to care about others is a difficult question. When people create a project together, or make dinner for each other, or spend time with each other year after year, they begin to care about each other. In a small village like Rosetta, Pennsylvania, when residents do things for the community and help others, they earn respect. And just like neighbors in a small village, cohousers earn a sense of mutual regard. While proximity helps to make this sort of co-care feasible, the "glue" is caring: There is no overestimating what people will do for each other when they care about one another.

If you've ever lived in a small town, you know that a community can take care of you. My grandmother, Dorothy Durrett, lived in such a town (Downieville, California, population 325). For her final years, about 15 of her neighbors and friends kept an eye on her and brought her food, medicines, movies, stories, clean sheets, and gossip. That's what happens in a community. Another friend, Geoff Quinn, died recently at age 77 in Goodyears Bar, a town in northern California with a population of about 90. Again, about ten people came by on a regular basis to stoke the fire, give massages, change his bed, take him to his chemotherapy sessions, and do a hundred other

things he needed help with. All of that supplemented the help he received from other institutions such as the local health clinic and HMO outpatient services. Again Geoff was born into that town and had contributed to it immensely over the years. This type of scenario is very rare today.

When 77-year-old Margaret in our Doyle Street cohousing community was diagnosed with breast cancer, it was an honor to drop in on her on my way to or from work, and take her a coffee, read the paper to her for a few minutes, and chat. Through her last six months we had several projects under construction around the country, and Margaret loved hearing about them in detail and comparing their experiences with ours at Doyle Street Cohousing.

As for senior cohousing communities in general, there are, practically speaking, 25 or so people nearby if a person becomes ill. In addition to the residents of the cohousing community, there are family, friends, medical organizations, the nursing establishment, and so on. In other words, 25 people above the norm — a small town worth of people — that live right next door. Five minutes here and five minutes there — all just a part of the ebb and flow of daily life — can mean the world to someone who is ill.

Dementia

Dementia is an increasingly common condition in our aging population. A cohousing group generally won't make a decision as to when someone has become incapable of living independently. More often, a couple of community members contact the person's children, or, if they can't find the kids, the Department of Social Services when they think he or she needs outside help or advice. These outside entities are the ones who decide the course of action. Usually, the combination of a spouse, in-house care, and cohousing community allows a person to remain at home longer than would otherwise be the case in traditional housing.

The subtility of the care is what gets the care done. "Let me give you a trim; I'll be over in an hour."

just sat and held her hand. But they did take better care of her at the nursing home because she had so many visitors — us. It was clear to the staff there that a lot of people cared about her — and so they cared too."

A third commented, "We have agreed to ring each other's doorbell if the curtains are not drawn back by 10 A.M. Most of us singles keep a key at our neighbor's house. This way, others can always get in, in an emergency. We also keep a phone list handy with the telephone numbers of those closest to each of us so that we will not have to look for them if somebody suddenly falls ill. It gives us a sense of security in our everyday lives that we would not have had if we had lived more traditionally."

As the Danes illustrate, in senior cohousing, people will only give the type and amount of care that they feel like giving. Some residents of senior cohousing say that those individuals who expect to be taken care of should find another form of accommodation. However, many residents find that they want to do a lot more than they ever imagined. Many residents enjoy the feeling that simple co-care tasks bring. Some even say it helps keep them young.

Existing senior cohousing groups found that they worried much more about these issues than was necessary in their early co-care discussions. Their concerns rarely came true; when they did, acting appropriately (whether it be caring for them or notifying social services) all came naturally. That said, one of the key reasons these established and successful groups did not experience their worst co-care fears was because they had worked through the issue prior to move-in. (Co-care agreements are discussed in detail in Study Group III). The individuals in the group all know the agreed-to limits, have contingency plans, and simply live accordingly.

Usually the approach to co-care in senior cohousing is three-pronged:

1. All of the things that you agree to: I'll pick up people's medicine, I'll take them to the doctor if I can,

I'll deliver their dinner from the common house, I'll help them or even cook their dinner when it is their turn, etc.

2. All of the things that you won't do. I won't give anyone a bath, I won't change anyone's diaper, etc.

3. All of the things that you do that you never agreed to, never imagined you'd do, but that you find yourself doing — not out of guilt or because it's required, but because it's easy and you appreciate these people at a level you hadn't expected to.

Once you care for people and it's easy, there is no underestimating how much you will actually do for one another. You can do more than you'd ever imagined.

Caregivers in the Common House

Normally when people plan for the care of increasingly frail seniors, they fully expect to hire professional caregivers for the more difficult nursing tasks. But cohousing offers an option that is far and away superior to traditional in-home nursing care. It's an option that is literally built right in. Senior cohousing groups can plan for professional care by including suites in the common house during the community's design and planning phases (Study Group II). These suites are

meant to serve as apartments for on-site caregivers.

The best place for this on-site residence is the common house itself. Therefore, it is extremely important that the common house operate comfortably as both a common space and a private space. Be careful here. This dual-purpose requirement, however, seems to present a huge challenge for most architects. Too many architects can't make these spaces warm and cozy. They err on the institutional side. A small handful of architects in Denmark do most of the senior cohousing projects there, for just that reason. It turns out that the more experience an architect has designing senior cohousing, the more likely it is that he or she will be able to accommodate this seemingly challenging request.

Suites in the common house are a convenient, temporary place for guests, visiting family, and live-in caregivers. Residents agree on how many suites they want to build during Study Group II. Sometimes, with only 20 households there will be as many as four suites. These common house suites are a key component for making the co-care environment work.

Take Bjorn, for example. He's a 22-year-old nursing student, likes hanging out with older people, and has

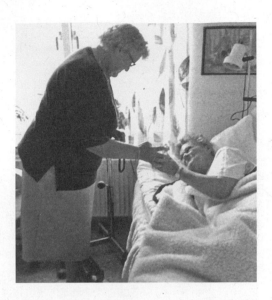

Visiting a neighbor in senior cohousing. People too often ask, "What if everyone gets sick at once?" They are used to seeing seniors in nursing homes. In any given neighborhood, in any given town, even in a conventional senior housing development, there might be one or two sick people — or none at all.

Living in community makes it easier for all levels of caregivers to do a better job — and at a lower cost. Nothing can be more economical than if a caregiver's clients live as part of some kind of community — as opposed to single houses spaced equidistant out across the landscape.

Co-Care Planning on the Fly

Nyland Cohousing (a mixed-generational cohousing community in Denver, CO) recently had a couple of its members diagnosed with cancer. The first sick person received total care from the community. But when others became ill, the community was overloaded. The group responded in a way that benefited both those who were sick and those who were healthy. They contacted a local assisted-living facility and obtained a list of real-world co-care tasks. They then went down the list and agreed to what they would do and what they wouldn't do. Once agreed, the group lived according to its new rules, thereby relieving each individual from being responsible beyond his or her comfort zone and level of competence. Professionals were called in accordingly, ensuring that each resident received equal care by the group and quality professional care, as needed.

a job in the nursing home down the street. He gets free accommodation in a senior cohousing community because he takes care of Mrs. Jenson for six hours each week. Soon, it turns out, Mrs. Olsen also needs help for four hours a week. Shortly after, Bjorn quits his job at the nursing home and is only taking care of people in the cohousing community — while finishing his nursing degree at the same time.

There is a plus here for everyone. Bjorn becomes part of the cohousing family, rather than being simply a caregiver living alone in an expensive apartment. He gets to know these people while they are still in good stead. He grows to care about them as individuals first and then, when they become more dependent on his care, he is more accountable to them as people, not just as clients. Moreover, when he is taking care of Mrs. Olsen he is actually accountable to the whole community, which means that the quality of his care dramatically improves. Just as important as anything else is that the residents hire and fire these long-term helpers themselves. In other words, they work for them — apparently all of them, even though Mrs. Olsen pays her particular share of her care. Nothing makes for better care than accountability. Glacier Circle in Davis California, the first senior cohousing community in the US, built a caregiver apartment above the common house thinking that within a couple of years they would need to hire a caregiver to live there (in the meantime, they'd rent it out). It turned out that they had to hire someone after just a few weeks.

A suite like the one that houses Bjorn can also be used for other purposes. Family members, for example, can stay in these common-house guest suites for weeks at a time, or longer if necessary. If Mrs. Jenson has a son, who himself has a wife and young child, the entire family can visit. Mrs. Jenson's son can then care for his own mother while his wife cares for their child, all without the entire extended family living under a single roof. And because the suites are in the common house, both Bjorn and the Jenson family will have use of a 3,500 sq. ft. facility and won't get in each other's way. On occasion, there is both a male and a female caregiver who move into the common house suites. One caregiver helps the women; the other helps the men.

Regardless of how any given group defines the co-care commitment, senior cohousing offers reasonable solutions to some of the most difficult problems associated with aging. This is where senior cohousing shines: it can present the highest of possibilities, rather than the lowest common denominator, expressing nothing less than society's full potential.

Cooperation Brings Down the Cost of Professional Care

Professional caregivers living within the community will be able to provide truly personal care to sick or disabled individuals, over and above that of a visiting caregiver or hospital staffer. All of this is much more affordable

> ## Other Topics Covered in Session 4: Co-Care and Outside Care
>
> Who says that your life will become completely consumed with concerns over bowel regularity and heart meds when you are 80, 85, or 90 years old? Some of the issues and question that the Study Group I Workbook looks at in this session are:
>
> 1. Why everyone in a community doesn't get old at the same time.
> 2. What are all of your care options? (Look for a resource guide for seniors in your town for in-home care or ways to supplement care if you live in cohousing.)
> 3. What are some of the options for co-care and outside care? What is co-care?
> 4. How would sharing a live-in caregiver work?
> 5. Describe the last time you got sick. Who helped you out?
> 6. Have you ever helped someone else out when they were ill?

than a traditional means of care ($4,000/mo for assisted care; $7,000/mo for in-home care). And the costs of *impersonal* personal care are staggering compared to *personal* personal care, if you can find it, or create it through something like cohousing.

Hearthstone Cohousing.

Session 5.
Co-Healing: Staying Emotionally Healthy through Community

Many studies have confirmed that there are three legs to long life other than genetics that you have control over:

Eating right (mostly light); staying active (mostly low impact); and staying connected (preferably to people who live nearby). The purpose of Session 5 is to establish the purpose and importance of staying connected and to figure out how you're going to easily accomplish this in the next 20 years.

Up until the beginning of the modern age, most people lived in small, generally self-sufficient communities. Today, however, it is much more difficult for people living by themselves to stay connected because community is based on the telephone, our date book, and our car if we are still driving. Without these things we are stuck. As one ages, having friends to share simple pleasures such as music, gardening, hiking, traveling, or just a cup of tea can mean everything in the world in shaping one's health. Looking at how isolated people become when forced to live out their

---

"The structure of our social networks, the support we receive from others, the quality and quantity of our social interactions, and our feelings of isolation and loneliness have all been identified as predictors of health and well-being."

— *American Psychologist*, Nov. 2004

"When asked what contributes most to living a long life, most seniors believe that having a supportive social network is the key to longevity."

— *Revisioning Retirement*, 2005

"Studying factors affecting healthy aging at age 70, I have found that a lack of bad habits (drinking, smoking, etc.) might be the most important factor, but social support is also important....Friends are always more fun than bad habits! Before and after age 50, cultivate the richest social network you possibly can. Your life will be better for it."

— George Vaillant, M.D.

The Small Town Effect

The impact a community can have on an individual is positive, powerful, and well documented. Here's what one senior cohousing resident had to say about her community:

"I wake up in the morning and look forward to a visit from at least one friendly neighbor. There's an element of surprise and interaction. Here, I feel a strong sense of belonging . . . of caring and being cared about."

The secret is simple. People thrive in a community that interacts and cares. The town of Rosetta, Pennsylvania has been the subject of numerous studies to discover why such a high percentage of its residents live to be well over 90 — an age significantly above the average. Surveys show the people here smoke at an average rate; they eat red meat and drink wine. It seems the number one reason for their longevity is the town's heightened sense of community. As one resident woman noted, "You have to get up in the morning — someone might come visit."

Other Topics Covered in Session 5: Co-Healing

Session 5 in the Study Group I Workshop continues with the process of planning for your future through discussions about the psychological well-being associated with staying connected.

1. How might your life be impacted by cohesion? Proximity to others? Companionship? Friendship?

2. What is the relationship between emotional connections and emotional well-being?

3. Exactly who is your community now? Where do they live? Exactly how often do you see them? How do you get there?

4. Why do elders tend to withdraw from others?

5. How did your mother and father age?

6. What would you like to do more of?

7. What do you wish you could do for your friends?

8. What is the menu of options for your future in terms of connection with others?

9. Have your relationships in the past helped you through times of loss? Painful situations? Regret? Times of celebration? Joy?

10. Have you considered the emotional differences between living alone, being in assisted living, and living in community?

11. When have you experienced community and thought it worked?

last days in an institutionalized system, it is no wonder that depression is the norm.

Healing is what happens when you talk about your issues with others. Co-healing is a term used to describe what happens when people get together to talk about the issues of the day and the issues in their lives — and not having to drive to someone else's house to see them is critical. In a cohousing setting, being in close contact with others will definitely help someone heal much faster than they would on their own. It just makes sense that co-healing is healthier, but this idea must be brought to the forefront in Session 5.

Dinner in the common house at Bellingham Cohousing.

Session 6.
The Economics of Getting Older

Living on a fixed income is a serious issue and an important topic for seniors. The threat that housing, medicine, and food costs will surpass fixed incomes is real and frightening. Aware that the incomes they once depended on are no longer available, seniors may become very protective of the fixed incomes they receive. In Session 6, participants step out of the box of familiarity to look at new, supporting ways to live gracefully and meaningfully within the boundaries of what they can afford.

Session 6 is about making a clear and honest accounting of expenses over the coming years in the context of different living scenarios. By the end of this session participants have a clear idea of the cost of living in their current situation, what it would be in other aging/housing scenarios, and how proximity and other factors can reduce spending and affect decisions in new ways. In other sessions, there was talk about denial — a factor that is also relevant in this session. Denial is evident when fear precipitates discussions, conclusions, and actions, and it can blind us to choices and options. To see this, take one of your bills and analyze it in comparison to different living arrangements. Look at what your potential for waste is in the various scenarios and then at what your potential for savings is. Unless you sit down and compare the costs, you're probably in denial about the real cost and the potential for escalating costs under the wrong scenario. Take the time to compare the costs and what you'll find is that this mundane exercise opens a lot of windows to the realities of the situation.

When Smaller Is Bigger

According to *E magazine*, the average house built in the US in the year 2000 was 2,300 sq. ft. By comparison, the average private house in senior cohousing is 1,100 sq. ft. However, the common house for a typical 20-unit cohousing community is about 4,000 sq. ft., including workshops and other outbuildings. This means, effectively, that the average cohousing unit is equivalent in size to a 5,100 sq. ft. house — big enough.

Katie McCamant with the Pleasant Hill resident group and their consented and extraordinary site plan.

The economics of aging are filled with trepidation and false economies. One woman at a workshop said that she couldn't order a copy of this book because she had so many expenses in her life, which she then proceeded to

Comparative Expenditures: Senior Cohousing vs. the World

Seniors often try to figure out how to make life more affordable. Shared facilities and proximity make senior cohousing one of the most economical options; comparative costs aren't even close. The following two examples show how much can be saved when buying into low-end or high-end cohousing. Then, the cost of senior cohousing versus assisted living is compared. The numbers are rough, and simply illustrate the differences among these three options.

Senior Cohousing vs. Single Family Housing: Very Low-Market

Consider the following, low-market 20-unit cohousing community:

- 1,100 sq. ft. private house x $125 per sq. ft. (sales price) = $137,500
- 4,500 sq. ft. common house x $100 per sq. ft. (additional construction cost) = $450,000
- $450,000 divided by 20 units = $22,500 for each unit's share of the common house
- $22,500 + $137,500 = a total cost of $160,000

By comparison, a 2,300 sq. ft. single-family house in a conventional subdivision selling for $100 per sq. ft. costs the purchaser $230,000. In senior cohousing, each individual household saves $70,000. It is important to remember that a 1,100 sq. ft. cohousing house comes with a 4,500 sq. ft. common house with gourmet kitchen, dining room, sitting room, guest rooms, etc.

Senior Cohousing vs. Single-Family Housing: Medium High-Market

Consider the following high-market 20-unit cohousing community:

- 1,100 sq. ft. private house x $300 per sq. ft. (sales price) = $330,000
- 4,500 sq. ft. common house x $100 per sq. ft. (additional construction cost) = $450,000
- $450,000 divided by 20 units = $22,500 for each unit's share of the common house
- $22,500 + $330,000 = a total cost of $352,500

This compares favorably to a high-end house in a conventional subdivision, in which a 2,300 sq. ft. house selling for $300 per sq. ft. costs the purchaser $690,000. Each individual household saves $337,500. This is just one way to look at it.

A mid-market scenario would, of course, be anywhere between the two scenarios above.

Senior Cohousing vs. Assisted Living

- The average cost per month for a mortgage and utilities in senior cohousing = $1,500
- plus $300 per month for food
- plus $400 per month for a visiting caregiver, once a week
- $1,500 + $300 + $400 = a total of $2,200 per month.

Compare this with the average cost for assisted living, which is about $4,000 per month (includes meals and light care).

Other Topics Covered in Session 6: Economics of Getting Older

Session 6 in the Study Group I Workshop helps people take a realistic view of life costs under various scenarios.

1. How will you finance your lifestyle after age 50?

2. Will you be living on a fixed income in your senior or retirement years?

3. How much of your expenses are paid by your children?

4. What might be your future expenses?

5. What would you like your lifestyle choices and options to be? Do you want to live in a city? On a ranch? In a village?

6. Neglect of care is an option — not a good one — that too many senior take simply because they don't have the support system to find the care they want. What are your possible care needs for the future?

7. What are the real costs associated with assisted care, retirement communities, and skilled nursing facilities?

8. What are your entertainment expenses? List every expense.

9. How much do you spend to travel to see friends? How much do you spend on hosting friends and family?

10. What are your food costs? How much do you spend on groceries? How much on eating out?

11. What are your energy costs?

12. What are your car costs?

13. What are all of your current expenses in terms of housing, phone, utilities, insurance, medical, and therapy?

14. What would it cost to renovate your house to make it mobility friendly?

15. How can costs be reduced or eliminated by living in community?

Nira, a resident in Nevada City Cohousing.

reel off. While listening, I couldn't help but think that most of her costs would be halved if she lived in cohousing and that she couldn't afford not to have this book. I ended up giving her a copy.

Session 7.
Mortality and Spirituality

Central to SG I is getting people out of denial (I'll be able and young forever); the most important aspect of Session 7 is coming to grips with mortality. Years ago, I spent 13 months interviewing people who live in multi-generational cohousing. In all those interviews, no one ever cried. By contrast, in two days of interviews with residents of senior cohousing, three people cried — all when discussing their experiences in working through the issues of mortality during their Study Group I. This discussion for them was both individual catharsis and recognition of common ground among their newfound friends in the study group.

Discussing philosophies, religion, and spirituality can be helpful in

Discussing Economics

Before discussing any specifics about the houses — how big, how many units, in what neighborhood — individual potential residents should work backward and figure out how much house they can afford (always keeping in mind the economies of scale that would come from being part of the cohousing community). After all, the size of each individual house or the location of the neighborhood is a function of how much the group can afford in combination with other financial goals. Each individual therefore should be extremely deliberate during this process and monitor his or her own ability to afford a house within a community. At this stage in Study Group I, individuals aren't asked to reveal details about their financial situations — many would feel uncomfortable being asked about their income and savings. As residents work through their personal finances within the group structure, a level of trust will likely develop within the group,

making specific economic issues easier to discuss when the time comes for the group to make decisions together.

To help the group members understand their own, individual abilities to afford a house, the group should contact outside financial experts such as mortgage brokers and financial advisors who specialize in the finances of senior citizens (including those on fixed incomes). As may have been done for the Session 3 discussion "The Realities of Getting Older," the group can invite professionals to speak at this session. Some people may also choose to include their own adult children in these discussions; such engaged third parties can be helpful in ensuring that everyone agrees that any negotiations between seniors and financial professionals are fair, honest, and open (the last thing a financial pro wants is to be accused of fraud or elder abuse).

addressing the issue of mortality, both for the individual and the community. Lots of people today are anxious to discuss spirituality, although traditional active-adult community marketers ardently avoid the topic. (Remember, these development firms are in business to construct units and sell property, not to build community.) But since community-building is the centerpiece of senior cohousing, discussions of this nature are not only entirely appropriate, if done right they can really bring people together. In some ways, they are essential to

Garden work in Strawberry Creek Cohousing.

Other Topics Covered in Session 7: Mortality and Spirituality

Elderhood is a time to discover inner richness for self-development and spiritual growth from a deep and meaningful point of view. This Study Group I Workshop offers questions and topics for philosophical and spiritual discussion.

1. What is your life's philosophy?
2. How do you implement your life's philosophy in your daily life?
3. How does your life's philosophy impact your life?
4. What are you passionate about?
5. Planning for aging in place includes planning for physical diminishment and death. What would you like your "exit strategy" to look like?
6. Elderhood can be a time to transition into a new phase of life and to prepare for dying.
7. Elderhood can also be a time to re-frame "senior years" to a time of "life completion."
8. Name three things that define you.
9. What gives your life meaning?
10. What do you value most?
11. What are your fears and strengths?
12. What have you learned about strength?

planning a successful project later. Some people would say that you have not had a successful Study Group I experience unless you have turned over this rock and examined it thoroughly. Appropriately, it is late in Study Group I because it is important that everyone in the group knows each other well when it comes to this topic. It's typical for people to tear up during these two hours.

Session 8.
Saging: What Do We Have To Offer the World?

"Elderhood is something that is earned. Anybody can grow old, but it is work to become an elder — one who embodies the experience and wisdom of their years."

— Senior cohousing resident.

The world needs to hear the wisdom of its elders. Cohousing provides a significant and supportive community environment in which seniors find opportunities to express and empower themselves. In a community, seniors are able to learn of opportunities from one another. They can remain socially engaged with their neighbors through simple and everyday activities, such as walking out their door, sitting on their porch, or sharing a cup of tea. This makes it much easier to be active and more engaged. This creates opportunities that help seniors to remain viable members of society — rather than become isolated and barely able to take care of themselves, struggling for their own life's maintenance.

A friend of mine, Chris Zimmerman, owns and operates a

couple of assisted-living facilities in Alameda, California. He inherited them at age 23. He's now 60 and has come to know a lot about seniors and elders. He makes a strong case that seniors today get very little respect, but he also adds vehemently that they have to earn the respect that they'd like to demand. He argues that seniors have abdicated respect because, while being an elder once meant earning respect by playing an active role in teaching others, today that doesn't happen. He argues that they can only earn elderhood by playing an active role in society.

When I was a kid in Downieville, California, you wouldn't imagine honking your car horn after dark (unless it was an emergency) without having an elder slam the hood of your car with an open palm and shout, "Hey, kid! We don't do that around here." No matter how long they'd known you. That's what elders do that garners so much respect: they enforce the mores and norms of society and the spoken and unspoken agreements. They enforce the social contract. Consequently, when I get together with the friends of my youth and talk about old Downieville days, we still talk about the elders of our youth. The same dozen names of elders come up over and over again — the people that we really respected. Sure, there were many more seniors than that dozen, but they were just

old people who didn't contribute; they were definitely not "elders." The promotion from seniorhood to elderhood must be earned.

Dr. Bill Thomas, a well-known geriatrician and social activist, suggests that the late- life tasks of elders are:

- Peace Making
- Wisdom Giving
- Legacy Creation

Bill's list points to the importance of the elder years not only for the "elder" but also for the wider community.

Seniors who live in proximity to caring peers (i.e., in cohousing) have the opportunity to continue to learn from each other and develop new interests. They also share in educating their peers about the values and responsibilities they promote as part of their legacy. They encourage each other to be "elders" and to give back to their families and the wider world the wisdom that they have acquired though their life experience. Seniors who live in community are able to affirm the importance of the "elder

New residents to Bellingham Cohousing after 2 years of planning and construction.

"Every life matters immensely; every well-lived and completed life helps in healing the world. Elderhood is a time to discover inner richness for self development and spiritual growth. It is also a time of transition and preparation for dying, which is at least as important as preparation for a career or a family."

— Rabbi Zalman Schachter-Shalomi

years" and empower each other to live meaningful and full lives. "My energy level is way up as a result of being with other people," said one resident.

This is all in contrast to the two prevalent media images of aging. The first depicts old age as being only about infirmity, decline, and inevitable isolation; the second promotes seniors who are "being footloose and fancy free." Neither of those images embraces the option that senior cohousing can offer: an elderhood spent exploring what life has to offer you and what you have to offer back.

Other Topics Covered in Session 8: Saging: What Do We Have To Offer the World?

Session 8 in Study Group I allows for time to recognize saging opportunities.

1. What do elders offer a town? A society? What is a sage?
2. What's the difference between a senior and an elder?
3. Where have you always wanted to contribute but couldn't?
4. What does living lighter on the planet mean to you?
5. How could support make it easier to be an elder?
6. How do others give you confidence and energy?
7. What has been important in your life?
8. What is your legacy? What do you hope leave behind?

Shared Home Option

One option that many people consider a "safe" one is purchasing a large house together with four or five friends. But even this is a risk. McCamant & Durrett Architects used to design a lot of shared homes for seniors. The situation does have some advantages. The home stays in the hands of seniors — so it's not being renovated as families move in and move out. A shared home is nowhere near as wasteful and is much more sustainable at every level. The risky part of this is that there are so few people. If you don't get along with someone, you still have to see him at breakfast.

Session 9.
Risk Taking

This session is all about risk. What is risk? What can I risk? Why risk anything? Just moving out of your house is a risk — you might ask, "How will I know if I will like it?" Remodeling your current house is a risk. I can give you countless examples of people who have spent five to ten thousand dollars to get ramps and grab bars put into their home only for that to turn out to be a band-aid; only to move out anyway three months later (and for the grab bars and ramps to be removed by the kids; only to waste money and the time that would have been better spent planning more comprehensive solutions. Moving in with the daughter is a risk. Moving to a small town is a risk. Even moving to assisted care is a risk. Staying where you are is a risk (albeit a little more like the proverbial water getting hotter and hotter under the proverbial frog).

Other Topics Covered in Session 9: Risk Taking

Study Group I is designed to help you become comfortable with making choices. Session 9 addresses the following areas regarding risk:

1. Define opportunities, and consider what risks are involved.

2. Consider how co-development and co-design for community involve risk — and mitigate risk.

3. Transform housing needs, wants, and desires into real options.

4. Look at what have you done in your life that was "out-of-the-box." What were the rewards?

5. Improve your skills in being open and communicative about risks and rewards.

6. The worst fear is fear of the unknowns. So — get rid of the unknowns.

7. When is not changing riskier than changing?

8. Replace the word "risk" with the words "expanding horizons."

The main purpose of Session 9 is to hear from everyone about risks they've taken in their personal and professional lives, and to hear about when risk served a purpose and when it didn't. Group participants also consider when it is a risk to do nothing at all. Then, when you look at alternatives in Session 10, you look at risks in terms of opportunities for growth and enrichment.

Session 10.
Fieldtrip: Looking at Cohousing Communities and Cohousing Designs, Assisted Care, Shared Houses, etc.

The cooperative life of senior cohousing offers residents a way to live independently longer and to have a

more practical, more convenient, more healthful, more interesting, and most importantly, a more vibrant life along the way. However, not all individuals are suited for the cohousing life. Other than moving into and living in a cohousing community, how does an individual find out if cohousing is

Passive cooling design precluded the need for air conditioning at Pleasant Hill Cohousing — even for seniors in this exceptionally hot climate.

Other Topics Covered in Session 10: Field Trips

There is a real benefit to seeing what types of communities others have chosen. Session 10 focuses on seeing such living dynamics in order to:

1. Get a real-life feel and preliminary understanding of life in a cohousing community.
2. Dissolve preconceived ideas and disillusionments about cohousing.
3. Create ideas and acknowledge preferences by seeing actual facilities, structures, gardens, and accommodations.
4. Witness interactions among those living in community.

Planning a new Senior Cohousing project.

right for him or her? In this part of the workshop, participants explore the issues of aging in place and refine their definition of what aging successfully means to them, especially in the context of the physical options.

During Session 10, participants will:

+ Meet people from established elder cohousing communities.
+ Meet older residents from inter-generational cohousing.
+ Participate in role-playing exercises designed to address specific living situations.
+ Learn about conflict resolution and effective communication.
+ Visit an assisted-living complex. (Although many will have already visited such places, when a group visits together, the experience is extremely focused, and even sobering.)
+ Explore all of the options.

Final Meetings

A visit to an existing cohousing community provides a perfect segue into Study Group II, where the physical community itself will be designed from the ground up.

CHAPTER 8

Study Group II:
The Participatory Design Process

Once the resident group is committed to a site for their community, they are ready to translate their theoretical plans into a concrete reality by working through Study Group II. Cohousing design begins with a participatory process that will sustain community long after the honeymoon has worn off, and it ends with blueprints for the physical community that embody a neighborly approach to living, while protecting individual privacy. The architect puts it all together and does the actual drawings, balancing the desires and needs of the group, the characteristics of the site, building codes and the project's budget to create a complete plan for the community, but the group makes the key decisions. By the end of Study Group II, the architectural design will be finalized. This start-to-finish design phase typically takes about four or five months.

> When done right, the group design process does not delay a project. In fact, it makes it go much faster, and it works socially. If it doesn't work socially, why bother?

A cohousing community's built environment either promotes or discourages interaction among residents, resulting in either a lively or lifeless place. After visiting and gathering a plethora of data on 285 cohousing communities, we found that the design can have as much as a 20-fold impact on the social viability and vitality of

Efficiency Means Progress

The biggest threat to the viability of cohousing is an ill-planned and inefficient design process. A disorganized design process threatens a cohousing project because it puts developers and other professionals in the position of wanting to do the job without input from the resident group, mostly because they think that they can be more effective. And without the resident group's input and ownership, the very foundations of the community are compromised.

Participatory site design. Nevada City Cohousing resident group in action.

the group after the first year of residency. Twenty-fold is at the extreme, but five-fold is well within the bell curve for impact due to design alone. That is, if designed poorly, people will talk together, be together, play together five times less than if it is designed well (though they may meet together more often trying to solve the problems that the environment has created and solving management issues inadvertently created by ill-conceived design). The environment very much has that effect on behavior. Future residents wanting to cut corners on architectural costs question the importance of design in the development process because the community may already feel strong and there is often intense excitement for the project in that period. It's not obvious that design is something that they have to take seriously. There is often the feeling that, somehow, community will take care of itself, but nothing is further from the truth.

Design Matters

People do not generally think about the impact of design on community life. Designed to ensure individual privacy, conventional senior-specific condominium and single-family housing developments rarely incorporate design factors that encourage neighbors to meet — much less to interact — in an organic way that builds and successfully sustains meaningful relationships. As a result, residents of many senior "communities" barely know one another, despite their close proximity. Sure, small gardens and comfortable, shared outdoor sitting areas make it easier for people to meet and talk, but the mere presence of these features does not mean residents will actually interact. Amenities alone are not community. To use those benches, you have to already know each other. You have to have an excuse to talk to each other, which will lead to asking: "What are you doing this weekend?"

The participatory development and design process is the best avenue I've ever seen for forging relationships among the residents in senior cohousing. Community is created prior to construction, and the environment that cohousers create together maintains these ties. The participatory development process gives residents a rock-solid foundation for daily interaction, and the pathway seating they share gives them the perch from which to survey the health and well-being of their community. A bench in a retirement project of a thousand units can easily see fewer butt-hours than a bench in a senior cohousing community of 20 units.

A Well-Trod Path

Resident participation in the development process is cohousing's greatest asset and its most limiting factor. It can be a huge task for a group of people to take on a project of this scale and complexity, especially because most people have little experience in collective decision making and little knowledge regarding housing development. A group can easily encounter problems with maintaining an efficient timeline, avoiding the domination of a few strong personalities, integrating new members without backtracking, and more. Fortunately, in addressing these issues today, we can benefit from decades of senior cohousing experience in Denmark.

The participatory design process has played an integral part in the evolution of cohousing. As cohousing became more clearly defined, the participatory process itself became more clearly defined. In senior cohousing,

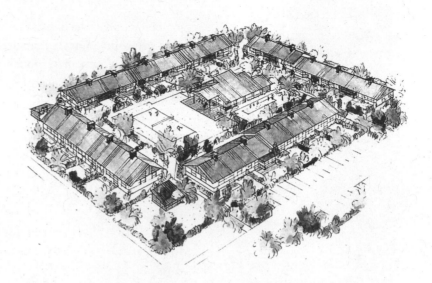

Ledøje-Smørum Senior Cohousing.

the group process and the design process are more coordinated than in the development of non-senior cohousing. As such, the greatest challenge in senior cohousing is to get enough input to get the design right and "owned" by the residents, but not so much input as to delay the process, thus making it too expensive and burning out the prospective residents and professionals involved in the project.

Building a viable community of this scale is a huge undertaking, to be sure. But when a resident group follows the well-worn path blazed by their Danish predecessors and commits to taking small, deliberate, well-planned, and incremental steps, what can otherwise be an overwhelming project instead becomes a very manageable and immensely rewarding experience.

Study Group II

The first step is creating the design program, which is broken into three parts: the site program, the common house program, and the private house program, and then there are three shorter follow-up workshops.

The process for developing these programs includes the following steps:

+ Site program and schematic site plan workshop.
+ Common house program and schematic common house plan workshop.
+ Private house program and schematic unit plans workshop.
+ Design closure workshop.
+ Submission to the city for preliminary approval.
+ Priority workshop.
+ Design development workshop.

Design Program

The enduring community is created through a collaborative and deliberate process that identifies and translates a group's visions and needs into design criteria. Design criteria are detailed requirements that provide the basis for the architectural design. The process is called programming. The

Site plan generated from participatory design for Nevada City Cohousing.

Community and Privacy

If I seem to focus more on encouraging the social side of senior cohousing versus the protection of privacy, it is because American architects and developers are conditioned to put privacy above all other social concerns. Groups that create a senior cohousing community must, in effect, break the old habits of all involved to give community as much consideration as privacy.

It's worth noting that the hundreds of cohousing residents we've interviewed almost never complained about the lack of privacy in their community, yet many readily pointed out design features that discouraged sociability.

Community design should encourage social interaction and at the same time allow residents to choose whether to be with others or to be alone. When you walk into cohousing, you should always feel that you have the choice between as much privacy as you want and as much community as you want. In typical suburban neighborhoods you feel as if you have the choice of as much privacy as you want — and little opportunity for community. One of the reasons cohousing works in America is because Americans like real choice.

building program outlines the goals, activities, spaces, and characteristics desired by a resident group, and thus clarifies the criteria on which design alternatives will be evaluated. An architect can facilitate a group's discussions by laying out the range of possibilities, outlining important considerations, and providing inspiration and resource materials. Field trips and analysis of favorite places can help to broaden the group's understanding of design alternatives.

Building on earlier decisions about goals and priorities, participants identify exactly what activities the outdoor areas, the common facilities, and the private dwelling should accommodate. What are the eating, kitchen, and entertainment needs of the common house? Of the private

dwellings? Are some households adamant about having their own washing machine? Is a workspace needed in some dwellings? The program requirements range from "warm and

Intimate spaces between buildings that contribute a warm atmosphere.

giving environments" to "outside dining for 40 people" to "two sinks in the kitchen, one 7" deep and one 9" deep."

Creating a Design Program

To assure the success of the social aspects of the community, and to best assure a deliberate and cost-effective design process, the group must create a cohesive design program (criteria) that defines the group's goals, priorities, activities, and design requirements for the project. A quality design program ensures that the actual design and construction phases of the project will be efficiently executed. Efficiency in this case means that everyone involved, from the group to the architect to the builders, will spend less time and money to complete each task. In addition, a cohesive design program, just as much as the community's social agreements, greatly helps to recruit and integrate new members into an existing group.

The actual creation of the design program should be considered a learning period for all participants, including the architect. Later on, the design program is the tool used to evaluate, and decide upon the actual design. In other words, residents can refer to the design program to answer the question, "Did the consultants actually design what we wanted them to design?"

Finally, having all of the design criteria in a single, cohesive document allows members of the resident group to relax; they won't need to tell the

---

Fill in the Blank

Questionnaires are useless: real information only comes from personal facilitation. To illustrate the point, in 2005 I attended a seminar on the housing preferences of seniors aged 55 to 75 in Orlando, Florida. One question in a survey carried out by staff and students of Harvard University asked senior respondents if they preferred a bedroom on the first floor. Fifty percent said "yes." An interesting result, because approximately 97 percent of the units built for seniors in this country last year have a bedroom on the ground floor. In other words, when it comes to actually buying a home, it seems the vast majority of American seniors want a bedroom on the ground floor. I should mention that every one of the 40 line items in this Harvard survey produced drastically different data than what we found when working with seniors in focus groups or other interactive settings. Surveys look in the rearview mirror. A facilitated process looks ahead. In another survey, I asked a couple individually, "How often do you eat in the common house?" She said, "Twice a week," he said, "Four times." After discussing it with them, they concluded, "About three times a week." After looking at the records, it turned out to be 3.25 times per week. The facilitated discussion always got me closer to the real deal.

consultants the same thing over and over again throughout the process or wonder if the design has strayed from their original intentions. Instead, they can just say, "Now, what does it say in the program?" Moreover, a solid design program prevents wasteful backtracking — new members to the group (joining after the design program is finished) will be able to see how thorough the group has been and won't be tempted to backtrack. For instance, when Larry, the new participant, asks, "Did you consider how big the front porches should be?" Sandra, who was there when the issue was discussed, can reply, "Yes, let's look at the program to see what decision was made." A membership committee should be charged with the very important task of carefully walking new members through the decisions that already have been agreed to. It's not enough just to hand them the program. It's best to take them out for coffee and walk them through each line item — that time spent really helps them to feel connected and welcome.

Goals and Priorities

In preparing the design program, the group will clarify and expand upon their agreed-upon goals and priorities to answer questions such as: Which shared facilities are most necessary, and which are less important? In order to keep costs down, which amenities can we do without? The development program requires trade-offs — few people can afford everything on their wish list. Groups can actually make such decisions efficiently and accurately in well-facilitated and organized weekend efforts.

There is always the temptation to increase unit size just a few square

Maximizing Potential

Organized and executed efficiently, a deliberate process gives the group the confidence to:

- Share their knowledge in a complementary fashion.
- Make firm personal commitments regarding recruitment, payment of initial fees, etc.
- Lobby the municipality to get the project approved, if necessary.

- Help keep costs down with careful planning.
- Maintain a non-institutional feel to the project.
- Push the percentage of common areas up and the sizes of individual houses down. This ensures that the project stays affordable and that the community operates at its fullest potential.

feet, to add just one more amenity. Cost control forces value to the forefront (especially in terms of quality and quantity). "Feature creep" has to be managed either by increasing the budget or by using low-end building materials and cut-rate services. The adage "you get what you pay for" applies here; in practice, construction materials and below-market labor will only increase headaches and reduce usability.

Rather than incur excessive debt or suffer through inferior materials and services, it's better for a group to keep unit sizes from creeping up, to keep amenities and construction costs within their original parameters of quality, and to establish clear development priorities and stay true to them.

Order of Design

The architectural design starts with the design of the overall site, determining where to place buildings, identifying areas to keep open, locating the common house, orienting the buildings. We address the site plan first because its configuration relates to key questions about feasibility and design, and it will be required for the city planning approval process. The site plan will show the location of the potential common amenities, the number and type of houses, the number of parking places, and so forth, and costs can be explored.

Once the site is laid out, we proceed to the specifics for the design of the common house. It is extremely helpful to have the common house design precede the design of the individual private houses because once group members understand the amenities featured in the common house, they will be able to see how the common house will supplement and become an extension of the private houses. People are much more comfortable with smaller private

Creating a hierarchy of spaces from the most private part of the dwelling to the most common, allows residents to choose how private or public they want to be at any given time, and makes transition between spaces more relaxed.

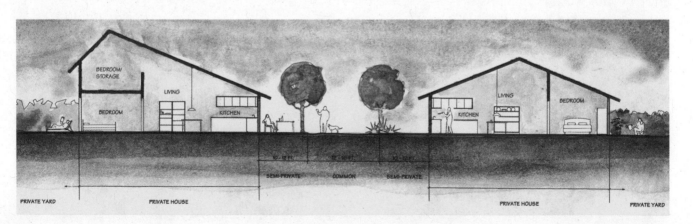

houses once they see that the common house will contain guest rooms or suites, laundry facilities, entertainment rooms, a sewing room, and other amenities, as well as a gourmet kitchen and large dining/living space that will accommodate a twice-a-year party or family gathering as well as community dinners several times a week. Once the common house is designed, the private house discussions typically go quite smoothly and rapidly.

In most cases, residents understandably want to be involved in the initial design of their project. Architects use various participatory methods specific to cohousing to help promote resident involvement, in particular, highly facilitated discussions and a plethora of images illustrating the various options for accomplishing their goals — goals such as community, living

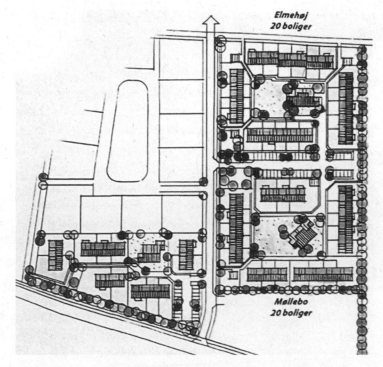

Two contiguous senior cohousing projects of 20 houses each and another of 16 houses. The project is big to keep the costs down, but broken into smaller projects to keep the social relationships optimal.

Distance between the Houses

In order to establish the "right" distance between the houses of a given cohousing community, we ask the group to form two lines and for two people to face each other 110 feet apart from each other (a common distance across a street between front doors of suburban houses). We have the group pretend it's Monday morning and that they are leaving their houses at the same time as their across-the-street-neighbor. As well, we ask everyone to pretend that they care about their neighbor across the street, imagining that the neighbor's daughter is sick and they want to see the neighbor's mood and perhaps ask how he or she is doing. Then everyone in each line walks toward their neighbor in the opposite line until one of them grows uncomfortable. When one person in the pair stops, the other stops. In a recent project, the end distances between "neighbors" ranged between 26 and 40 feet; and those were the distances between the front doors that we designed for their community. I live there, and I usually can tell the mood of my neighbor and whether I should stop by or just say "howdy."

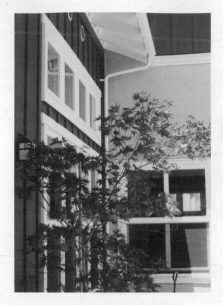

FrogSong Cohousing community house entrance.

lighter on the planet, affordability, and privacy.

Working Relationships

A good architect will educate the group about the social, ecological, and cost consequences of various design decisions. The residents, new to the collective decision-making process, must trust the professionals to be frank, honest, and open during each phase — and as interested and dedicated in creating a quality cohousing development as the residents themselves. The architect earns this trust through demonstrating his or her competency in facilitating the development process itself. The architect obviously must be fair and efficient and must possess a good understanding of the cohousing concept itself.

Experience also teaches that the success of a senior cohousing project does not solely depend on the quality of the relationship between the resident group and the distinct design professionals — the residents themselves must have developed an effective working relationship among themselves. If not, any design professional will have more difficulty working with the group.

Once trust is established — within the resident group, between the residents and professionals, and among the various professionals themselves — it is maintained only when all parties

learn when and how to challenge each other, always seeking the highest common denominator.

The architect must sometimes challenge a group's decisions or priorities, because only through this dialogue will a resident group clarify its objectives and priorities. When it comes to real people's lives, only honest, face-to-face discussions and challenges will produce a design that everyone will actually want to live with.

The most effective participatory design processes recognize both the value of resident input and where it should be limited. How much influence residents want over the design, and where they should step back, is the art of the process. The group should, of course, be involved in the establishment of design criteria. Many past participants, however, recommend leaving most technical and aesthetic decisions to the architect, since it is almost impossible for most groups to agree among themselves on these more subjective issues, and the architect must be kept solely on the hook for the technical solutions.

Looking at Accessibility Options

There are many special design considerations that separate senior cohousing from regular cohousing, and also from other types of senior living. Senior cohousing is different from other types of senior housing in that prospective residents directly discuss the issues of accessibility and mobility and how to incorporate solutions to these needs in the design — decisions that ultimately affect their quality of life. Some of the most important means of sustaining individual health are visitors, social interaction, a sense of identity, and a sense of belonging. In other words, community. Making sure that residents can visit each other's homes may be the second priority after a fully accessible common house.

Before such discussions happen, group members generally visit other senior housing projects to see how the "experts" have responded to these issues. What seniors say in response to these visits often boils down to the notion, "I want my cohousing community to be at least adaptable without looking or feeling accessible or institutional." This sensibility is important, and is something that American architects often overlook (unless prodded by the actual residents). It is another reason why a senior cohousing group must be proactive in creating their design. The group also must establish how accessibility features fit in with their budget priorities. Senior cohousing communities in Denmark typically first decide the price they can afford and what their accessibility goals are, leaving it to the architects to optimize the solution, with accessibility features that foster a sense of community and encourage independence. (See Appendix D: Universal Design.)

Building Upon a Strong Foundation

Study Group II should prove to be an exciting experience where friendships are formed, tested, and made stronger. The group, building upon the foundations of the group process that were laid in Study Group I, together will design the landscape, common facility, and home designs that will house and nurture the community. The process should be fun and rewarding.

Site Design

There is a distinct sense of neighborhood that all senior cohousing communities share — it is the payoff for the time spent putting it together. Outsiders quickly recognize and appreciate each cohousing development as a community with the strong neighborly bond that's usually missing from a typical seniors-only development.

A large window provides good light for the kitchen counter but more importantly facilitates ongoing social contact.

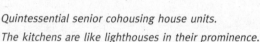

Quintessential senior cohousing house units.
The kitchens are like lighthouses in their prominence.

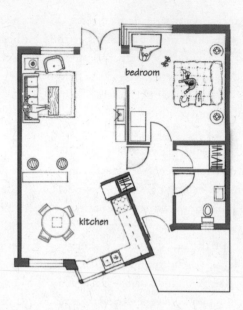

To keep affordable, many seniors planning cohousing projects have chosen small units.

This is no accident. A senior cohousing development requires a special set of design considerations that, in turn, support this special kind of neighborly community.

The Site Program Defined

At McCamant & Durrett Architects, we dedicate four days with the group to come up with a schematic site design. We:

+ Establish a common language (using slides of completed projects to educate and inspire). This helps the group to visualize their concepts and to broaden and communicate their ideas.

+ Agree on goals for the site plan (e.g. community friendly, easy to know your neighbor, living lightly on the land, good solar orientation).

+ Brainstorm, discuss, and decide on the activities between the houses that facilitate community and individual goals (sitting and talking, gardening, washing the car, playing games, hanging out the clothes, drinking a pot of tea, laughing, etc.).

+ Establish which activities require their own place (e.g. parking lot, gathering nodes, common terrace, clothesline, swimming pool, bocce ball court, common garden, private front porch, private front yard, or private backyard).

- Establish where activities occur that don't need their own place (e.g. car washing at the car park, basketball court at the overflow car park).

- Create clear design criteria for each place (e.g. for the garden: fruit trees and raised beds, a watering feature, compost, greenhouse, tool shed, south facing, gathering place, picnic table). More specific decisions are usually established later by a committee; the type and quantities of fruit trees, for example, would be a gardening committee decision.

- Establish the character of each space, where each space is located in relation to other places, and the details of each place.

- Establish optimal distances between houses (front door to front door).

- Use wooden blocks to represent houses on a scaled survey of the site to locate houses, parking, garden, picnic area, bocce ball, etc., based on the above criteria. This is often done in two different groups in order to explore different alternatives.

- Evaluate the block designs until they merge into a solution that fulfills the program requirements and therefore represents a first pass at a viable schematic design. Presuming that the education process along the way is smooth and thorough, this phase is both a fun and valuable basis for community building, and also leads to the best and most thoughtful plan.

We've used this method for every cohousing project we've built since our first project in Davis, California, in 1990, and it really works.

Number of Households

The size of a senior cohousing development is generally discussed in terms of number of one or two person households (there consistently seem

Preliminary schematic design sketch for Munksøgård senior cohousing by Martin Rubow.

The central path in elder cohousing is where people meet; where life between the buildings eminates. This is why the parking is at the periphery and the common house is on the way to parking.

"The relationships are what make it all work and all worthwhile" — a common quote from cohousing residents. Having the car next to, or even worse, in my house, short circuits the community.

pedestrian lane; or, as in some older cities, it might be focused on a plaza-like courtyard. A resident living in the Munksøgård senior cohousing community explains:

> What I like most about the design of this place is that when I walk out of my front door someone will say, "Hello Anna. Come for a stroll with me." It's easy to bump into people and usually that's enough for me. Usually I like the casual contacts more than I like the formal activities, except common dinners. I love common dinners.

Circulation to the individual houses from the parking areas and the main pedestrian entrances into the development should be centralized along a limited number of paths in order to increase the chances for neighbors to pass one another and to help maintain privacy on the back sides of the houses. Site plans with the clarity of a central street or courtyard work particularly well at promoting such encounters. When houses are scattered around the site, connected by a multitude of small pathways, no single route gets used enough to ensure that people will actually meet other people. With centralized circulation, life unfolds between the houses.

to be about 1.3 people per household). Senior cohousing, dealing with a smaller number of units than found in mixed-generational cohousing developments, usually features 15 to 30 households. A community of 24 or 25 is widely considered the best size in Denmark, small enough that everyone is heard, large enough for everyone to have three or four good friends. (See Chapter 6 for more on number of households per project and its impact on community.)

Circulation

Pedestrian circulation can serve as an organizing element for the layout of buildings. Like the main street in a small town, circulation can be organized along a spine, as with a

Nevada City Cohousing.

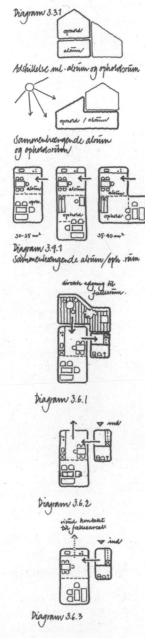

The Site Plan

Mixed-generational cohousing and senior cohousing have been built in many forms — attached row houses, dwellings clustered around courtyards, rehabilitated factories and schools, and even high-rises.

The majority of cohousing takes the form of one-, two-, and three-story attached houses, often referred to as clustered or medium density, low-rise housing. This building type has many advantages over both detached single-family houses and high-rise apartments. It uses land, energy, and materials more economically than detached houses and the relatively high density of clustered housing supports more efficient forms of public transit. In rural and semi-rural areas, clustered housing can help preserve open space, an increasingly sensitive issue in high-growth areas where demand for housing often conflicts with agricultural needs. This practice can be beneficial in general and is particularly compatible with cohousing.

While high-rise apartments use less land, living four or more stories above the ground creates feelings of anonymity in many people as well as detachment from the outdoors. Everyone in a well-designed community benefits from easy access to outdoor spaces that, in turn, accommodate people with differing abilities. All residents are therefore able to take part in outdoor activities such as gardening, or simply sitting around and chatting. To sustain healthy lives, the design of outdoor accessibility is just as important as indoor accessibility design.

Diagrams illustrating spatial relationships within the dwellings in a cohousing community.

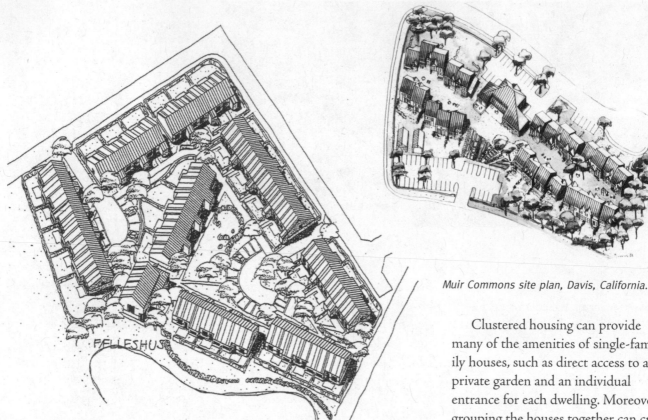

FÆLLESHUS

A senior cohousing community site plan.

Muir Commons site plan, Davis, California.

Close Proximity Fosters Community

Americans always look at a cohousing site plan and say, "Wow, that feels like a village." In practice, they do operate as a village, and a visit to any well-designed cohousing community will prove this out. In the case of senior cohousing, the seniors themselves often argue most forcefully for a tight village-like street or courtyard design. An intelligently crafted site design creates proximities that foster community for many years to come.

Clustered housing can provide many of the amenities of single-family houses, such as direct access to a private garden and an individual entrance for each dwelling. Moreover, grouping the houses together can create larger, more usable open spaces for such things as community gardens and sitting areas. Modern building techniques can prevent sound transmission between shared walls, a concern people often mention in regard to attached dwellings in the planning phase. The ability to provide both privacy and community is what makes clustered housing such a popular solution.

In cohousing, the treatment of spaces between buildings contributes to the quality of life as much as the buildings themselves. These outdoor spaces can be used for sitting, pedestrian travel, spontaneous encounters, gardening, and socializing. The site plan, because it defines how the site is used (where buildings sit, how they relate to each other), largely determines how well these activities are accommodated.

Some site plans are formal in their organization, while in others the dwellings are situated very informally. With sensitive handling of the relationships among all spaces, either arrangement can work equally well. Which approach the group chooses usually depends on their goals, the site itself, and the surrounding context.

A Living Place without Cars

Car access and parking have a major impact on every site plan and are often the first aspects considered in an architectural design. Almost without exception, cohousing developments are pedestrian-oriented, with the parking relegated to the periphery of the site. Car-free pedestrian lanes and courts are essential to creating places where everyone can move about relaxed and worry-free. Clustering the parking also frees up the orientation of the houses, allowing them to optimally relate to people, the sun, and the terrain.

Residents or their caregivers may want to drive to an individual house

to deliver groceries, drop someone off, or move furniture, but cars should not be parked just outside the front door all of the time. One resident exclaimed while gesturing down the pedestrian lane, "There is no reason for automobiles to occupy the most valuable areas of our site and separate us from our neighbors, and lots of good reasons why they should not."

People who live in cohousing communities have clearly stated that they would rather have a short walk in snow or rain than compromise their immediate living environment with cars. Given the often harsh winters of the American West, Midwest, and East Coast (and Northern Europe), this is no small choice.

The primary reasons residents give for preferring a car-free site are community, safety, and ecological considerations. However, the personal

"When cars don't dominate the space between the houses then there is a life between the buildings," said one cohousing resident. "The cars live in the parking lot, they won't get lonely out there, and we live here in between, as well as in the houses." When cars are elsewhere, the outdoor "room" works.

encounters that occur while going to and from the parking area serve important social functions. When people meet in the parking lot going to and from errands, they can plan outings and maintain friendships through casual chats on the way home. "Hey, I'm headed to the store, do you need anything?" is a common refrain. Along those lines, the common house ideally should be placed between the parking area and the houses so residents need to walk by the common house to and from their car and their own home. It's all about community on a human scale

"But wait!" outsiders stammer. "Shouldn't older folks live close to where their car is parked because of mobility issues?" My response: "Seniors will not include any feature that they themselves don't feel is important. It's their community; it's their choice. I'm always amazed by how many seniors who live in cohousing are so clear about parking. One resident echoed many voices when she said, "In the end, what matters is my relationship with my neighbors, not my relationship with my car." And she knew that if she put her auto anywhere near her house, her relationships with her neighbors would recede precipitously. I live 700 ft. from my parking place; this may sound like an inconvenience, but the real amenity is seeing, on a daily basis, the faces and the smiles of neighbors that I care about, running into them and staying connected over the years.

Whether a group chooses to place their parking area in a single central

FrogSong Cohousing grand opening.

Considerations for General Site Design

- Number of units.
- Site amenities to preserve (views, trees, etc.).
- Location of common facilities, residential buildings, open space.
- Building type and form (two stories, clusters, detached, etc.).
- Building materials (general).
- Energy considerations (electric, gas, solar, wind, conservation, etc.).
- Accessibility considerations.

Outdoor Areas:
- Parking (location, how much covered/uncovered).
- Car access on site (traffic-free, access to houses when necessary).
- Open space.
- Shared amenities (sitting areas, gardens, etc.).
- Transition between private residences and common areas.
- Private outdoor functions (sitting areas, gardens, etc.).
- Fences, hedges, plantings.
- Personalization.

Good Design Can Make Small Sites Work

About 15 years ago, working on a cohousing project in Sacramento, California, Susan, one of the group members, called me up and said, "Chuck, it looks like we're not going to go for that 1.25 acre site. We think 25 units on a site that small won't work." Most of the future residents were moving from modest, but single-family homes and were not used to quality clustered housing. I asked, "Wait before you finalize your decision. Please bring the entire group to Berkeley, and I'll show you how density can work comfortably."

I knew that at that time there was almost no quality multi-family clustered housing in Sacramento, at least nothing that anyone who could afford to buy, or even rent, a detached house would want. They were sure that clustered housing that dense would look cheap, that you'd be able to hear your neighbors breathing next door, and that it would degrade their self-image.

Two weeks later, most of the group made the 70-minute trip to Berkeley in several cars. In the morning we visited some poorly designed clustered housing developments. I noticed (and later pointed out to them) how they would walk up to windows, brim their eyes and peer in. They stepped onto people's front stoops, basically feeling they had free reign. These were good, upstanding citizens who would never intentionally disrespect someone.

During the afternoon, we visited four well-designed clustered housing developments, but this time I noticed how, from the very first step onto each property, the group appeared to stop and think, "Oh, someone lives here, I have to be on my best behavior." The difference between the housing developments we visited during the morning and those we visited during the afternoon was in the transitions and other architectural signals that proclaimed, "Somebody lives here, is taking care of this place, is accountable for it, and you should feel accountable for your behavior too."

We headed back to our studio and dissected the differences between good and bad design. Since they hadn't previously seen good multi-family housing design, they hadn't realized how positive that density can be. Several days later they made an offer on the property, which was ultimately accepted. Two years later they moved into a wonderful cohousing community.

location or several depends on the site, the community size, and the preferences of the residents. Usually one or two centrally located lots are adequate. Using pervious, structurally supported lawn or gravel surfaces and including trees in the design can make parking areas attractive. Wouldn't the social life of any neighborhood be enhanced if cars were parked at the end of the street? Pooling the parking keeps the unecological and unfortunate impacts of asphalt to a dead minimum.

The amount of parking per resident depends on many factors beyond the residents' ability or inability to drive — the site's size and location and the availability of public

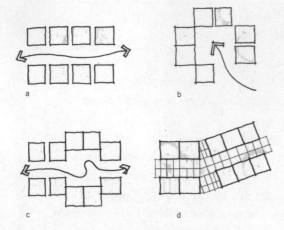

Different types of site plans: a: pedestrian street;
b: courtyard; c: combination of street and courtyard;
d: one building (glass-covered street).

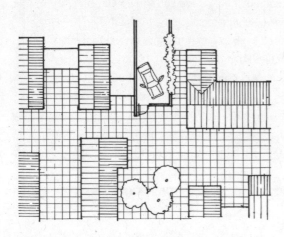

Automobiles are as much a part of our
culture as they are a practical necessity.
A community car wash area has both
practical and social benefits.

transit are also key determinants. Cohousing reduces the need for separate cars by promoting the possibility of sharing. A couple who needs a second car can easily arrange to share one with another household. Cohousing projects sometimes have a shared van and recent projects are looking at shared electric cars and other options. American condominium planning codes typically require parking for more than one car per dwelling, but officials usually allow a parking reduction if an actual car count for future residents can be provided and/or if residents show how parking can be expanded at a later date, if needed. In fact, senior cohousing developments often average fewer than one car per dwelling.

It is absolutely clear that placing cars close to the houses short-circuits sustained relationships. People-hours at the common house and people-contact between the buildings drop many-fold when parking areas are placed adjacent to the houses. As a

direct result, community, physical, and emotional health deteriorate. Special circumstances, however, can be accommodated. Inevitably, just by virtue of how a site plan works out, some parking spaces end up relatively close to residences. These residences are usually chosen by folks who have mobility concerns.

Location of the Common House

The location of the common house greatly affects the frequency of its use. For the common house to be an integral part of community life, residents must pass it in the course of their daily activities. The three most important (and sometimes conflicting) requirements for the location of the common house are:

1. Residents pass the common house on their way home from their car or the bus stop.
2. The common house is visible from each house, or from just outside of it.
3. The common house is roughly equidistant from all dwellings.

The first of these considerations is the most important. Passing the common house on their way home, residents can see if anything is going on. You stop in to check for Hannah — you've been wanting to chat with her, see what's for dinner, or look at the

The common house focuses on the common terrace which really is the focus for the entire community.

Nevada City Cohousing common house side view.

bulletin board. Because the common house is along the path home, visiting it becomes part of your daily routine.

Likewise, if residents can see the common house and the terrace from their own homes, they are more likely to join in when there is an activity there. Finally, no dwelling should be so far from the common house as to make someone feel isolated. Naturally, some residents will prefer to be farther from the central action than others.

Transitional Spaces

The transitions between the private, common, and public realms affect residents' ease in moving from one to the other, and they also define the relationship between the community and the surrounding neighborhood. There should be a hierarchy of spaces, from the sanctity of the private bedroom to the openness of the common plaza. Each transition — from the private dwelling, to the community plaza, to the public realm — helps support community life and the relationships among people. If these transitional spaces are not well organized and perfectly designed, there will be missing links and fewer opportunities to continue the relationships that keep a

This gathering node in Strawberry Creek Cohousing supports spontaneous social atmosphere and community life.

The easier it is to step outside, the more outdoor space will be used. Corridors, extra doors, and level changes should be avoided.

group of houses a community. The omission of any of them makes the appropriate use of spaces ambiguous, inhibiting people's activities. These links and thresholds should be indicated physically, although the demarcation can be as subtle as a change in ground cover.

In cohousing, there is less need for territorial definitions, and the relationships between private homes and community areas can be more relaxed (but still clear) than in other housing types. A resident's front door faces a common area shared by friends, rather than a public street crammed with cars. This traditional community space can support the spontaneous social atmosphere and community life that residents value. Generally, the kitchen/dining area is the room most people "live" in, and the area of the house that people don't mind being seen in. A door and window connecting the private kitchen to the common area allows a resident to call out to a passing neighbor. Locating this room at the front of the house increases opportunities to observe the common area from inside while tending to domestic activities. Visual access to the common areas, whether indoors or outdoors, allows people to see activities they may want to join. As one resident said, "I can't decide to join the neighbors sharing a pot of tea if I don't know they're there." Casual surveillance is also a highly effective form of building security, with neighbors "watching out for each other" and taking notice of strangers.

Direct access between the dwellings and a semi-private garden patio increase the use of outdoor space. When it is easy to just "pop out," people flow between indoors and outdoors many times during the day. This threshold to common areas is a particularly important element of cohousing. In order to make it as easy

The Backyard Shed

The two most unfortunate mistakes in designing transition areas are: providing only a hard edge between the individual residences and the community realm, and placing storage buildings in front of dwellings. We have seen that a soft transition between the private interior and the common areas encourages informal movement from one to the other, with more time spent outside. Storage sheds are often used for extra household wares, since cohousing dwellings often lack garages. When these sheds are placed in front of the house, they block views of passers-by or activities in the common areas. They impede the "conversation" between houses, just as holding your hand in front of your face would impede a conversation with another person. Once built, it is difficult and expensive to correct such mistakes. Storage sheds are usually better placed out back. Like fences, residents can build them after moving in, when they have an understanding of how the areas between buildings are actually used. Basement storage areas eliminate this problem altogether, but they are not always economically feasible.

as possible to pass from indoors to outdoors, the design should avoid corridors, extra doors, and level changes. If a vestibule is desired for winter entry, a secondary entrance can provide direct access from the living area to the outdoors.

A "soft edge" — that is, a semi-private area or garden patio between the front of the private dwelling and the common area — further increases opportunities for casual socializing. Like a front porch where people sit for hours on summer evenings, this semi-private area provides an easily accessed, comfortable place to be outside and "watch the world go by." Here residents may set out tables and

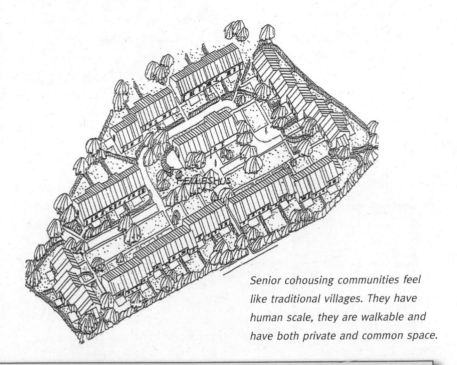

Senior cohousing communities feel like traditional villages. They have human scale, they are walkable and have both private and common space.

Body Language

With all the discussion about design to encourage casual socializing, someone who hasn't lived in a cohousing community might wonder whether a resident can take out the garbage without getting sidetracked. Cohousers told us they quickly learn to use and read body language in a variety of situations. "It's easy enough just to say 'howdy' and walk on. People know that everyone has their own lives — it's natural and accepted," explained a resident. Body language readily signals approachability. One resident told us that some people might not be approachable for months because of how things are going on in their lives, but soon enough they will open up again.

"People in cohousing tend to be very honest with each other," said a cohousing resident of sixteen years. "In my old house, when a neighbor used to ask to borrow a tool, I felt obliged to loan it, even if I felt uncomfortable doing so. In what might be a rare contact, I didn't want to come off as un-neighborly. Here if someone wants to talk, or have coffee, or borrow a tool, and I don't feel like it, I don't hesitate to say no. They know me, and there is less likelihood that they will be put off by my honesty. In fact, it's a sign of respect and intimacy to be able to say no." It's reminiscent of when the cash machines first came out. No one had to tell you to stand ten feet behind the person using the machine in front of you. A new and unique body language emerged.

"Like a Volkswagen, cohousing homes need to be sensual, small, and well engineered" — Jim Leach, Cohousing developer and resident.

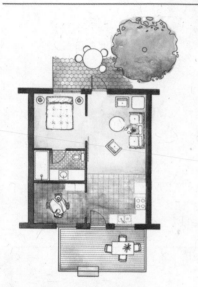

With a soft edge design, semi-private front yards are used more than twice as often as private back yards in senior cohousing.

A "soft edge" in senior cohousing.

chairs or plant a small garden. Set apart from footpaths by plantings, low fences, or changes in paving, this area need not be large; a space only eight feet deep will suffice. In fact, a front yard more than 15 feet deep will actually deter the flow of activity between the house and common areas.

A study by Danish urban designer Jan Gehl compared outdoor activities in two Danish clustered housing developments (not cohousing). He found that when a soft edge was provided, residents used the area in front of the houses 68 percent of the time they spent outdoors, compared to 32 percent in the more private backyards. When there was a hard edge and no semi-private area, residents spent only 12 percent of their outdoor time in front. Even more importantly, the total number of hours spent outdoors increased four-fold when there was a soft edge.

Our findings show that people's preference for sitting or working in front of their houses is even more pronounced in cohousing; approximately 80 percent of the time people spend outdoors near their residence is spent in the area in front of their own house, compared to 20 percent in their backyard. Be it a "front porch" literally or

figuratively, the area immediately in front of a house allows people to observe and take part in community life from their own perch as they choose. Cohousing's 80 percent front/20 percent back design proportion is the exact opposite of the typical American single-family house, which is 20/80.

Enclosed Streets

A few cohousing communities in cold climates have enclosed interior streets and courts, and the transition area between dwellings and common space, though reduced, still plays an important role. Not having to worry about putting on shoes or warmer clothing in order to go outside their home, people can move more casually from private to common areas. Private entrances can be set back from a covered street to provide vestibules for storing shoes and other outdoor clothing. Casual sitting areas along the street are well used all day long.

A private outdoor space is usually provided in the rear of the house, although even here there has proved to be little need for barriers such as fences or hedges. Usually, once residents get to know their neighbors, they find it unnecessary to define territory with fences. Visual privacy can be provided with plantings, and if at some point later residents feel the

In both Europe and the United States, clustered housing is preferred when attempting to create a social environment, as in this design for senior housing by the architectural firm of C.F. Møller.

need to install fences, they will have a better idea of where and how high they should be.

Transitions within Common Areas

The common areas themselves should be designed to provide a variety of gathering spaces (architects call them "gathering nodes"), from sitting areas shared by five or six private dwellings to a "community plaza." Again, sensitive transitions from the most intimate to the most public gathering spaces encourage active community life. For example, along the pedestrian streets, picnic tables can be placed where neighbors can

> ### Considerations for Common Facilities
> - Functions to be accommodated (dining, visitor's short/long term suites, etc.).
> - Priority of functions (in case all can't be afforded).
> - Desired characteristics (warm, comfortable, easy to maintain).
> - Light (daylighting, solar access, visual access to private houses, site, etc.).
> - Acoustics (acoustic ceiling treatment, quiet dishwasher, etc.).
> - Indoor/outdoor relationship (access to terraces, etc.).
> - Possible future needs.

gather over a pot of tea. And from these picnic tables, residents can have a view of the common house and patio, where people often gather on sunny afternoons. The Danes often place mailboxes and bicycle sheds

Nevada City Cohousing.

An enlarged balcony with a love seat, coffee table, and reading lamp provides a secondary private space in a scaled-down dwelling. Large front porches are the least costly part of the house, but can be one of the nicest areas in the house.

near gathering nodes to create a nexus of activity.

Prior to move-in, some residents have expressed concern that local gathering places promote cliques, thus diminishing the quality of the overall community. Although it's natural for people to initially become better acquainted with their immediate neighbors, in practice, such gathering places benefit the whole community because they bring residents out into the common areas. Stopping and resting places should be located where there is the greatest chance that they will be used. Besides benches and tables, low walls make excellent perches.

Equally important is a community plaza for larger gatherings. When located just outside the common house, the plaza functions as the community's "front porch." Here residents gather before and after dinner, have summer barbecues, and hold other community celebrations. Ideally, people should be able to pass by the common plaza on their way out, or on their way home, and be able to see whether others are there.

Living as Community
Spatial relationships among the individual dwellings and common spaces don't so much define a cohousing community as they express its possibilities. A good site plan fosters a

lively neighborly community spirit that not only enhances individuals' quality of life, but also allows them to actively contribute more positively to the larger group. Most importantly, the design sustains the community. It will never wane if the design helps stitch it together.

Common House Design

If the single-family house is designed to spread people out across the landscape, then the common house is designed to bring them back together. You could say it bridges the gap between home and neighborhood. Moreover, while a single-family house design consumes energy, time, and money, the common house can be seen as a way of conserving all three. To create the right common house, we start with a good common house program.

Common House Program Defined

At McCamant & Durrett Architects, we dedicate two days to planning the common house with the resident group. This has proven to be quite adequate. We:

+ Brainstorm, discuss, and decide common house goals. After all, none of the residents has a common house, and they cost $300,000 to $400,000 to build, so the first question we ask is why? Individual goals for a group's common house

usually include things that supplement the private houses, making life easier, healthier, more convenient, more practical, more economical, more interesting, more fun, and supporting many other goals. Each group seems to find 20 to 30 main community goals that their common house should strive to foster.

+ Show images of common houses and amenities from around the world, which in turn helps everyone visualize and articulate the possibilities for achieving their goals.

+ Brainstorm, discuss, and decide the activities that directly serve those previously-stated goals — dining, laundry, playing cards, hosting guests, cooking, dancing, reading, and much more — activities that are better done together than at home. Usually groups list 80 to 100 activities that they would like to see accommodated in the common facilities. It's at this stage when groups begin to see exactly how cohousing can enhance their quality of life. We all have a private realm (for sleep,

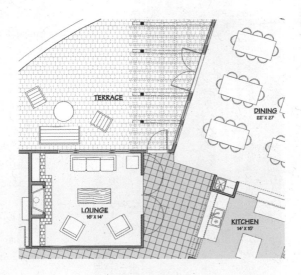

When the lounge/sitting area is directly adjacent to the dining area, community members will use it as a gathering place. When the sitting area is located down a hall, isolated and away from the action in the dining area, it will likely be underutilized.

Hearthstone Cohousing common house interior.

respite, reflective time) and a public realm (schools, roads, hospitals, etc.), but a woodworking shop, for example, is hard to outfit adequately in the private realm, and rarely seems manageable in the public realm. In cohousing, a woodworking shop is a popular amenity to a common house because there are enough people to afford the space and tools, and (this is key!) because people know and care enough about each other, they will not leave a mess or misplace tools. I have met a lot of folks (including myself) who tend to leave a mess in their own woodworking shop but wouldn't dream of leaving a mess in the common realm because they feel more accountable to others.

• Decide when these activities will be done (time of day, how often, with how many people).

• Determine which activities need their own space. Obviously dining does, but dancing can happen in the dining space at a different time, and meetings can happen at yet another time.

• Settle on a list of 15 to 20 places within or around the common house that are dedicated to a main activity and several ancillary activities. Each area must be designed for one primary activity.

Multi-purpose accomplishes no purpose well. As the Danes say, "If you try to do everything, you won't do anything."

• Prioritize the places. If a group can only build a dozen places (which is likely), then the group should build that dozen with the highest priority. If a group has this discussion now, these decisions can be made in 90 minutes. Groups that don't settle their common house priorities at this stage might never settle them and can spend hundreds of people-hours not settling them.

• Program each space starting from the most important one. What main activity will happen in that space; i.e., how many dinners and on which days of the week? What other common activities would happen in that space? Groups who have this discussion now will only spend a few minutes on it. For those who wait, it will take forever.

• Define which details matter most (light and acoustics are paramount). These details will determine the size and shape of the common house. What is the character of the building (warm, cozy, natural?). Groups will state the obvious as well as particular qualities they hold dear. We like to define these design criteria in as specific terms as possible. Unlike a more conventional design program, clearly defined functions to be accommodated are much more important than assigning square footage requirements. In other words, we recommend that a resident group figures out how many to seat in the dining room, or what activities the visitor's suites should accommodate, and then they should let the architect determine how much square footage different design solutions require. The completed design program documents these desired physical characteristics and design requirements and objectives.

After these two planning days, we take the resulting criteria, establish a schematic design, and later present it to the group (just before the private house workshop). We make changes as per the consensus of the group (usually about 10-15 percent changes).

Spatial Relationships

As with the site plan, the relationships among the spaces in the common house — kitchen/dining area, lounge, workshop, visitor's suites — and their relationship with the site largely determines how well the whole works. Specific activities, such as attending common dinners or

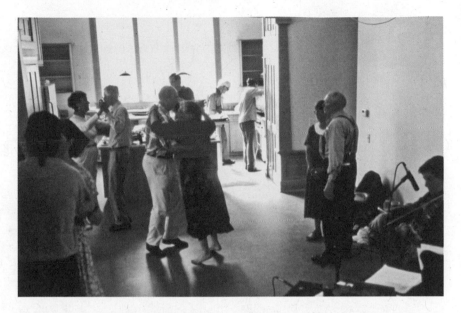

Planned from day one of the design meetings — dancing happened after the first common dinner on May 13, 2001 and after the second common dinner on May 14th.

using the laundry facilities bring people to the common house, and the design should work so they will see other people who are there. The location and design of the kitchen can be a great asset in this regard, since the cooks are usually working throughout the afternoon and evening. In a well-designed common house, one walks by — but not through — the kitchen from any of the entrances.

The relationship between the sitting and dining areas is also important. Although these spaces should be within hearing distance from each other, they need to be separate enough so that people have a place to relax before or after dinner. With this in mind, sometimes people use the common lounge to get away from people, or as a place to stretch

Typical Common House Kitchen Characteristics

A. If there is a **happy interface,** a warm and inviting space open to, but not within the kitchen activity, then this will be the most utilized place on the entire site. It makes for a more open kitchen where people will come to talk to the cook, but not go into the kitchen and get in the way.

B. The **countertop** is open and unencumbered, making room for dishes ready to go out to dining and dirty dishes coming back to the kitchen. This eliminates unnecessary walking around the bar, especially when two people are working together. One person puts things on the bar, and another puts them on the table.

C. A **cart** takes things to the table and brings them back efficiently. Clean dishes go from the dishwasher to the cart, ready to go directly to the table the next day. There is no extra motion of putting the dishes onto the shelves, only to take them out again. No shelves, no wasted motion.

D. The **four activity triangles** (prep, cook 1, cook 2, clean) should not overlap; separating these areas makes the kitchen safer and more efficient.

E. A **central island** brings people and activities together — it facilitates community. You'll find folks there drinking coffee 'til the wee hours if the kitchen is warm and cozy and attracts people. You'll find the lights on there when they are out everywhere else (except maybe the sitting room). Common kitchens are designed to be centripetal, that is to bring people together, to make cooking social and fun.

F. **Open cabinets:** If there are no doors on the upper cabinets and if most utensils can be seen, working in the kitchen is much easier. We have stayed in the guest rooms of many common houses. In half of them, you could always tell when it was 4 p.m., because you could hear the noise as people went through the cabinets, trying to remind themselves where everything is because the last time they cooked was a month ago. Having things open and accessible, with a French utensil bar, pot rack over the island, or pullout shelves facilitates a j.i.t. kitchen (j.i.t. means "just-in-time," in manufacturing parlance).

G. **Floor drain**: This saves the cook or assistant 15 minutes at the end of the evening — just when one needs it most. The last thing done is mopping the floor. The floor drain makes that a lot easier, and therefore helps keep the kitchen sanitary, too.

H. **Industrial appliances**: This is important. When it's a quarter to six, you're expecting 50 people for dinner, and the pasta water is not boiling, that "wooff" of the 15,000 btu/hr burner is music to your ears. The dishwasher needs to take less than three minutes to get 20 dishes spotless, etc. But this in no way implies that the kitchen needs to feel cafeteria-like or institutional.

I. **Refrigerator** is near the entrance to the kitchen, so it is easily accessible to cooks as well as to people who want to access the refrigerator (to see if that orange drink they left there yesterday is still there, for example). Accessing the refrigerator will be the number one reason a non-cook/assistant will enter the kitchen. Non-cooks/assistants walking around the kitchen can be dangerous (sharp knives, hot pots, etc). Keeping them out of the cooks' way is important.

J. **Wet bar** to keep the thirsty out of the kitchen. Grabbing a glass is the second most common reason someone will wander through the kitchen. Placing glasses and drinking water just outside the kitchen, but close to the refrigerator and the dishwasher, is the most efficient solution.

K. **Storage** above the work areas for less frequently accessed items like salad and punch bowls.

L. **Phone and cook books** at hand.

M. **Plate rack** over the door to store and display large platters.

N. Probably most important is a **cozy feel.** People will want to be in an extraordinary space — and it is essential to the success of the kitchen that people will fundamentally want to be there. To accomplish this, the kitchen should be:

1. **Open:** To see and be seen. The pleasant distraction of saying hello to a passer-by. To be appreciated: "It sure smells good." The cooks need to see folks and folks need to see them. Seeing them will attract other activities. Not seeing them facilitates an otherwise empty common house. When cooking in an open kitchen, the cooks feel like the heroes for the day. In a closed kitchen, they feel like the servants.

2. **Warm:** Lots of natural wood; rounded wood edging at the countertop; wood cabinets (upper and lower). Besides the custom upper cabinets, I recommend a shaker lower, of which there are many reasonable manufacturers on the market; a deep, rich-colored linoleum for the floor; natural finish at the door to the pantry; wood baseboard; and other warm aesthetic touches.

3. **Light:** Natural light and supplementary lighting. Lighting needs to be strong at the task sites (100 foot candles) and softer for general lighting (50 foot candles). No ceiling-mounted fluorescents.

4. **Gourmet in feel:** "Wow, what a great kitchen," — like you would find in a nice house, never commercial. Commercial kitchens are designed to keep everyone separated and task focused. Cohousing kitchens are designed to bring people together, to make cooking fun — like a French country kitchen — yet also very efficient.

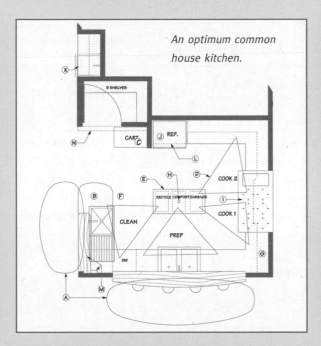

An optimum common house kitchen.

or practice a musical instrument. The common house can be a place to go when one needs to "get out of the house."

Making the Most of Available Space

Nearly every existing cohousing community contends that they need a larger common house, regardless of whether theirs is 3,000 or 8,000 sq. ft. Residents often cite the need for extra guest rooms, which can be rented out to extended-stay visitors or used by live-in professional caregivers. Building costs usually limit the space and amenities a community can afford. If saving money while retaining community is a goal, then making the common house bigger and the private houses smaller is a better financial decision than making the common house smaller. It is critical that the design is efficient and provides maximum use of the space available.

In many cases, certain spaces in a common house are underutilized. The best example is that of a separate library. Why go to a common library when a cozy chair sits at home and another in the sitting room? Moreover, set off on its own, a library does not encourage interaction and the public library is much better outfitted than a common library can be. Don't try to duplicate the public or private realm; the common realm is a unique genre.

During the planning process, residents may envision using the common house like a neighborhood café, where they can read the newspaper, relax after chores, or meet with friends. By putting a casual sitting area at the edge of the dining area or near the main entrance, a separate space isn't needed and the sitting room will be used more frequently. Voilá, an instant neighborhood café. People will gather there before and after dinner and will likely take advantage of whatever reading materials happen to be lying about.

Creating an Intimate Atmosphere

Designing for multiple uses (not multi-use) is one way to take maximum advantage of available space. For

The Beating Heart of the Community

More than just a nice place to have dinner with friends, the common house is the heart of every cohousing community. It is where you break bread together and, just as important, it is over dinner that you might decide to go bird watching together on Saturday, or to take a walk after eating. In other words, dinner is the number one place where relationships are built — not necessarily at the dinner table itself, but from all the activities that stem from dinner conversations. The common house is also the place where people drink coffee and play chess on a Sunday afternoon. It is inviting and friendly to the point where residents feel as if they are in their own space. Coziness, good lighting, good acoustics, good design, good company, and good food — now that's living!

example, the dining area can double as a meeting room. Although it is difficult to create an intimate atmosphere while at the same time providing for the needs of a large group, the dining area must be comfortable, not cafeteria-like. There must be places in the common house dining and sitting areas for both a few people to gather informally and for the whole community to meet.

The kitchen should be a professional facility adequate for efficiently preparing large meals, but it should not be institutional. Some communities have gone overboard to provide a professional kitchen and have consequently failed to create a "homey" atmosphere. Fundamentally, residents have to ask, "Do I like being there?" and "Is this a place where I will enjoy spending my time?" There is no reason to not make it warm and cozy.

Cooking and serving should be as convenient as possible, even fun. Visual access between the kitchen and dining areas helps create a residential feeling, as do the choices of interior finishes and light fixtures. For example, natural wood finishes and warm lighting (rather than plastics, and ceiling-mounted fixtures) make spaces cozier.

Acoustics

Because large groups of people will be gathering and conversing in the common house, good acoustics are necessary to create a pleasant atmosphere. If residents cannot talk in a normal conversational tone during dinner, they are likely to eat at home. Uncomfortably noisy areas are often

A comfortable and relaxed common dining experience is literally designed down to the tables and chairs in senior cohousing.

Caregivers in the Common House

Common house suites are the cutting edge of senior cohousing in Denmark. Twenty years ago, in an effort to house professional caregivers on-site for an extended period of time, Danish senior cohousers installed one suite in the common house, then two suites, then three. They found that by having several suites, all of the under-utilized square footage in the common house was better used. And because the professional caregivers became more integrated into the community, residents who needed professional care received better quality care. These suites were designed with privacy in mind and with the minimum space required for a comfortable extended stay.

A Question of Choice

I'm often asked, "How can you afford to spend all this time with the group?" It's a good question, but I think the real question is this: "How can we afford not to?"

By choosing to make a better life for themselves — one that fosters human-scale community while lessening their collective consumptive demands — each resident group actually accomplishes much more than their expressed goal of establishing a cohousing community. They are helping to create a viable society. How can we afford not to spend our time building our communities?

Space efficiency can be achieved by having an open house plan such as this house in senior cohousing.

the result of having too many large, flat, hard surfaces. Sound absorptive surface materials reduce noise build-up.

The bounce-back time of conversational noise should last about 0.5 to 0.7 seconds. Longer reverberation times lead to the "cocktail party" effect where people must keep talking louder and louder in order to be understood.

If the reverberation time is kept to less than one second, and the background sound level is moderately low (less than 40 dBA), it should be possible to carry on a normal conversation with someone 3 to 5 feet away.

In the design of the common house, we avoid introducing loud noise sources such as televisions, regular dishwashers, window air conditioners, high-speed supply or exhaust fans, or an oversized refrigerator unless these sources can be managed so that they don't interfere with the ability to converse. Control of noise at the source is usually the most cost-effective approach.

Sound absorptive materials added to the walls and/or ceiling help avoid problems with reverberant noise. There are many types of these materials. Don't rely on your intuition for which materials provide good sound absorption; you may be wrong. In general, look for materials that have a NRC (Noise Reduction Coefficient) of 0.7 or greater.

Dining Tables

Even small details, such as the size of the dining tables, significantly affect the atmosphere of the common house. Two communities we know of felt it necessary to have extra-large tables. The result is that people sit farther apart, which means they must talk more loudly to be heard across the vastness of the table. This, in turn, raises the ambient noise level, which means that others must talk even louder.

A 2'-8" x 6'-10" table seats six to eight people and will permit comfortable conversation and promote a relaxed, enjoyable atmosphere. A smaller table or two provide alternatives for individuals or couples who may wish to be by themselves.

Laundry

When located in the common house, laundry facilities generate the second highest number of people-hours spent in that place (the only more-utilized space is the dining/kitchen area). As a result, this lonely chore instead becomes an opportunity to socialize, be it for a few minutes or an entire afternoon. You don't have much of a community unless you have things in common, and like the washing rock by the river, common laundry machines help achieve that sense of community.

In terms of economics, it's more cost effective for a group to purchase a bank of machines than it is for each household to purchase its own set. Fewer machines purchased means less money spent, not to mention the per-household savings in construction costs. Common washers are also a cost-effective way to collect gray water for irrigation purposes and

conserve water. As well, the highest quality biodegradable detergents are affordable only when purchased in bulk (I've only seen these used when laundry facilities were located primarily in the common house). Laundry machines generate heat, and it's more difficult for each household to eliminate (or cut down on its) air conditioner usage when washer-dryer heat is generated inside. Finally, the sound of a washer-dryer in your house is like a diesel truck idling in your living room, whereas the noise can easily be isolated in the common house.

All of this is not to say that individual households in a senior cohousing community can't have their own washer-dryer; many communities have made laundry hook-ups an option in the private residences. However, a truly usable, readily available, common laundry maximizes use of space while fostering community and ecological goals.

. . . And Finally

The common house supplements the needs of individual houses, but its primary purpose is much greater: It transforms a neighborhood into a community, and in so doing, it enhances the quality of life for everyone.

Hearthstone Cohousing common house interior.

Private House Design

Just as each common house and shared outdoor areas in a cohousing community foster livability on a human scale, so do the interior spaces of each individual residence. Architects need to work closely with residents so that each home reflects the residents' actual needs, desires, and priorities as agreed on during the private house workshop.

Private House Program Workshop

At McCamant & Durrett Architects, we dedicate three days to creating the private house program and finalizing the schematic designs with the group. We start this workshop by presenting the common house schematic design for discussion. Before we launch into the private houses, we want the common house amenities to be fresh in the minds of group members. While the group discusses their common house design and suggests modifications, they are reminded of the extent to which the common house supplements or potentially duplicates

the features in their own houses. For example, residents might decide that since the common house has two guest rooms, they might not need a guest room in their own home after all. The grandchild who visits from college can just as easily camp out in the common house guest room — and really experience cohousing.

When we consider the goals of the private houses in the context of the larger cohousing community, we look at:

- The house matrix: how many studios, one-bedroom, and two-bedroom units will the community contain?
- The number of stories for each house and building type.
- House zoning issues: living areas versus private areas (such as bedrooms).
- Accessibility, adaptability, and visitability needs.
- Kitchens — the size of refrigerators, sinks, range, etc.
- Fireplaces.
- Acoustics.
- Heating and cooling.
- Architecture and image.

We often use slide images to help visualize and articulate possibilities.

Although house planning is the task at hand, people will interject

Front porch view of the Pleasant Hill Cohousing private houses. The passive cooling in this project works so well that it has eliminated the need for any air conditioners in this exceptionally hot climate.

comments like: "But I've got to have tile countertops like my daughter has." These details can be accommodated, but in their due time. For the moment, toss all extras into one big hopper and put them aside in order to focus on the basic house plans. Solar power, alternate building materials, attic access, built-in sound systems, bathtubs, and yes, tile countertops will be decided on in the design development phase.

In the evenings, we make an architectural tour of the neighborhood to look at good architecture — both historical and contemporary. We seek cultural architecture that respects the architectural heritage and climate of that particular place, as well as architecture that contributes to the built environment as a whole and our sense of place in it. By understanding the context, we can add architecture that, once built, will feel like it was always meant to be there. Cost, climate, and culture are the three "c"s that our company lives by, and we do our best to share with the group what that means.

After the first day of collective design work, our architectural office begins design of the four or five house plans that fit the private house program. About three or four weeks later, on a Saturday, we meet with each house-group (one-bedroom, two-bedroom, etc.) for one and a half

> ## Considerations for the Private Houses
>
> - Distribution of house types: number of studios, one-bedroom units, multiple-bedroom units, shared households, etc.
> - Functions to be accommodated: dining, sleeping, work, etc.
> - Desired characteristics : combined kitchen/dining/living room, open floor plan.
> - Acoustics and light: solar access, visual access to common house, neighbors, etc.
> - Indoor/outdoor relationship: access to terrace, etc.
> - Flexibility and future additions .
>
> ### Construction Phase Upgrades
> - Individual upgrade options such as washer, dryer, wood floors, or tile countertops etc.
> - Post move-in options such as built-in bookshelves, an extra skylight etc.

hours. The next day we meet with each house group a second time to go through plans that reflect their suggestions from the previous day. We discuss cost ramifications that more square footage will have, and we explain the basic principles of how to maximize limited space.

Unlike much architecture built today, cohousing communities aren't machines designed for making money (though cohousing units often appreciate faster than similar real estate). As Danish architects found, designing cohousing with the future residents is the only way to produce a meaningful community. It's also the fastest way to do it. While this deliberate three-day

Build Now, Customize Later

Cohousing communities can save money by limiting the number of floor plans to one for each house size and by keeping finish options (flooring, cabinets, bathroom tiles, etc.) to a manageable number. Residents may be able to accept such limitations if the units are initially designed so they can be easily expanded or customized later.

Cohousing communities often develop four or five house models to fit the different needs of residents.

and sharply focused private house programming process can lead to heated discussions, if done right, it avoids any serious acrimony and eliminates backtracking. We have done many projects without any arguments — and created great houses in the process.

Special Design Considerations

As important as community and togetherness are, people still spend a majority of their time in their own houses. As one woman put it, "The beauty of cohousing is that you have a private life and a community life, but only as much of each as you want." Dwellings in senior cohousing reflect special design considerations because of shared facilities, the variety of residential needs, and the relationships among residents.

Adaptable Interior Design

One of the primary problems with conventional senior housing today is its monotonous and impersonal feel. By contrast, new senior cohousing communities usually agree together on four to six different house plans for residents to choose from, and those who prefer a specific model work with the architect to refine that design. Individual households often make additional changes (by selecting options and upgrades such as flooring and appliances), so that in the end, every house is slightly different.

Being realistic about what the future may hold, senior cohousers can choose which features to include at construction and which may be added later. The design should be readily adaptable for sudden and unexpected needs of residents, including the possibility that residents can easily swap units. While it is not essential to make every unit conform to the highest accessibility standards from the beginning, it is important that there be contingency plans.

A variety of dwelling sizes allow residents to move within the community as their needs dictate. One resident commented just after swapping houses, "With the help of neighbors, we exchanged houses on a single Saturday afternoon. Of course, the paperwork took a little longer."

Standardizing Designs

Custom construction is typically twice as expensive as production construction, so to make cohousing affordable, we use a production approach. The custom home experience can be seen as the opposite of the cohousing experience. Custom houses usually start with a standardized lot subdivided — along with many others — and then a custom home is placed on it. In other words, what starts off as production housing (one of many), ends up as individual custom houses. Cohousing is just the opposite; it is unique in its inception, being designed with the residents to meet their specific objectives, but each of the houses ends up as one of many.

A truly effective way to keep prices down is for residents to consciously limit the number of custom features incorporated into the design of their individual houses. The price of a custom house is substantially higher than that of production housing, where a few floor plans are repeated over and over. As one contractor explains, "If the builders have to think too much about what they are doing and keep track of what goes where and in which house, they charge more."

If not carefully planned for, "individualizing" can add considerably to construction costs. Undisciplined design efforts have been known to increase unit costs beyond some people's reach. Unfortunately, some cohousing groups have only discovered this the hard way. Minor custom touches such as an extra wall or different bathroom fixtures, though relatively inexpensive when viewed one-by-one, have a cumulative effect that can increase the cost of construction exponentially for everyone, since they effect larger design considerations and construction timelines. Several communities that allowed residents to incorporate numerous additions and changes into the design were shocked in the end by a construction price $5,000 to $10,000 higher than they had anticipated. Residents later calculated they would have been much better off if they had kept to standard designs, even if every household had later customized with its own contractors.

Once construction begins, any subsequent changes, no matter how minor they appear, will increase the final price of the units. It takes a lot of self-discipline to impose limitations on what may be the residents' only chance to design their own homes. Yes, it is difficult for architects, builders, and developers (as

Doyle Street Cohousing private house interior. Mezzanines, high ceilings, and creative design make small dwellings seem larger.

An example rendering of a comfortable small house plan. Fresno Cohousing, Fresno, California.

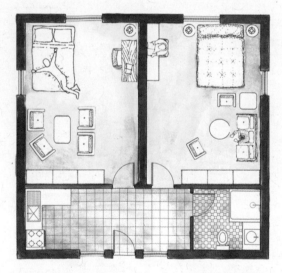

Guest or visitor suites are well used in senior cohousing communities.

well as owners), to say "no" to future neighbors with whom they have been working with for months. But it can be done — when people see the tradeoffs.

Setting a careful budget from the start and trying to stick to it can keep the conflict — and the prices — to a minimum. The reward to homeowners for such self-discipline can be lower mortgages, more money for later renovation, and even better houses, since complexity detracts attention from quality.

Designing Small Residences

The small dwelling sizes often necessitated by today's economy, the group's specific goals, and the needs of seniors to age in place as comfortably as possible for as long as possible require residents to be careful in establishing priorities, and designers to be creative in the use of space. It is easy to accommodate many different functions in a large house, but a small house must do more with less — small housing must fit like a glove instead of a grocery bag. In addition to avoiding overlap with the amenities provided in the common house, residents need to work with the architect to clarify and decide the functions that are the most important for their homes to fulfill. Residents can also establish priorities for construction quality. Speculative developers may choose to spend less money on sound insulation between units, in order to spend more on flashy kitchen cabinets that have more immediate selling impact. When residents are able to make decisions themselves, they are more likely to consider long-term trade-offs, and therefore may choose simpler kitchen cabinets so they can afford better sound insulation. After move-in, it's a lot easier to upgrade kitchen cabinets than it is to rebuild walls and floors for better sound insulation.

The use of mezzanines, high ceilings, light, and the juxtapositions of spaces can help make small areas feel larger. Ceiling height and window placement can have an enormous effect on how a room is perceived. The subtleties also add up: acoustics, storage, and even paint colors take on great importance. Making a small house work requires attention to these types of details.

Breaking from the long tradition of locating the most formal rooms, typically the living room or parlor, toward the front of the house, cohousers have discovered many advantages to locating the kitchen on the public side of the house, nearest to the shared outdoor space. This layout creates a stronger link between indoors and outdoors and between private and community areas. Conversely, the private side of the house is usually toward the rear or upstairs, where there is as much peace and quiet as in a detached house. A small supplementary sitting/reading area can sometimes be provided in a corner, a balcony, or hallway without taking up much space.

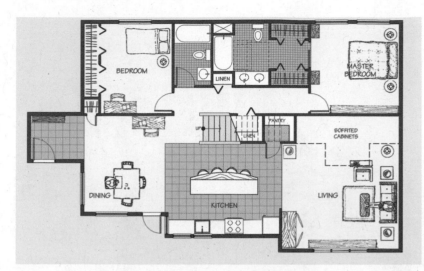

An open floor plan saves space by "overlapping" rooms or borrowing space from adjacent rooms, even if only psychologically. Local lighting, low walls, and/or flooring changes, rather than full-height walls, define areas in this house in senior cohousing.

Multi-Story vs. Single-Story

Another important consideration in senior cohousing design is whether some or all of the units should be one-story flats. While it is true that most American seniors prefer single-level housing, this is not an absolute. Some residents may want to live in a townhouse-style unit and only move to a flat later on if the stairs really become a problem for them. For example, in a 16-unit senior cohousing project that we recently designed, all but six units had either loft or basement spaces. At the time of design, the residents of this community were looking to the future, but didn't feel it necessary to omit stairs at the start. The lofts and basements

were designed as non-essential spaces — if or when the residents themselves can no longer manage stairs, those space will still be useful for visitors (caregivers, family members, etc.).

In the case of Munksøgård, stairs were important to that group of 20 households. I was startled to find half of the houses in the development upstairs, and, as it turns out, the residents were weary of being queried about it. There is a long story behind the decision, but the short answer was finally provided by one resident over a glass of wine at about ten o'clock in the evening: "It was the most economical way of getting this project built, and we needed the most economical way." And as if to rationalize

Direct access from the entrance to the downstairs bedrooms allows for temporary boarders or live-in caregivers to have greater autonomy, or in this senior cohousing in Boulder, Colorado, the downstairs is a basement for storage.

At Munksøgård senior cohousing, the top units are accessible via stairs. This is indeed counter-intuitive but with cooperation, swaps occur when necessary. If someone upstairs twists an ankle they can move into the common house short term, or if they break a hip they swap a house with someone who lives downstairs. They proclaimed that what was important was the community that they brought to the table as people, and that the physical limitations could be readily mitigated through cooperation. They had a mechanism in use — cooperation — that most of us are not familiar with.

it a little, he added, "Besides, walking up and down the stairs keeps us younger." The Munksøgård seniors found that in their case, if all the houses in their community were single story, the building costs would increase along with the building footprints. Indeed, if single-story houses had been built, the square footage of each unit would have been smaller than usual, and each would have cost 25 percent more.

Munksøgård's residents, of course, recognize that they are aging. Therefore, when they made the decision to build two-story housing they also considered their community co-care agreements. In Munksøgård today, when a mobility limitation becomes a reality for someone in the community, the affected person will move to a downstairs unit. And if that is not necessary, an oversized guest room is to be made available for them in the common house. And if that isn't possible, other residents take turns caring for the disabled person in an upstairs home until a downstairs unit becomes available. Although most Danish senior cohousing features easily accessible ground-floor units, thus sidestepping these specific co-care issues altogether, Munksøgård shows what sort of exceptions can be made when affordability is an issue. In senior cohousing, community trumps design constraints every time. And it's not always a physical design solution — sometimes it's an issue of cooperative social mechanisms that most of us have never envisioned until we get into the discussion. That said, even in Denmark, most senior cohousing units are single story. The true story here is that of listening to the group and not underestimating the power of cooperation. In the last eight years, they have had only one person become less than fully capacitated.

Bathrooms

While the houses in senior cohousing typically run on the small side (averaging 800 or 900 sq. ft), the bathrooms within the units are quite large, often 6 ft by 9 ft (54 sq. ft.). In contrast, a standard bathroom size for other housing types is 5 ft by 7 ft (35 sq. ft.). In addition to increased size, bathrooms in senior cohousing units are designed to be exceptionally flexible, functional, and easy to clean.

Although it is rare for an individual to move into a senior cohousing community while in a wheelchair, a good design plans for that possibility. A flexible design provides living spaces that meet a resident's needs at move-in and will accommodate their needs in the long-term. In practical terms, a bathroom can keep its "desired feel" and still provide optimal utility. If optimal utility is not incorporated initially, the design should be adaptable, such that the necessary utility can be added economically when it is actually required.

A Word about Architects and Architecture

The discussions here about design should be used to broaden and guide — not replace — the dialogue between architect and residents. When residents and architects consciously consider the activities they want to occur easily and naturally later on, only then will a community emerge that's designed to emphasize a community approach to living while protecting the privacy of individuals and families within the community. A bad design program guarantees bad architecture, but a good program doesn't guarantee good architecture.

A good architect needs to be skilled in provoking and inspiring the group to new architectural heights from a social and aesthetic point of view. Good architecture comes from the heart and a heartfelt appreciation for what a resident group is trying to accomplish. Find a good architect — one who truly appreciates the cohousing concept and understands the needs of today's seniors. The end result is worth the search. That said, in Denmark a predictable pattern emerged regarding two distinctly different types of cohousing architects.

One type was the group of architects who had come up with an extremely organized method of walking a group through a design process. All of the rocks (design considerations) were turned over without sacrificing an extremely efficient process. In fact, it was efficient and organized *because* the rocks were turned over and discussion was exhausted. I mean *really* organized. Each of six design workshops, which lasted three hours to three days, was organized in 15-minute increments. The group always knew what they were doing and what product they were going to get out of it. And good records were kept so that the architect could always know what decisions were made. You could always tell when you walked on the site how much cohousing experience the architect had. Since time was not wasted,

Note the roll-in shower and the sink that can accomodate a wheelchair. Wait to put in grab bars later, only if and when they are needed. Utilitarian bathrooms do not have to be without charm.

A bathroom in Senior Cohousing with an easy to access shower.

it could be used to make good, well-conceived and well-executed architecture. It was usually pretty good-looking, if not beautiful. The front porches were big enough, the windows to the kitchens were big enough, and the flow of the house made sense, not to mention ample natural light and a frequently used common terrace. In one case, we noticed that 10 or 12 people were at the common terrace at 10 a.m. when we walked onto the site, and a different 10 to 12 when we left at 4 p.m. And out of the corners of our eyes, we noticed people there throughout the day.

I've also witnessed the work of a different type of "cohousing architect," the type that gets hired after acquiring something of a green and groovy

reputation by designing custom, expensive houses that might or might not be truly "green" (a house isn't green just because it's straw bale or uses something recycled). These architects thought that their "green" experience qualified them to design a cohousing community. Their process was unorganized and inefficient. They lost money and never wanted to do another cohousing. And the design suffered.

One of the things I like most about designing cohousing is that it takes architecture to the people (historically reserved for the rich). Indeed, the private houses in a cohousing community can be more beautiful and more functional than any home the residents have ever lived in.

Finally, good architecture doesn't necessarily emerge from a particular process. But if the senior cohousing design program is efficiently and clearly accomplished, the architect will have the time, energy, and motivation to make beautiful buildings — to focus on designing something that the residents will love. Meaningful places are missing from most institutional settings (and most private settings for that matter). Beauty takes time.

A new cohousing community grand opening.

CHAPTER 9

Study Group III: Policy

The core resident group is strong, has had its say during the design of the project, and the final architectural plans are being drawn up. During the time it takes the architects to compile construction documents, take bids, negotiate with contractors, get permits, and actually get the construction done, it's the residents' job to decide on critical issues, raise additional funds, and probably gain a few more members prior to moving in. This is the process of creating the social community that makes cohousing different from condominiums. How will we maintain the place, what are the final agreements regarding who will take care of whom? Exactly how will we run our meetings? What finally, and exactly, is the cooking agreement?

Forward Progress via the Participatory Process

The participatory development process has evolved into an established, efficient, and most importantly, effective procedure for creating successful cohousing communities, and it is only through this process that senior cohousing communities have optimally been built. Otherwise they cost too much, take too long, create too much acrimony, or — worst of all — don't work very well.

To progress forward, it is very important to keep to a timeline and avoid backtracking. Once decisions have been made at each phase, the group must move on to the next phase. If everyone understands the issues and the agreed-upon solutions at the time, old issues are less likely to resurface. But most importantly, if the group backtracks, they will inadvertently chase away the can-do people who they need to get the project done. It is discouraging (and disrespectful) for members of a group to make a decision one Saturday, only to have it raised again five Saturdays later. If 12 people sat through a discussion for 20 minutes, that's four people-hours that went into that discussion. The person who had a great deal to say during the first discussion might not be present

Pre- and Post-Construction: Cost Estimates, Tasks

Because the site, common house, and private residence design workshops are complete, and the program has been compiled, the project's costs can be updated. Reasonable estimates now can be projected for:

- Site improvement costs.
- Construction costs per sq. ft. for houses.
- Costs for common areas.
- Development timeline.

This updated information is critical for individual households to secure their necessary financing, and for the group to evaluate bids on the project and negotiate with a builder.

Pre-construction, the professionals will:

- Complete working drawings and building specifications.
- Obtain building permits.
- Solicit and negotiate construction bids.
- Select contractor.
- Finalize construction contract, loan, and schedule.
- Secure construction financing.

Pre-construction, the residents will:

- Complete recruiting efforts, if necessary.
- Finalize community participation ownership agreements.
- Do financial estimates. The group needs to ascertain what their monthly association fees are (maintenance, tools, insurance, hired help, if any, birthday cakes, etc.) The entire replacement costs of roofs, water heaters, etc., are done separately.

During construction, the professionals will:

- Monitor contracted work.
- Help secure mortgage loans.

Post-construction, the residents will:

- Complete any resident-built work.
- Finish Study Group III.

After occupancy, once the community is a living reality, our architectural firm spends a considerable amount of time studying how we might have reflected group priorities even better, and what design aspects might have been accomplished even more successfully.

for the second. Of course, no one wants to close the door on good ideas, and some groups agree to re-raise an issue if two-thirds of the people there for the original discussion agree. It doesn't happen very often — once or twice a project. In the context of trying to get others to re-raise a question, usually it becomes clear why the original decision was reached.

Respectful Dissent

What do you do with the problematic person who's never learned the art of discussing issues with other people and finding the best solution for everyone, not just for him or herself? This concern has come up at every single cohousing seminar I have ever given. What to do? Respectfully say your piece. Hold your ground. Listen attentively. Be willing to compromise. Remind yourself it isn't about "who wins" and "who loses." Be willing to accept a solution or approach you don't 100 % agree with. Call for consensus. Make the decision. Then move on.

In a group setting, people are much more dynamic than simply "cooperative" or "non-cooperative." If an individual storms out of the room when he doesn't get his own way, he probably won't last long in the group. But cooperation can be learned. And while people may have less than perfect skills when they join the group, if they are willing and motivated and

Nevada City Cohousing group meeting.

work hard, they might become the most giving, thoughtful, and considerate neighbors you've ever had. Or they will soon figure out that cohousing is not for them and move on. Group members might also drop a hint:"Look, if you don't want to try to cooperate with your future neighbors, then you might want to check out some of the other options available." Elders often aren't afraid to point out the difficulties that someone is having with others:"You know, if you spent more time asking others what they thought before the meeting and didn't just charge into the meeting with all the answers, people might be more open to your ideas." Remember that an individual who initially seems non-cooperative may turn out to be a

great community member. Sometimes, it just takes a few months to figure out who's who, and under what circumstances.

Recruitment: Before Move-In

How the group recruits and orients new members affects a group's ability to stay on track. New members need to learn the history and status of the group, which decisions have already been made, and which are still open for discussion. Sitting down one-on-one and going through the previous materials over coffee or over lunch works well. That time spent is respectful to the current members and is a great group-building/community-building experience because people make real connections with individuals who make them feel welcome — not always easy in a group setting.

Turnover of participants is inevitable. Someone might land her dream job on the other side of the country. Family matters might intervene. As long as at least six members participate at any given time (post site selection), turnover does not seem to affect the final success of a project. The backbone of the project is the organizing group and the participatory culture it creates. The momentum of the people committed to it, because they intend to live there, carries the day. While people are in the group (even those who later move on), they contribute to it and each member in turn helps to build the community — a community responsive to real people's needs because real people were involved to solve real-life issues.

Recruitment campaigns should be organized at key points, such as before site purchase and before taking a construction loan. If, by the time you are in Study Group III, a core group has not filled out its ranks with a full roster of households, that is the time to do so. Make no mistake, since the resident group itself is ultimately responsible for ensuring the success of their project, if there are not enough households, then the group needs to put their recruitment efforts into overdrive at these key points.

The first public presentation for the Nevada City Cohousing community.

Resident Committees

Committees come and go as necessary. As work needs to be done, interested individuals set up and join a committee, then disband once the particular project has been seen through to completion.

Committees at Work

Whatever the problem, a committee first brainstorms with the whole group. For instance, let's say the group is in Study Group III and finds it needs more members. The following might be the scenario for finding a solution:

- A 10-minute brainstorm on recruitment — how many open household spots need to be filled; where to place ads; where to place posters; ideal commitment timelines for new prospects; who to contact for publicity and when; what angle to take per outlet; what lists do we already have to follow up on; etc.

- The committee goes away, does some research, creates a proposal, comes back, and presents it. Brief and to the point is best.

- The whole group discusses the relative merits of the proposal.

- Straw polls are taken, consensus is reached, and then the committee takes over. Soon, it has something to hand to the local newspaper's lifestyles editor for the Sunday paper and the ball is rolling, with the buy-in and participation of the entire group. The committee will request cooperation from the entire group as needed.

Potential residents may (and do) drop out during the Study Group III process for any number of reasons. The group needs to maintain its numbers in order to retain its social and economic viability; it must be able to meet expenses for the architect and project manager, including fees for civil, structural, mechanical, soils, and sometimes acoustic engineers, landscape architects, and even interior designers.

There are many ways to go about filling in open spaces, tactics the group will probably be quite familiar with by this point: placing local newspaper ads, getting the ear of a sympathetic local journalist, and any other number of schemes. Get creative. And don't forget to tap already friendly local officials and senior organizations for a helping hand. The good plans already in place will make the project a compelling opportunity.

The recruitment goal at this stage is to inform as many prospective households as possible about the senior cohousing community under development — what it is, what it isn't, what it could be. Since the group already has as sense of the sort of community it desires — mixed income, number of households, co-care responsibilities, and so on — the purpose now is to find others who might share these same views. An informational meeting that is designed to attract others interested in the basic sort of community that the core group has already envisioned is the self-selecting process.

What the Danes have found to be one of the most effective marketing techniques — by far — is to have continuous Study Group I sessions in the town where the new cohousing project is planned. It often becomes the future residents themselves who facilitate the ten sessions, with guest facilitators for certain sessions. You can ask a physician or nurse to come for Session 3, a non-violent communication expert for Session 2, a philosopher for Session 7 and 8, a financial planner for 6, a psychologist for Session 5, anyone who has taken

Nevada City Cohousing where 22 seniors moved in 2006.

risks to accomplish something for 9, and a cohousing resident for Session 10. Be careful with Session 4. The best person to facilitate will be a person who lives in senior cohousing; someone who works at an assisted care or nursing home often will be too dire.

New Residents: After Move-In

What about people who move in after the group is all together and everyone else has been living there? Although turnover in cohousing is much lower than in regular neighborhoods (if you've spent two years putting together a custom-made neighborhood, you're motivated to stay) things happen, and people do move.

The established community itself will go a long way toward attracting potential new residents. A highly functioning neighborhood is very palpable and very attractive. Communities often request prospective buyers to attend a couple of common dinners, a couple of workdays, a couple of common management meetings, and, with a guided tour through the participation agreement (the outline of how each member will do his share), potential new residents will know exactly what they are buying into *before they make an offer*. Showing prospective new residents early design plans and decisions will help them understand

how the community came to be, and where it likely is headed. That said, most resales go to people who have been familiar with the project for a long time; while the upfront familiarizing sometimes seems redundant, there are always revelations. Why is it that people who say, "Oh, I know all about cohousing," always seem to be off the mark? Because cohousing is about the agreements these particular neighbors have made — and the agreements are never quite the same.

Lest one think it is difficult to attract cooperative-minded people to an established group, know that many existing cohousing communities in the US today have waiting lists of potential residents. In this regard, demand exceeds current supply.

Pleasant Hill Cohousing under construction.

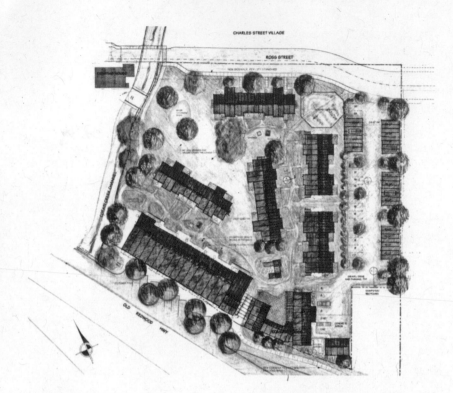

Site plan of FrogSong Cohousing, Cotati, California.

Changes during Construction

Groundbreaking is an exciting time for all cohousing groups. All the months of planning and long meetings finally begin to take tangible form. Generally, the group can relax. Typically, a "building committee" is delegated responsibility for bi-monthly contact with the architect (the project manager earns his or her keep here) and for making many decisions.

Caution! Do not allow changes during construction! Allowing virtually no changes (except for the bare minimum necessary to accommodate local code updates) is the only way to avoid complicating the building process — and complications virtually always mean additional costs.

The terms of the construction contract should be carefully worked out beforehand, with no changes allowed during construction. Residents may swear at the contractor and the committee for not allowing "just this one little change," but the defined set of "options" determined earlier by the entire group (usually no more than 20 options for choice of countertops, flooring, appliances, and so on) defines the mechanism and time-frame for individual unit choices. In the long run, a firm "no-changes during construction" policy will save the community a lot of grief and money.

As for the order of what should get built when, the rule here is: Finish the common house first. It is a great asset to have a place to meet, eat, and do the laundry while the houses are just being occupied and people are still moving in (and usually the equipment there is better than you could ever afford at home). More importantly, having a functioning common house from the very beginning establishes community; the pattern of daily use helps break old habits for people used to having one of everything. The common house works like a dream if it is designed effectively and built early on, because it gets the cooperative culture started.

Finance Essentials

From the outside looking in, the number and variety of economic issues confronting a resident group may seem considerable. However, when broken into component parts (which may not be obvious), these issues are straightforward and easy to solve with basic policy choices.

In the US, banks typically require purchase commitments for at least 70 percent of the units before they will approve a construction loan. Those residents who put up the initial investment for consulting fees (and cover the uncommitted shares) are reimbursed later from the construction loan. This is a critical stage in that members are now taking a greater risk. Should the partnership decide to dissolve, a portion of the individual investment will have already been spent and could be lost. I should point out, though, that to the best of my knowledge, every cohousing community that has started construction in the US has been successfully completed and occupied.

Fannie Mae and Personal Mortgages

A bank can handle personal mortgage loans in two ways. With a portfolio loan, the bank keeps the loan in-house, holding on to the 30-year note and absorbing the risk itself. However, many banks prefer to sell the loan to a federal mortgage company that buys loans from banks on a scale large enough to minimize its own risk. The loans available through this secondary loan market often (though not always) deliver the best rates and certainly broaden the choices of an individual shopping for a loan.

There is a catch: A new development must be approved by the Federal National Mortgage Association (nicknamed Fannie Mae) before any bank can offer a secondary market loan on it. Many banks, and even portfolio lenders, will not loan on projects that have not been

Community gathering at Skraplanet Cohousing in Denmark. This cohousing was first occupied in 1972 by young families motivated to make childrearing more practical and more fun for children and themselves. Today, they are retooling the community with ramps and handrails to accomodate for those who are becoming seniors.

approved. They fear losing money if they should have to foreclose on the unit and fail to find a buyer. Historically, single-family houses are considered a safe bet because there is theoretically a confirmed market for this type of housing. Few banks are willing to be adventurous with their loans. They look to Fannie Mae to weed out the bad risks. Banks typically want to see 20 to 30 percent of the project's cost already invested in equity before they will loan the remaining 70 to 80 percent. This

Flexibility in Tasks

Since seniors tend to have relaxed schedules (they're either retired, or about to retire), they usually have time for getting things done. As such, seniors typically need fewer rules for many ordinary tasks than do residents in multi-generational cohousing, where people are often kid-driven, career-driven, or recreation-driven — and just seem to have less time to devote to community chores. In those circumstances, you need rules to get anything done. In senior cohousing, if the lawn needs mowing and you're able-bodied, you'll probably just mow the lawn — unless you hate mowing the lawn. In that case, someone who likes to mow will do it, and you'll tend to the planter boxes and flower gardens instead. Senior cohousers typically recruit help from their fellow neighbors for these tasks, not because they need to, but because it's more fun.

I also have noticed an encouraging thing about the policy-making and community meetings. You can participate as much or as little as you like. You come to realize that your neighbors will do "almost" as good a job with or without you. You might even determine that the process will go just as well while you are fishing, or finishing furniture, or bicycling — or whatever else you might be busy doing.

The Danes in senior cohousing rely a little more on organic methods for chores and have less lengthy formal agreements than any congregate housing situation. Their less formal methods usually have worked. However, working this way requires a little faith. People who haven't lived in cohousing before are sometimes nervous about leaving things to chance. It seems overly optimistic. But as one Danish senior cohouser told me: "Our approach is that whenever we have a specific need, we put it on the agenda, brainstorm, discuss, and decide. Usually very quickly." The result is a custom solution for a given task, at the moment it's needed, forged by the group. It is not quite as necessary to absolutely fix the level of cooperation ahead of time, provided all members of the community can agree on a plan for working out issues in an ad hoc fashion, whenever problems arise. A smart list (an agreed-on plan) covers basic issues like who maintains what and when and who belongs to which committees (finance, social, kitchen, etc.). What agreements the Danes do have, they hold close and dear: "You have to cook dinner every six weeks; you have to belong to a management committee; you have to participate in four work days per year. In other words, once it's agreed to, we adhere to it — and if there are any exceptions at all, we have agreed to those as well."

equity is amassed from a number of sources: money already spent on land purchase and project approvals, cash from investors both resident and non-resident, and any amount the current landowner is willing to carry until the completion of the project. The commitment of the future residents is essential. Their money invested in the project shows that they are serious and able buyers. It's important to note, in light of recent record numbers of house foreclosures, record bank losses, and waves of misfortune that, to our knowledge, there has not yet been one house foreclosure of a cohousing house in the United States. In fact, cohousing units seem to be beating the national average in terms of increases in sales values. In 2007, real estate values decreased an average of 7% in Nevada County, California, and are expected to decrease 10% in 2008. But when the first two units of the Nevada City, California cohousing development were sold in early 2008 (two years after move-in), they went for $115,000 more than the original purchase price. (They were bought for $325,000 and sold for $450,000.) Both units sold within a couple of weeks of being put on the market, and were sold entirely by word of mouth — no realtors. This makes sense — there were over a hundred people on the waiting list to buy into that community. (In March

2008, 60% of house sales in the state of California were to banks. As far as I know, not a single cohousing house in California [out of more than 2,000], or in the entire US, has ever sold to a bank.)

This kind of enthusiasm is what makes banks in Denmark — and increasingly in the US — so interested in cohousing. A custom neighborhood is actually much less

Work days are usually one Saturday a month. There are often two or three coaches — that is, those who organize the projects and buy the materials.

Unlike the body language at an ATM machine, people do approach residents in their back yard — their private space.

The better the layout, the less management. Issues get solved along the way.
Southside Cohousing, Sacramento, California.

risky than a custom house, which, of course, is much less risky than anything built to sell on speculation. Oddly, of the 830,000 or so houses built in the US in 2008, the vast majority were speculative (over 90%) and therein lies the risky part for banks. "Build it and they will come," is the kind of simplistic approach that gets people in trouble. Custom neighborhoods have proven to be the safest real estate investment in the United States. Again, it makes sense. If, for some reason, you have to move somewhere else, there is an entire neighborhood to continue the momentum to successfully occupy

Who Does What?

The more able-bodied, say those 55-65, tend to assign themselves the more physically-demanding tasks; the healthy 65-75 year-olds might do mid-range chores like tidying the workshop or cleaning the shelves in the common house; and those 75 or older might mend the curtains. Of course, we know that many abilities are not age specific.

This scenario is reminiscent of any small town or village. This timeless fashion of managing our own needs is the only sustainable solution. There just isn't enough money to hire all this out, not to mention that, if done right, it's not an imposition on anyone — and in fact, is great community building.

While a group's social policies will be specific to that group (the social policies of two senior cohousing com-

munities are at the end of this chapter), there are a few issues that every senior cohousing group will take up at some point during the planning and development process. We have found that it takes longer — much longer — to use another group's management policy as a point of departure than it does to brainstorm, discuss, and decide on your own. The most far-reaching and personal of decisions have to do with co-care. What can and should residents expect in terms of co-care? Conversely, what should be the limits? Since aging gracefully includes the possibility of aging suddenly, certain basic co-care issues have to be resolved in advance of move-in.

the empty home. And who better to sell a neighborhood than the other future neighbors? The end of suburbia may finally get this message across in the United States.

Sources of financing outside the large banks can be found. Small local banks might step up to finance local projects when larger banks take a more conservative stance. Innovative energy-saving measures might provide a group access to low-rate, government-sponsored mortgages. One of the key points about financing is that where there is a will, there is usually a way.

Policy Agreements to be made in Study Group III

Co-Care

Codified co-care issues should address who does what and when, and what each member commits to doing, or not doing. It's about boundaries. Most residents just want to be neighbors, after all, not health aides.

Separating neighborly care from professional care is not a colossal task in senior cohousing, for two reasons. First, people who live in cohousing readily learn to say no — they know each other that well. Second, the size of the community means that co-care burdens are easily distributed as a natural, normal part of everyday life. Picking up someone's medicine while

you're picking up your own is just not that big of a deal.

After living in a senior cohousing community for a while, residents will likely find that their agreed-upon co-care tasks are not an undue burden. Rather, they will be naturally easy to do and immensely rewarding. Said one resident: "I love the support I get from this small group of people — but it also works because I don't depend on it. I could live without it, but then again why would I?" Co-care basically comes in three categories:

1. Care that you have agreed to do. For example, bring dinner to people when they can't make it to common dinner, pick up medicine, check on folks in the morning — easy stuff.

2. Care that you have agreed that you will not do, for example

Single women find particular harbor in cohousing.

Living room in Otium senior cohousing.

administer medication, give baths, change diapers — hard stuff.

3. Care that you never imagined you would do before you cared about a person, but it turns out to be easy because he or she lives just next door. There's lots of small, easy things like making a cup of tea, having a conversation, reading someone the paper — tasks that aren't critical but are somehow very important and very giving at the same time.

Some of the issues about eventual co-care that might be addressed are:

- What are the extents and limits to care that residents should be expected to provide to other residents? At what point can an

---

The interesting thing about community rules is that each community's rules are different — each one fits. Here is one community's set that was given to me by resident Olaf Dejgaard.

Munksøgård's Rules & Regulations

During construction, the senior cohousing group at Munksøgård devised a set of rules to address:

A. Community relations.

B. Residents' payments to a common fund for paying expenses for equipment, plants, etc.

C. Rules for administering the waiting list for people who would like to live there.

D. The frequency of general meetings and establishing a coordinating committee of three members who prioritize current issues for the general meeting.

E. Committee meetings held according to need — initially once each week, later, once every other week, and then once a month.

F. Ad hoc working groups that are formed when needed, for both management and practical tasks such as house maintenance, lawn and garden maintenance, snow removal, common house matters, etc.

These special rules have proven particularly useful:

1. Decisions of special importance must be presented at one cohousing group meeting, but not decided on until the following meeting.

2. New group members must be between 50 and 65 years of age and cannot have children living with them.

3. At least one-third of the community should be male (at the time this was decided, Munksøgård had 17 women and 6 men).

4. When an apartment becomes vacant, it is first offered to the other cohousers. If none of them wants the apartment, it is offered to those on the waiting list, which usually has between 40 and 80 people on it. Usually between five and ten people show an interest, so the first five are invited to an interview with all of the current members of the group. Everyone tells them a little about living in a senior cohousing community and the candidates are given the opportunity to explain how they think they can contribute.

individual say, "No, I can't do that"?

+ How are the costs of outside caregivers shared?

+ When residents become seriously ill, under what circumstances should they move out?

+ What amount of work (chores, etc.) should be required of each resident. Should it be dependant on age? Length of residence in the community? (Often it averages about 20 hours a year of required time.) Usually, everyone can do — and enjoys doing — something, from telephone reminder calls, to shopping, to physical work. If residents can't do all of their hours, can they pay an hourly fee, and if so, how much?

+ How often can ill residents expect to have people checking in on them?

+ What are the rules for new residents entering senior cohousing? Are there age limits? Health requirements?

+ How does the money work (dinners, supplies, insurance, guests, etc.)?

+ Who pays for the rental unit that one person's caregiver has occupied for two months?

These are examples of the kinds of issues to address. Residents should consider enough scenarios to feel comfortable. That said, I often argue that people who are new to the cohousing concept should just take a deep breath and relax. After they experience the upside of living in a cohousing community, they often discover that, in retrospect, they worried too much about these issues. But, since it takes time to get a project built, talking over these items gives an excuse to get together.

Planning for Acute Disability

If the group wants to, it is sometimes helpful to consider hypothetical cases

Crossing paths at Pleasant Hill Cohousing.

Andedammen Rules

Karen, Tua, and Kirsten (women who are all over 70) have written down the following rules of their cohousing community, Andedammen in Birkerød, Denmark. Decisions about the committees are made at the common meetings, which are held on a monthly basis. Membership of the committees is not fixed; members can move from one committee to another. This is a good way they found to split up their work:

The Basic Committees:

- The Outside Committee Responsible for:
  - Maintaining the outdoor areas: lawn mowing, hedge cutting, pruning and planting.
  - Upkeep of the driveway and parking lot.
  - Sweeping the flagstones on the footpath and the square.
  - Buying sand for the sandboxes and gravel for the road.
  - Cleaning the duck pond and the hedge around it.
  - Clearing snow.
  - Buying and maintaining the garden tools.
- The Garbage Room Committee Responsible for:
  - Cleaning the garbage room: removing old newspapers, cardboard boxes, sweeping the floor.
  - Ensuring that the garbage truck has clear access each week.
- The Vegetable Garden Committee Responsible for:
  - Sowing, planting, weeding, harvesting of vegetables and flowers.
  - Beekeeping.
- The Shopping Committee Responsible for:

- Pricing and ordering of supplies, including beer and soda.
- Keeping supplies in order, maintaining accounts
- Cleaning and maintaining the common refrigerator and freezer.
- The Kitchen Committee Responsible for:
  - Buying and maintaining the service machines and cleaning supplies for kitchen and basement.
- The Common Living Room Committee Responsible for:
  - Maintaining the hall and common rooms.
  - Washing sofa covers.
  - Keeping flowers and decorations in the common rooms.
  - Maintaining the furniture, lamps, and plants.
- The Laundry Committee Responsible for:
  - Maintaining the machines and clotheslines.
  - Purchasing detergent.
  - Keeping the laundry and drying rooms clean.
- The Social Committee Responsible for:
  - Organizing common parties and get-togethers, Christmas parties, etc.
- The Workshop Committee Responsible for:
  - Creating and maintaining a workshop for the residents of the cohousing community.
  - Maintenance of the common tools.
  - Assigning a resident to be responsible for overseeing the cleaning.
- Cleaning Rules.
  - All common rooms, on the ground floor and basement must be cleaned every Sunday morning.
  - The cleaning team makes sure that everything has been cleaned thoroughly, including the 🐁

kitchen, tables, floors, and window sills in the common living room, the staircase, and the bathroom in the hall.

- Kitchen Rules
  The cooks:
  - Decide the menu and post it on the kitchen message board as early as possible. The cooks shop for, cook, and serve the meal, and keep receipts for reimbursement.
  - Set the tables.
  - Clean and do the dishes; put crockery and cutlery back into place.
  - Ensure that the dining room is cleaned up, floor swept, and tables wiped clean. The cooks put buckets of soapy water out on the tables, and the residents clean their own tables. The chairs are put back after the floor has been swept. Empty beer and soda bottles are put in boxes under the kitchen table, and wine bottles are put in the bottle containers.
  - Toss out the leftovers, if none of the residents want them. Feed for the chicken must be put in their respective bowls and taken out to them.
  - Clean the kitchen floor, and the big trash bag must always be taken to the trash room.

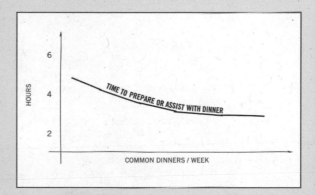

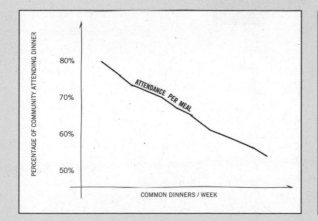

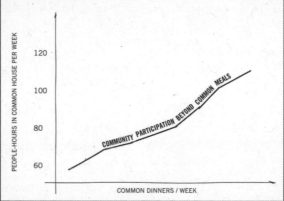

Nira and Hazel on the sidewalk playing go-fish at Nevada City Cohousing.

around to other seniors? Must Joe hire an outsider to mow the lawn?

Of course, these are minor issues compared to Joe's healthcare needs. But when Joe gets out of the hospital and wishes to return home, does co-care in senior cohousing include requesting, or assigning, another person or two to help him to dress in the morning and undress in the evening? Can Joe make it to the common house for dinner? Can he cook for himself? Who might bring him three meals a day, or stock his fridge with microwaveable frozen dinners as a fallback? Who will take charge of installing the extra safety bars for the shower? Does he need a wheelchair? Who is going to take him to physical therapy sessions at the medical clinic two or three times per week, perhaps for months? Maybe it will be someone from the group or maybe not. While it's key to avoid overburdening the individuals within the group, it is encouraging to see how in a village, it's just natural to help out.

While the questions are many, the answer is straightforward: yes, cohousing residents can be counted on to do some of these tasks — which ones depends on the agreement. Most likely, the cohousers will take care of a couple of tasks; relatives and friends will do others; insurance will take care of a couple; some will be hired out. After eight years,

based on plausible "fourth quarter" scenarios. For example, consider Joe Smith, a previously healthy 60-year-old in a senior cohousing community, who has a sudden stroke. With his right side paralyzed, he can't dress himself. He may not be able to talk coherently for a while. He cannot do anything that requires the coordination of both hands. All maintenance tasks are out for him, perhaps permanently. How do the routine tasks that he was happily performing get shifted

Munksøgård is having its first seniors who are not fully capable, and the group easily helps out with their needs. Some tasks need be done only long enough to organize a permanent solution. This community approach is tantamount to carry-over care, and will give Joe's family enough time to find more permanent assistance for him (an HMO provider, for example), and it can play a huge role in keeping Joe out of institutional care. Senior cohousing's built-in intermediate co-care feature is perhaps the most important — and certainly the most tangible — method for successfully aging in place. Again, I have a lot of faith in a group to come up with the right thing — even without a policy. Interestingly, I've found it is impossible to predict who will come through more often — it may be the person who patiently sat down with others to consider all the possibilities or it may be the person who didn't have a minute for any of that discussion.

Joe's story brings up important questions: What sort of agreements should a resident group make about allowing a disabled senior into the community early on, and when does someone become too sick to remain? Where does a group draw the line? It may not sound politically correct, but it can never be assumed that it is OK for a community member *not* to do his or her share. No one is obligated

to take care of another member, and everyone is obligated not to take advantage of the good will of others. That said, I'm so often amazed how those who might appear at first blush the least capable, in fact may do more than their share and get the most done. In our community, we have 21 seniors, one with multiple sclerosis and one with Parkinson's disease — and they are two of the most capable people in the community.

Entry into the community would not be a problem for a person like Joe, since he was fine before his stroke. But should someone with severe Parkinson's disease, severe MS, Alzheimer's, or other long-term diseases that are increasingly debilitating be admitted? How does the community make sure that there are enough caregivers? Answers to these questions all depend on the group and their individual and collective sensibilities. When these issues get addressed, it has to be done openly, honestly, and without righteousness or guilt-inducing language.

But what seems clear is that while you can't manufacture caring, loving feelings, you can predict timeless, village-like patterns. My grandmother died in a village, a little hamlet of 325 people. During her last ten years, she was entirely bedridden. Fifteen different townspeople played a significant role in providing for her quality of

Being silly in the common house.

Preparing common dinner in Bellingham Cohousing.

Dinner Policy

Dinner is important; we have to eat. And especially in the context of senior cohousing, it is not only where residents get physiological sustenance, it is where they get emotional sustenance as well. So many seniors say that, especially after 70, they have to make a very conscious choice, a choice that is not that easy, every day. That is the choice to either get up and be active, or to think "maybe I will just lounge around today. I don't have much energy."

In senior cohousing residents have to get up — someone might come visit; there might be something really good to eat in the common house; someone might want to do something fun, and, oh yeah, there is someone else to do it with. Senior cohousing is for people who don't like to be alone, at least not all the time. Residents can have dinner at home — that choice is always available — but Munksøgård residents say that they eat in the common house more than they thought they would. As proof, common dinners at Munksøgård are available and enjoyed five times a week.

life. Only one person was paid — for about ten hours per week— to check in and do things for her. My grandmother had been a member of the community for over 40 years. She was known as a great cook, a quilt-maker, and an incurable gossip — an elder in the community who had accumulated a lot of good will.

Part Four
The First Wave — Pioneering Senior Cohousing in America: The Beginnings of an American Movement

Senior cohousing development in the US is getting off to a great start. And we have already learned lessons that will make it far easier for future communities to be built. In this section, we present five of these communities: Glacier Circle in Davis, California; ElderSpirit in Virginia; Silver Sage in Colorado; Wolf Creek Lodge in Grass Valley, California; and Artisans Plaza in San Juan Bautista, California. These are five very different communities, but they have similar mandates — to make a community that is supportive for the real lives of active adults.

CHAPTER 10

The First Wave

**Glacier Circle: The First Senior
Cohousing in America
Davis, California
8 units
Architect: Julie Haney,
Macaulay + Architects
Completed: 2005
Tenure: 8 ownership units**

(Case study originally written by
Marysia Miernowska, McCamant &
Durrett Architects)

Glacier Circle courtyard.

Rich Morrison walked into the common house and took the gong off the wall. "Have you seen our common table?" he asked proudly, "We designed it ourselves." He smiled and began walking up and down the courtyard, summoning his neighbors to their weekly meeting. Rich's neighbors slowly began trickling down the curved path, surrounded by blossoming flowers and birds feeding on seeds.

Conversation was lively as everyone gathered around the round common table for the weekly two-hour business meeting. When all of the seats were filled, the members began the meeting with their covenant, which is read aloud before every meeting.

After the reading, neighbors had time to share personal comments with their group. "Perhaps you should define 'sharing,'" suggested Stan to his wife, remembering that our standard culture does not allot a special space and time for this type of communication. "When we share, we sit together, listen with intention, and take turns sharing something that is either happening to you in your life or something that you are feeling," she stated.

The business meeting was fun. The neighbors covered their agenda with care, and reached consensus on the issues presented. Stan pointed out that the fountain in the courtyard was often low on water. "How can we fill the fountain with recycled water?" "Well, I can collect about a pail's worth each time I do my laundry," Ann offered. "I'll bring it down to the fountain after I drop off the paper for you," Ray volunteered. "I can also collect some water from my shower." Others agreed to do the same; others offered to collect water if someone else could help carry it down.

After resolving each issue, they opened up the agenda. Rich reminded his neighbors that he would be away for a week. Right away, somebody volunteered to water his plants and another neighbor volunteered to feed his dog, the community mascot, Fergie. "It was arranged for Fergie to be walked each day, and if anyone else wishes to give him some company, a pat on the head, he would love to see you." Rich offered to leave his keys in the common house office and everyone agreed to stop by and visit Fergie while Rich was away.

The two hours flew by. There was so much grace and easiness to the meeting — not to mention laughter and lightness! When one of the residents from the health committee reminded her neighbors to get a shingles shot,

---

We, the members of Glacier Circle, covenant:

- To listen deeply and thoughtfully in our dialogues, mindful that our relationships are sacred.

- To be patient with each other, appreciating our differing gifts and welcoming creative ideas. When necessary, we will confront courageously with love.

- We agree to assume appropriate leadership roles and to participate fully in the group process.

- While we value our time together, we also respect our members' need for privacy.

- We will remember to assume the good intent of others and to strive to treat other members as well as ourselves with loving-kindness.

Nancy remembered that she had a case of shingles last year. "When did you have shingles last year? How could that be without me knowing it?" Lois asked. The best of friends, they both realized that they weren't able to keep up on each others lives before becoming immediate neighbors. "I don't know, but I did," Nancy replied. "Remember?" Ellen piped in, "You had shingles last year before your trip!" "What trip?" asked Nancy as she burst into laughter. Albeit good friends, this was before they moved into a senior cohousing community together. Everyone laughed, and as they closed the meeting, they arranged to carpool to the Chinese restaurant where they traditionally go out for dinner after the Thursday meetings. Rich and his wife Sue joined John and Nancy in their Prius, and a group of four hybrids drove to the restaurant where they gathered around the large, circular table that had inspired the design of their common house table.

A Unique Community Planning Process

From their first design meeting in Ellen's home in March 2002 to the completion of construction in 2006, the Glacier Circle community underwent a lengthy and organic process of definition and design. Because of the group's initiative, hard work, and

vision, they live in a vibrant cohousing community today. The sunshine that shines back from the smiles and eyes of the residents comes from their unique planning process: a process of coming together with friends and peers to determine what housing arrangement would best support successfully aging in place. "We explored what we wanted for our futures and how to create it," said one resident. This process of exploration and discovery made peers into friends, residents into developers, neighbors into confidants, and this group of seniors into pioneers.

Old-time Friends and Explorers

Before we describe *how* this group of 80-year-olds began their quest for a high quality of aging, or *what* they did to make their dream a reality, it is

Residents partake in a round table group meeting.

Glacier Circle Mission Statement:

The mission of Glacier Circle Senior Community is to create and maintain a small cooperative-style housing community of seniors who share some expenses, skills, and visions in mutual support and friendship. We are committed to being a welcoming community of independent outlooks and shared values.

"At one point we even considered buying bungalows together. We also looked into renovating a huge house. We had various ideas, and we invited specialists to come and teach us about our different options. We had someone come to talk to us about co-ops. But we decided that a co-op was not what we were looking for either; we wanted more autonomy, and we wanted our children to inherit our homes."

— Glacier Circle resident

important to say *who* they are — mostly to appreciate their can-do attitude. Their success wasn't due to their having a lot of money (obviously, they had to have some) but was mostly about their self-deterministic attitude.

Who are the residents of Glacier Circle?

They are a group of retirees (age 74-92) whose professions include:

+ Schoolteacher and watercolor painter
+ Physicist
+ College professor
+ Environmental health scientist
+ Psychotherapist
+ Psychologist

The majority of the members are also members of the Unitarian Universalist Church. Many of them have known each other for 40-50 years. Many of the women were in a women's group together, and once the husbands saw how much fun the women were having, they started a men's group.

Not only did these social activities bond the future residents, many of the couples were also the founding members of their church. They were used to being pioneers and doers. They shared the empowering experience of creating something based on their vision, and when the time came to explore what was needed for their old age, they knew who to turn to. For this reason, their project never required any active recruiting.

A Quest for a "Better Way"

As the empty nesters planned for their retirement, they considered different options. Many of them shared the frustration of taking care of a large, empty house. "The lawn was just too much to take care of, and I easily imagined feeling isolated in that house. So a few of us signed up for the university retirement community. They had even agreed to put us near each other. But that development was so large." They did not want to feel anonymous in a sea of homes. "There had to be a better way," said Ellen.

The women's group became a safe place for Ellen to share her concerns about isolation and institutionalization. Nancy remembers Ellen being the one to bring up the question of "who would take care of us when it got to that point." "So we listened to her concerns and we started talking about it," said Nancy. None of the friends knew the perfect solution for their retired years, but their friendships were strong, so they agreed to explore the issues of aging together. Ellen made invitations for a gathering at her home, and she invited the women and husbands of her women's group and some other folks from the UU Church. "That first day, two dozen people filled up my living room." Among the attendees was Muir Commons Cohousing developer Virginia Thigpen (also a UU member) who became an advisor to the project.

An Informal Study Group I: Successful Aging

The group got together regularly and shared their concerns about the realities of aging: becoming isolated, driving, providing care for a spouse who needed assistance. To understand what it would mean to care for an elder, they invited a woman from hospice, who went through all of the details, explaining the reality of care. "We did not all come to the same conclusion, but we all became more aware of what we wanted," Ellen noted. Some of the original members decided to move closer to their kids. The group that went on concluded that they wanted to stay independent, for as long as possible, avoid isolation, and that in proximity, they could better support and care for one another. Then, after seeing Muir Commons

Cohousing, it was clear to them what they wanted to create, and they set out to do it.

They concluded that senior cohousing gave them both the independence and the proximate community they needed to age in place successfully. They participated in facilitation training at the local university. This program included personality tests, which helped members learn more about each other's strengths and challenges. They decided they were ready to complement each other's strengths, to work together, and to learn from each other. Thus, they had created and completed the Study Group I process of exploring the issues of aging in place, all on their own. This group had actually started their group process 30 years earlier in their women's group and 20 years earlier in their men's group. The Danes created the organized SG I process to compress this 30-year process to a 10-week process.

Having gone through the process of choosing the housing solution that would best serve their needs and aspirations, they embarked on a journey as developers, hiring a developer consultant and an architect, Julie Haney. Julie facilitated the site programming, common house design, and the programming for the private homes — the process otherwise known as Study Group II.

Landscaping at Glacier Circle.

Residents at Glacier Circle, Davis, California. A sense of entry, a sense of place. The physical environment feels embracing, like the social environment.

Interior of a unit at Glacier Circle. The houses are open and airy.

The Site

Glacier Circle is within walking distance of a greenbelt area with a walking path and wildlife pond. A medical building is adjacent to the property and a major hospital is four blocks away. Mass transit and shops are also nearby.

Gardening space was included in the site design, both within the courtyard and in the rear of each home. Knowing there would be a garden made it easier for some members to leave their existing homes and move to Glacier Circle. Flowering plants and a common garden with vegetables, citrus and fruit trees unite the buildings. They chose native plants — no grass — and drip irrigation to conserve water.

One of the biggest challenges of the project was parking. City planners insisted that the parking lot accommodate a large turning radius for big cars, as they had pre-conceived notions about old ladies driving Cadillacs. In reality, the group members were all driving hybrids and small compact cars.

The Common House

The residents decided to include an affordable second floor apartment of 900 sq. ft. above the common house, and they offered it to a couple in exchange for house-cleaning services for the community. They thought that in the future the apartment would be used for an on-site nurse to help residents age in place. They actually hired a caregiver within a month.

The common house also includes an office, a meeting room, and, of course, a large kitchen and dining area. A gracious common terrace faces the common courtyard. The residents have potluck dinners once a week, go out to dinner once a week, and have a professional chef that cooks common dinners twice a week.

The Private Homes

The eight homes, which range in size, are placed along an east/west access; all face south for maximum solar gain. There are three types of residences: the bungalow (1023 sq. ft.); the cottage (1204-1348 sq. ft.); and the townhouse (1536 sq. ft.). Three homes have photovoltaic panels and solar water heating with a tankless gas water heater for a backup. All of the buildings incorporate daylight from skylights and sun tubes and use fluorescent lighting for general room illumination.

They've Paved the Way

Four years after they began their planning, the residents were able to move in. Now, they enjoy the fruits of their labor and the rich relationships that are so close at hand. As 79-year-old Rich told me as we chatted in the courtyard one day, "Emotionally, there's no reason why I can't continue to grow until I'm 100, if I'm lucky." Indeed, the residents feel that by living in community, they are able to be more supportive friends; the support that they receive helps them grow in wisdom.

Nancy told me how her long-time friend Peggy began losing her eyesight before they moved in. "I couldn't be as supportive of my friend Peggy as I wanted to be because I lived across town, and you have to make a real arrangement to make those

Interior of a Glacier Circle unit from the upper level.

Age-in-Place Design

- 3-ft. wide doors.
- Low profile floor coverings and easy-to-negotiate concrete sidewalk textures.
- Wheelchair-accessible bathrooms and showers.
- Flat foundations.
- One-story homes (all but two).
- Two-story homes that can be retrofitted with an electric stair chair and a first floor plan that can be adapted to include a master bedroom.
- All units have two bedrooms so, if necessary, one bedroom can be used for a live-in caregiver.
- Bright lighting.
- Extra storage space.
- Parking connected to homes.

This last item would usually be a concern in cohousing, since an important intention of the cohousing site plan is to have neighbors meet on their way home from the parking lot. Across the board, all others planning a senior cohousing community have told me that a relationship with their neighbor is sustained by walking from parking to house and does not occur if parking is at the home. However, since this group is small and the particular site plan is so centripetal and so focused around a small central courtyard (you can see from one living room into another), the cars at each house don't compromise the relationships much.

Glacier Circle Economics

- Total cost: 3.2 million, or about $400,000 each, plus $350 per month in dues.
- About $850 per month to be collected in rental income.
- Each residence is individually owned; each property includes a private yard and patio.
- Of course, everyone owns the common house, common yard, driveway, and gardens.

View from courtyard.

helps me further myself in my old age," says Stan, who studies ethics in his free time.

As the sun began to set, Nancy and John brought out a bottle of wine and sat on their porch facing the common yard. A neighbor walked by and joined them for a drink. The water level had risen in the fountain (somebody must have brought a pail down already) and the water was making the stones glisten in the sun. Laughter and lively conversation filled the air.

The Glacier Circle community is a living example of the vitality that senior cohousing supports in the lives of elders. "We have more to do than people in retirement communities. Having to work and think, even if it doesn't help you live longer, it helps you live in a healthier fashion."

Much credit is due to the lively and caring residents of this community who figured out the Study Group I process of exploring issues of aging in place — all on their own. Just as it is intended, this process of exploration and discovery led them to establish a strong foundation upon which they built a thriving community.

Lessons Learned

The example of Glacier Circle is unique, and it provides great lessons for other senior cohousing groups. This group of friends was the first group in the US to build their own

connections. I couldn't be the friend I wanted to be. With this proximity, I can check in really easily. I wasn't able to do that before, because it was all such a production." Peggy's husband Stan feels the difference that living in proximity to caring friends has had on his life as well. "Feeling supported senior cohousing community. They accomplished it with the average resident age being 80. Their strong friendships and faith in finding a better housing solution carried them through to the successful completion of their community. The process that this group developed organically is possible to accomplish in a more economical and timely fashion using the process suggested by cohousing professionals. "It took a lot longer than we thought it would," said one resident. "Had we used a more efficient process, we probably would have saved $40-50K on each of our houses."

When we asked founding members Ellen and Ray what they would have done differently, they concurred:

"We really wish we would have started this earlier. It would have been great to start aging in community by the age of 60 or 65. If we could share one piece of advice to those considering senior cohousing, that would be it: Just do it!"

ElderSpirit: The Second Senior Cohousing in America
Abingdon, Virginia
29 Units
Tenure: 16 condominiums,
13 rental units
Completed: 2006

Spirituality can be an incredible source of strength for seniors and a great common focus for a community.

Standing in awe of the future ElderSpirit community during construction.

The Spirit Center at ElderSpirit Community at Trailview.

ElderSpirit Mission Statement

Spirituality:

Members believe that spiritual growth is the primary work of those in the later stages of life. Members encourage one another in the search for meaning in life and commitment to a spiritual path. Freedom of religion is fundamental.

Mutual Support:

Members develop face-to-face relationships through which they offer and receive support. They express their needs and convictions, listen to each other and strive to act responsibly, considering their good and the good of the other.

Simple Lifestyle and Respect for the Earth:

Conscious that over-consumption by persons in wealthy countries threatens the earth's living systems, members seek a simplified lifestyle that reflects a respectful relationship with the environment.

Arts and Recreation:

Leisure, recreational activities, and travel contribute uniquely toward refreshing the mind, body, and spirit. The arts form an integral part of the community. Members share and develop their gifts and talents through such activities as music, dance, theater, storytelling, gardening, crafts, weaving, etc.

Health:

The word "health" comes from the same root as "heal," "whole," and "holy." Recognizing this, members pay attention to nutrition, rest, exercise, and social interaction.

Resident members also commit to the following values:

CARE DURING ILLNESS AND DYING:

The common goal of the ElderSpirit cohousing community is to offer care to one another in the later years. It affirms home care and dying at home. However, when institutional care occurs, a member of the community stays in touch with the person and closely follows her/his condition. Members recognize that the process of living involves one's desire for tolerable health and a capacity to be generative. Within the community, the process of dying raises one's awareness that all surrender physical life, not in isolation, but as a sister or brother of the human community.

Mutual Assistance

Sharing of goods and services is the norm in the ElderSpirit cohousing community. When members have needs beyond the individual and family group, they are encouraged to make their needs known. Community meetings and common meals provide opportunities for open discussion, sharing, and mutual assistance.

Many seniors use spirituality to reach greater insight and self-awareness, either through established religions or through activities like yoga or tai chi. ElderSpirit is a senior cohousing community that is based on the desire to explore the potential of late-life spirituality and mutual support.

The idea behind the ElderSpirit community came from a committee of the nonprofit Federation of Communities in Service (FOCIS). FOCIS was started in 1967 by a group of women working with community service and development organizations. When some group members reached retirement age they decided to explore the possibilities of creating a senior community, and in 1995 they formed a committee named FOCIS FUTURES. I worked with them and encouraged them in their decision to create a cohousing community specifically for people over the age of 55. They wanted to attract seniors who regarded their senior years as a phase brimming with possibilities, not a boring and depressing end to a long life. The result is ElderSpirit, a senior cohousing community designed to enable residents to explore all the opportunities the senior years afford. Late-life spirituality and mutual assistance are the keywords that express the sensibilities of this group of people, and in order to better realize their vision they defined these terms and, in turn, formed the social framework of their community (see "Mission Statement" sidebar).

After extensive research in the Appalachian area, the group decided to place their community in Abingdon; with the help of Dene Peterson they found a 3.7-acre site along the Virginia Creeper Trail. A corporation (Trailview Development Corp.) was formed to purchase the property and FOCIS received a three-year grant from The Retirement Research Foundation of Chicago for predevelopment expenses. They established a board, hired a part-time

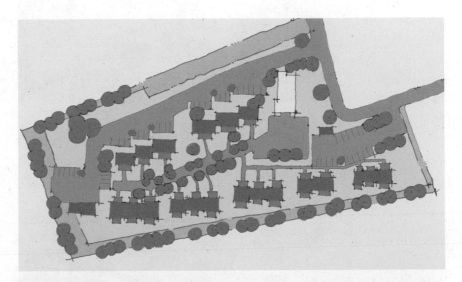

Site plan of ElderSpirit Community.

Planting Time.

Enjoying a common meal at ElderSpirit.

Chatting over lunch.

Dene Petersen

"From a public policy perspective, the preventive value of a cohousing community, which reduces isolation, encourages social activity, and supports members through illness or bereavement, is inestimable."

— Maria Brenton,
Cohousing Communities Consultant

staff, and engaged an architect. Project manager Dene Peterson contacted government housing agencies to find ways to make affordable housing a part of the project. A community coordinator, Jean Marie Luce, worked on getting the word out about the project and gathering prospective residents. This was done primarily through classes for older adults taught at the local college.

During the programming process, the architect collected input and ideas for the design from a building committee and future residents. The result is a community consisting of 29 homes: 13 privately owned one- and two-bedroom attached homes, 16 income-restricted rental homes, a common house, and a spiritual center. The private houses are laid out along a pedestrian path, with the common house and a plaza in the center. Parking is behind the houses on the edges of the site. Construction began in 2004 with move-in the summer of 2006. ElderSpirit is the second senior cohousing community to be built in the United States.

ElderSpirit Community is now a separate organization that works with seniors interested in forming new senior communities and spiritual programs. The untraditional values of ElderSpirit Community in Abingdon have created a lot of interest in the project, inspiring people to start creating similar spiritual communities all over the US and Canada.

Silver Sage: The Third Senior Cohousing in America
Boulder, Colorado
16 units
Architect: McCamant & Durrett Architects
Co-Architect: Brian Bowen
Completed: 2007
Tenure: 16 ownership units

More and more intergenerational cohousing communities are faced with the question of how to accommodate their senior residents as they grow older and their needs and physical abilities change. Some of the first cohousers to actively address the issue were the residents of Nyland Cohousing in Boulder, Colorado, ten years after their own community had

been built. Their first idea was to extend their community with units especially designed for the needs and preferences of their senior residents. They also considered subdividing their 42-acre site to create a second cohousing community for seniors, but unfortunately, that didn't work out.

In order to find out more about the possibilities of making senior cohousing, they hosted the two public presentations about Danish senior cohousing that I did during two winter holidays. Then, the Nyland residents found more interested seniors, and in 2003 they had gathered a group. Their vision was a small-scale, participatory cohousing community where everybody knows each other and amenities are close at hand.

The developer who had built Nyland, Wonderland Hill Development, proposed a ¾-acre site in

Monica Appleby enjoys a fruit cornucopia.

Gathering in the common house.

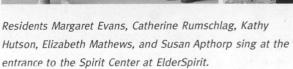

Residents Margaret Evans, Catherine Rumschlag, Kathy Hutson, Elizabeth Mathews, and Susan Apthorp sing at the entrance to the Spirit Center at ElderSpirit.

Visions and Values of the Silver Sage residents:

- Nourish body and soul with good food, good health, and good company.
- Live mindfully in community, encouraging wisdom, compassion, and interpersonal growth.
- Experience stylish living with thoughtfully designed interiors.
- Share inviting outdoor spaces such as gardens, courtyards, decks, patios, and views of the Flatirons.
- Enjoy North Boulder's urban options, including hiking, biking, cafes, and public transportation.

the new, urban Holiday Neighborhood (two miles north of downtown Boulder) that includes community gardens, a park, bike trails, artists' studios, pedestrian walkways, and a (projected) new Boulder Public Library branch. The prospective site was located just across the street from Wild Sage — an existing intergenerational cohousing community built in 2004, also by Wonderland Hill Development. Working with a local nonprofit housing advocate, the developer put together a varied-income project and worked through the steps for creating senior cohousing: Feasibility and Study Groups I and III. They engaged our firm, McCamant & Durrett Architects, to work with the group in the participatory design process in Study Group II, and part of Study Group I

The common house has a large kitchen, a dining area, intimate living room, guest rooms, and crafts and performance areas. A variety of common activities take place there, including common dinners, lectures, films, house concerts, reading groups, fitness

Future residents planning for Silver Sage Senior Cohousing, Boulder, Colorado.

Street elevation of Silver Sage by MCamant & Durrett Architects (MDA).

classes, and more. Like ElderSpirit, Silver Sage residents share an interest in spirituality, although this was not the emphasis of the community's planning.

✳

Interview with resident, Arthur Okner, during the planning stage of the Silver Sage project:
March 2005

Arthur Okner MSW is 62 years old. After a successful career in business, which included five years with the US General Accounting Office (a congressional auditing arm); four years in the US Air Force; and 25 years as a self-employed small business consultant and expediter, Art turned his attentions to community building. In 1999 he relocated to Boulder from Greenwich

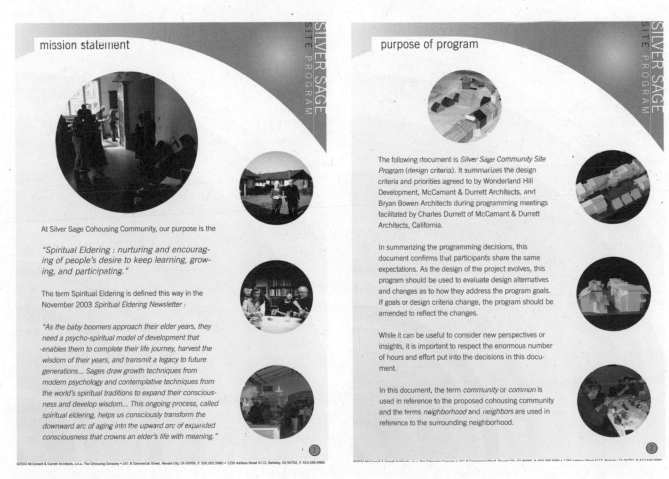

mission statement

SILVER SAGE
SITE PROGRAM

At Silver Sage Cohousing Community, our purpose is the

"Spiritual Eldering : nurturing and encouraging of people's desire to keep learning, growing, and participating."

The term Spiritual Eldering is defined this way in the November 2003 *Spiritual Eldering Newsletter* :

"As the baby boomers approach their elder years, they need a psycho-spiritual model of development that enables them to complete their life journey, harvest the wisdom of their years, and transmit a legacy to future generations... Sages draw growth techniques from modern psychology and contemplative techniques from the world's spiritual traditions to expand their consciousness and develop wisdom... This ongoing process, called spiritual eldering, helps us consciously transform the downward arc of aging into the upward arc of expanded consciousness that crowns an elder's life with meaning."

①

02004 McCamant & Durrett Architects, a.k.a. The Cohousing Company • 241 B Commercial Street, Nevada City, CA 95959, P. 530.265.9980 • 1250 Addison Street #113, Berkeley, CA 94702, P. 510.549.9980

purpose of program

SILVER SAGE
SITE PROGRAM

The following document is *Silver Sage Community Site Program* (design criteria). It summarizes the design criteria and priorities agreed to by Wonderland Hill Development, McCamant & Durrett Architects, and Bryan Bowen Architects during programming meetings facilitated by Charles Durrett of McCamant & Durrett Architects, California.

In summarizing the programming decisions, this document confirms that participants share the same expectations. As the design of the project evolves, this program should be used to evaluate design alternatives and changes as to how they address the program goals. If goals or design criteria change, the program should be amended to reflect the changes.

While it can be useful to consider new perspectives or insights, it is important to respect the enormous number of hours and effort put into the decisions in this document.

In this document, the term *community* or *common* is used in reference to the proposed cohousing community and the terms *neighborhood* and *neighbors* are used in reference to the surrounding neighborhood.

②

Sample program.

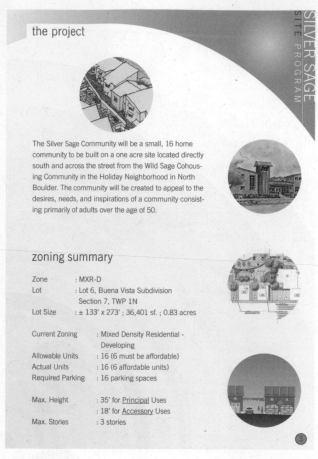

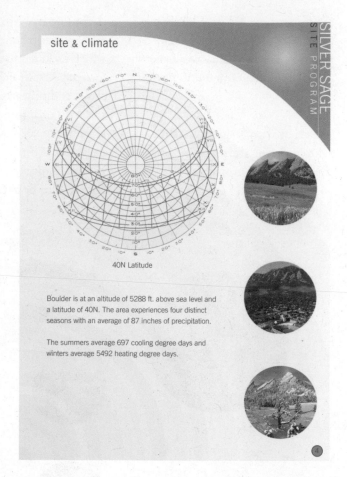

Sample program.

SILVER SAGE SITE PROGRAM

the project

The Silver Sage Community will be a small, 16 home community to be built on a one acre site located directly south and across the street from the Wild Sage Cohousing Community in the Holiday Neighborhood in North Boulder. The community will be created to appeal to the desires, needs, and inspirations of a community consisting primarily of adults over the age of 50.

zoning summary

Zone	: MXR-D
Lot	: Lot 6, Buena Vista Subdivision Section 7, TWP 1N
Lot Size	: ± 133' x 273' ; 36,401 sf. ; 0.83 acres
Current Zoning	: Mixed Density Residential - Developing
Allowable Units	: 16 (6 must be affordable)
Actual Units	: 16 (6 affordable units)
Required Parking	: 16 parking spaces
Max. Height	: 35' for Principal Uses : 18' for Accessory Uses
Max. Stories	: 3 stories

③

site & climate

40N Latitude

Boulder is at an altitude of 5288 ft. above sea level and a latitude of 40N. The area experiences four distinct seasons with an average of 87 inches of precipitation.

The summers average 697 cooling degree days and winters average 5492 heating degree days.

④

Village, New York. He then became very active in affordable housing issues; for two years he extolled the virtues of affordable housing to low income passers-by at the Boulder Farmers Market. The next year, he discovered cohousing and became a founding member of Wild Sage Cohousing in Boulder. He moved into Nomad Cohousing in North Boulder during the planning stages of Wild Sage. On a Wednesday or Sunday evening at Nomad, you can share dinner with the community and meet Arthur's gaggle of adopted grandkids. And get beaten in pool.

Interviewer: Kurt McCulloch, McCamant & Durrett Architects

Kurt: Tell me a little bit about how you live — are you retired? How do you spend your time?
Art: I retired when I was 50 and began to really search for a community,

an ecosystem to live in. This eventually moved me to go to graduate school in the early 90s when I got a masters degree in community organization at Yeshiva University in New York City. After living in Greenwich Village in New York from 1975 to 1999, I moved to Boulder, Colorado. I was very lonely here, and to overcome this I began doing volunteer work for the City of Boulder's Dept. of Affordable Housing.

Kurt: Okay, so how exactly did you get involved in cohousing?

Art: I met Jim Leach and Chuck Durrett in April of 2000 when I was asked by the director of the department of housing to attend what she thought was an informational seminar on cohousing — it was actually a kick-off meeting for what became Wild Sage Cohousing. After this experience, I thought there was no better place on earth to live than cohousing. Since then I've been working on developing cohousing communities. I try to have as much leisure time as possible. I'm interested in cohousing because cohousing makes sense in so many ways and is an important movement as well as a wonderful place to live.

Kurt: You live in cohousing at the moment, right?

Art: Partway through the Wild Sage development process a unit became vacant at Nomad Cohousing and I thought I would live there temporar-

ily until Wild Sage was completed. However, two little girls at the time 2½ and 3½ — my neighbors at Nomad — started coming over to my house every day. I couldn't leave them. However, since then, Silver Sage has taken my interest and I've been involved in this community's development. Senior cohousing suits me even better than cohousing and those girls will be near enough that I'll still be able to see them. They will be 8½ and 9½ when I move.

Kurt: What are your goals and expectations for Silver Sage Cohousing? How are they different from Nomad, the cohousing community where you live now?

Art: My goals? Well, even though I love being with children, I'm not involved in raising children full-time or in the capital-formation period of my life, as working parents are. There is a certain period of people's lives when it's important to earn money, focus on a career, and children who are in school. Work and children. That's not where I am right now, and so it's better for me to live with people where these things aren't central. I'm comfortable financially, and retired. In a senior-targeted community where people are finished raising children, they're around for a drink at 4:00 p.m. It's easier for people to reach out to each other when they're in the same place in their lives. In other words, I need more people to "play" with.

Kurt: What about the fact that you'll only be living with older people?

Art: Consider the alternatives. The location of most senior living facilities is determined by the affordability of land. Silver Sage, however, is intentionally located in order to allow for

Perspective sketch of Silver Sage Senior Cohousing. MDA

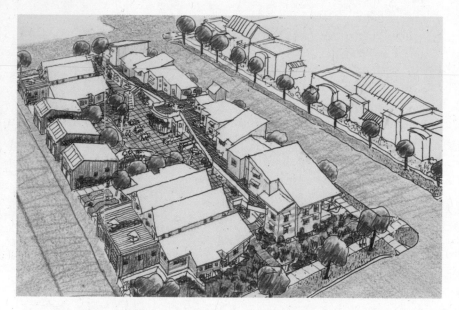

wider interaction. And much energy will be spent in reaching out to all generations through mentoring programs and a coffee shop, among others.

Kurt: Tell me more about the alternatives for seniors.

Art: I just got back from the National Conference on Aging. There are many institutions ready to take on the emerging senior demographic — but they are institutions where a resident follows the rules and is managed. At the conference there was much talk on the Dell Webb model of elder life. This is an illusion-based advertising campaign that paints a picture of a white-haired couple playing golf and tennis and sitting around the pool. In this model there is nothing to support life. There are only things. Things are bullshit. I'm not interested in paying to live at a place where I'm asking, "where's the management?" — I want to be the management. Besides, it's only a very small percentage of the

Courtyard elevation of Silver Sage. MDA

population that can financially support this way of life — for most people this illusion is something that they'll never have the money to buy.

Community is about getting closer and closer to each other. The Dell Webb model tells us that our lives as contributing members of society are already finished. In cohousing there's something more than just things, there's a shared sense of values and purpose. Institutions kill people. They make people sick, and eventually kill them off before their time.

Kurt: How does cohousing operate when someone's health begins to fail? How does cohousing address this?

Art: The design of senior cohousing provides people with the ability to age in place for as long as they possibly can. For example, there may be an extra room in your home where a professional care provider could live, and walking distances to the common house have been designed to be minimal. There's a suite in the common house for caretakers to work and live. And cost-efficient cluster care will be encouraged. As a community we've agreed to make such arrangements before we're faced with these realities. Aging sneaks up on people and then slams them into reality. However, we're thinking ahead. We're not in denial of our own mortality.

Kurt: Do you have any concerns or fears about living in senior cohousing?

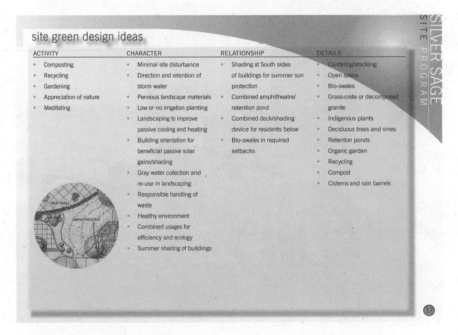

common courtyard

ACTIVITY	CHARACTER	RELATIONSHIP	DETAILS
Gardening	Pedestrian oriented	Porches, decks, and patios open onto court	Community garden
Performances	Beautifully landscaped		Bocce ball court
Bocce ball	Shaded areas	Links via pedestrian paths to all houses, to 16th street and to 17th street sidewalks and to rear alley	Casual amphitheatre and platform
Playing instruments	Sunny areas		Gathering nodes
Concerts	Colorful		Paved exterior extension of workshop/ arts/crafts building
Meditation	Fragrant	Bocce ball court to be near Common House patio	
Reading	Accessible		Raised beds for accessible gardening
Outdoor gathering		Retention pond and swales to act as landscape elements	
Casual meetings			Planters
Conversations		Stairs to podium level to act as landscape elements (trellised entry, bridge or gate) if possible	Trellises
Strolling			
Arts, crafts, and woodwork			

(SILVER SAGE SITE PROGRAM — 15)

site green design ideas

ACTIVITY	CHARACTER	RELATIONSHIP	DETAILS
Composting	Minimal site disturbance	Shading at South sides of buildings for summer sun protection	Clustering/stacking
Recycling	Direction and retention of storm water		Open space
Gardening	Pervious landscape materials	Combined amphitheatre/ retention pond	Bio-swales
Appreciation of nature	Low or no irrigation planting		Grass-crete or decomposed granite
Meditating	Landscaping to improve passive cooling and heating	Combined deck/shading device for residents below	Indigenous plants
	Building orientation for beneficial passive solar gains/shading	Bio-swales in required setbacks	Deciduous trees and vines
	Gray water collection and re-use in landscaping		Retention ponds
	Responsible handling of waste		Organic garden
	Healthy environment		Recycling
	Combined usages for efficiency and ecology		Compost
	Summer shading of buildings		Cisterns and rain barrels

(SILVER SAGE SITE PROGRAM — 17)

Sample program (design criteria).

Art: I'll miss the youth. I'll miss having people in their 30s and 40s in close proximity. But everything's a

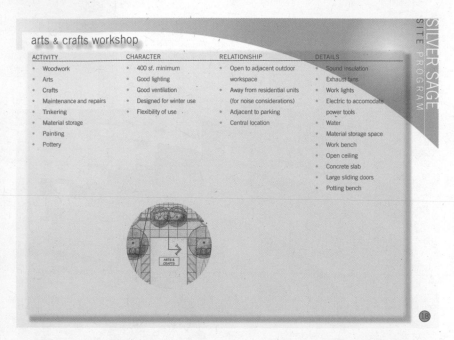

arts & crafts workshop			
ACTIVITY	CHARACTER	RELATIONSHIP	DETAILS
• Woodwork	• 400 sf. minimum	• Open to adjacent outdoor	• Sound insulation
• Arts	• Good lighting	workspace	• Exhaust fans
• Crafts	• Good ventilation	• Away from residential units	• Work lights
• Maintenance and repairs	• Designed for winter use	(for noise considerations)	• Electric to accomodate
• Tinkering	• Flexibility of use	• Adjacent to parking	power tools
• Material storage		• Central location	• Water
• Painting			• Material storage space
• Pottery			• Work bench
			• Open ceiling
			• Concrete slab
			• Large sliding doors
			• Potting bench

Sample program (design criteria). MDA

Residents enjoying the newly completed Silver Sage Cohousing.

trade-off in life. The place I live currently isn't specifically engineered for seniors. And as I stated previously, the vast majority are very busy raising their children or earning money.

Kurt: What sorts of people live in senior cohousing?

Art: People who aren't in denial. People who are proactive, intelligent, and caring. People who want to laugh at the world and themselves. All of the institutions for seniors are talking about "aging in place." These days families are geographically spread out, making it difficult for children to care for their aging parents. So many people have bought into the "subdivide and conquer" housing-tract lifestyle. Erik Utne of the Utne Reader has said: "give up your dream home place, for your dream community." We've coined a phrase here in Colorado that means something more than "aging in place." It's "aging in community."

Interview with future resident, Silvine Farnell, during the planning of the Silver Sage community.
March 2005
Silvine Farnell, 62, currently lives with her husband Stewart, a financial planner, in a townhouse in Boulder, Colorado. Both are retired college professors, and they have no children. She works as a freelance

copy editor and has been very involved in the growth of the Silver Sage Cohousing group for about ten months.

Kurt: How did you hear about cohousing? How did you become interested in joining a group?

Silvine: I have known a little about cohousing for a while and chose not to become involved until recently because I was put off by the idea of meetings, the fact that most groups consist mostly of younger people, and my own shyness. What really caught my attention was seeing an ad in the Spiritual Eldering newsletter, put out by Rabbi Zalman Schachter-Shalomi's organization, about Silver Sage, an elder cohousing project with a spiritual angle. The thing that appeals most to me about Silver Sage is the awareness of the spiritual dimension. The spiritual dimension is so practical, and so important.

Kurt: What is it about the spiritual dimension that's so important to cohousing?

Silvine: One thing I've learned about cohousing is that it isn't about living with people who are all your best friends. In fact, you want diversity — but then it's crucial that you build community effectively.

We can learn about the practice of spirituality as an effective community-building tool from the work of Rachael Kessler, who has developed a

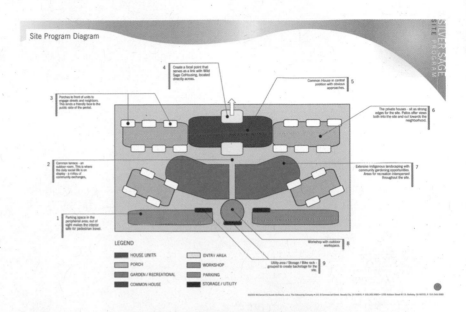

Sample program.

Entrance gateway to Silver Sage.

way to bring spirituality into the public schools that is well received by everyone from fundamentalist Christians to atheists, partly because she makes obvious how spirituality speaks to basic human needs. Just take a look at the title of her book, *The Soul of Education: Helping Students Find Connection, Compassion, and Character at School*. We just have to discover the deep connection we have, simply because our deepest nature is to give attention and space to each other — which is another way of saying, to give love to each other. If we are given the right kind of activity to encourage the giving of attention and space, to ourselves and to others, love will happen, and we will find it deeply satisfying. We will become a community.

Kurt: Compassion and attention to others sounds important for all cohousing groups — is it especially relevant for elder cohousing?

Silvine: The best way I know to answer that is with a few lines from a poem by Yeats.

The site plan at Silver Sage. The activities and the life in between the houses (gardens, bocce, eating, talking, music, outside workshop space, etc.) took on an importance as significant as the life in the houses.

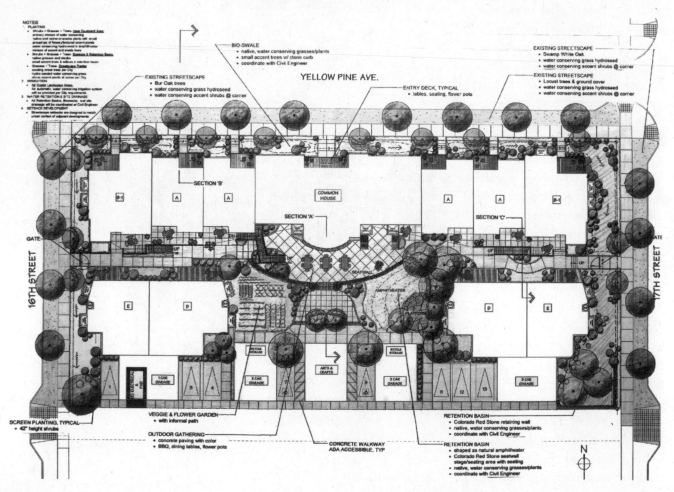

An aged man is but a paltry thing,
A tattered coat upon a stick, unless
Soul clap its hands and sing, and louder sing
For every tatter in its mortal dress

Kurt: Is this poem about how the man's tattered clothes visually expresses the trials he has gone through and the inner wisdom he has gained from that, and his enduring joyful spirit even as his body fails?

Silvine: The joyful spirit part, yes, absolutely, but Yeats did have a tough time with getting old. I think this poem is mainly about how getting old and deteriorating physically is pretty rough, unless your soul is growing at the same time, unless aging becomes saging. Your soul can't help growing when you're willing to engage at a deep level in a community and work through whatever comes up.

Society is much more prescriptive for those people with developing

Early conceptual sketch. MDA

Detail of courtyard elevation. MDA

View from 17th Street.

careers and growing families. The world isn't so clear in telling older people what to do. So what do we do as seniors? Go off to Tucson and play golf for the rest of our lives? For some people being retired, with the children gone, is depressing. They're at a loss; it feels like society has told them their life is over. Rabbi Zalman Schachter-Shalomi, who's the spiritual leader of the Jewish Renewal Movement, found himself in deep depression

17th St. Elevation. MDA

after he turned 60, and he realized it was because our society didn't have any kind of positive view of aging to offer him. Out of his exploration of the wisdom of other societies and his

View of courtyard at dusk.

BEN TREMPER PHOTOGRAPHY

The elevator tower and street scape at Silver Sage. MDA

own spiritual work came a different way of looking at the whole process, and that's the heart of his book, *From Age-ing to Sage-ing: A Profound New Vision of Growing Older.* Do your inner work, harvest the wisdom of your life, and you'll become a true elder and people will want to listen to you — you'll have something to give. And much less to fear.

Kurt: So, I can see how senior cohousing with a spiritual angle can be a path to individual development. And you've started to address what senior cohousing may have to offer those outside the immediate community: to the neighborhood, Boulder, and beyond. What will this look like?

Silvine: Well, the answer to this question starts small and works outward to the greater communities. We have Wild Sage Cohousing right next door. There are many of us yearning to be surrogate grandparents for some of the children there. I plan to host a reading-out-loud time that kids can come to. Most of all, I believe that people can get deeper into poetry by performing it, and that poetry has real gifts for anyone who does go deeper into it, and so teaching people to perform poetry is my main way of giving back. Silver Sage provides a platform for me to do this; the common house is a perfect place to host poetry performing workshops. And in the same way, it will be a focal point for all kinds of activities. Our members have so many gifts.

Kurt: Knowing what you do about the architecture of Silver Sage, how do you think living in cohousing will change your daily patterns?

Silvine: For one, the common house will really be an extension of our individual home. Our actual home will be smaller than the one we will be leaving, but having a common house will provide us with a chance to expand. We won't have to spend money going to movies because of the home theater that's planned — and we'll be watching those movies with people we know and care about. I'm looking forward to coming down to the common house to do laundry, and there will be a cool deck that I want to do my stretching exercises on. Then there'll just be much more bumping into people and chatting than we experience in our current neighborhood. There are people who you want to chat with for a little while, or to eat dinner with, but not necessarily have over for the whole evening — but our current situation doesn't allow for this at all. We have older neighbors right now who need more attention than they get, people I'd really like to spend some time with, but I'm just not the kind of person who can make things like that happen. You know the majority of people in cohousing are introverts, and I certainly am, so I

Physical architecture like front porches and the social desire to cooporate begins to bring us back together as a society.

Remote parking at Silver Sage. MDA

love the idea of interactions being made easy. In cohousing, everyone expects you to behave like old-fashioned neighbors. The design of Silver Sage supports community as opposed to working against it. I'm also looking forward to common meals. I don't think we can have them too often.

Kurt: Don't you have some concerns and fears about moving into cohousing?

Silvine: Sometimes I get cold feet. Life now is very comfortable. I live in a secluded place that's very comfortable indeed. Everything is under con-

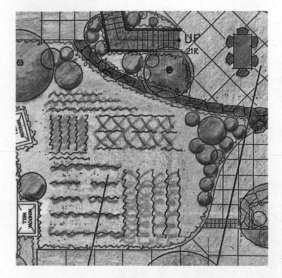

Detail of site plan. MDA

Conceptual sketch. MDA

trol. I'm drawn to the growth that comes out of spontaneity and not always being in control.

Kurt: How do you feel about living with people who will be aging and, like all of us, eventually dying? Isn't this depressing? How will you take care of each other? Is that something you want to do?

Silvine: At a very personal level, if I want people to support me as I get older, I need to be ready to support them. We'll also have a relationship of mutual support with our neighbors at Wild Sage. I can think of babysitting for the kids of the young parents at Wild Sage as a long-term investment — some day they may do some babysitting for me! Any way you look at it, aging is going to happen. Senior cohousing is for people who are not in denial about aging and dying. Living in a nursing home would be a hell of a lot more depressing than living in senior cohousing, and we're expecting to be able to stay in our own home much longer this way. It's also true that we want a broad age range at Silver Sage. Currently we're mostly in our early 60s. It is easier for older people to take care of other older people because we're moving at the same pace, and it's even better if there's a diversity of ages within the category of "senior," so that not everyone is experiencing exactly the same stage at the same time. A lot of us don't want to be a burden to our children, and are happy to help others if that means we get help when we need it.

Kurt: How do you feel about the roles the community group, architect, and developer played in the design and development process for Silver Sage? Was the process successful in creating a community? Why?

Silvine: This process is so much more trouble than simply buying a typical townhouse. It's also so much more worth it. It's fantastic to have an impact on the design of the community. It's fantastic to form a community of people before moving in. I have been on the board of my HOA in my current neighborhood; in fact, I've even been the president of the HOA, and still I don't get to see very much of my neighbors. There's really zero community here. There may be some tough meetings during the development of the design for a cohousing community, but there's a payoff. People end up feeling good about themselves and about each other in the end. I think we felt rushed at times; as you get older your decision-making process slows down. The developer's leadership and early involvement in this project created some tensions as we worked out our common house design, but having experienced professionals on board also made it possible to get this complex project finished with everyone feeling good, because the professionals listened to us members.

Kurt: What sort of a role do you play as an individual in the community-building process? Are you a leader, a facilitator, an active participant, or more of an observer?

Silvine: I'm definitely a big mouth in meetings, and recently facilitated a meeting. I've pretty much taken on a leadership role. I have a lot of ideas and really enjoy expressing them. My husband has also taken a leadership role, in perhaps a quieter way — he's great at sending out eloquent emails when the need arises. One thing that's great about cohousing is that it can accommodate all sorts of personalities — there's a synergy.

Kurt: It sounds like you have people with a variety of skills in your group, and there's a strength in diversity. We can be greater than the sum of our parts.

Silvine: Yes, and things really work when we get rid of the garbage that prevents our love from coming to the fore and being expressed. We're going on a retreat in May, and this will give us some concentrated time for really listening to each other and for strengthening the compassion, connection, and inner growth that Rachael Kessler talks about. We've already had some great experiences of deeper connection, and I love that we're focusing on strengthening that.

Wolf Creek Lodge
Grass Valley, California
30 units
Architect: McCamant & Durrett Architects
Developer: Cohousing Partners with Wolf Creek Lodge, LLC (Cohousing Group)
Status: Start construction 2009
Tenure: condominium units

In the fall of 2005, local landowner Marilyn Pendola invited McCamant & Durrett Architects to look at her beautiful 8-acre wooded site with 1,000 feet of creek frontage in Grass Valley, California to advise her on the most "sustainable" development solution for her property. The site was zoned commercial and flanked by shopping centers, but all three of the previously proposed designs (a big-box drugstore, the Department of Motor Vehicles, and a gas station) fought the natural features of the site with seas of asphalt and 22-foot-high retaining walls. By contrast, a cohousing community could fit within the

The Development Scenario

Lots of people consider starting new senior cohousing communities. It is not an easy process. They need to know how to do it: how to organize a group of strangers, how to find other investors, how to negotiate for a piece of property, how to get through the city entitlement process, and how to hire consultants. They need to know how to pull it all together and how to hold it all together — and how to stay on schedule and on budget. Someone has to wake up each morning and ask themselves "What do I need to do today to move this project to the next square?" Real estate development is not for the faint of heart — one needs to know how to stay encouraged when times get tough and how to encourage others when their faith is waning. Developers need to know how to see the biggest of pictures — countering climate change, fostering community, and creating decent urban design, while simultaneously focusing on the small picture. "*Consumer Report* says that a 26-gauge stainless steel sink is just as good as a 24-gauge. Let's use the less costly one."

In a context of rising costs and falling home prices, the role of Cohousing Partners, LLC, is optimizing the success of this project. The firm is a cohousing development company founded by Jim Leach and Kathryn McCamant. After getting the property under contract in 2006, the firm facilitated the formation of two cohousing groups — the intergenerational "Commons" and the active adult "Lodge." Through a series of design workshops, the architect and each of the two communities defined their visions for the neighborhood they wanted to create. The Lodge members continued to refine their expectations in Study Group III, discussing how they'll live together.

Cohousing Partners literally partners with cohousing communities, providing financial systems, community process, and developer expertise through the entire development process.

trees and slope of the site, and the convenient shopping and proximity to downtown would work especially well for seniors. After doing the preliminary arithmetic for miles driven, energy use, affordability, accessibility, carbon footprint, complementary uses (housing next to commercial), social ecology (support for the individuals living there), community and cooperation, and all of the other cradle-to-cradle issues, it became clear that a senior cohousing community next to an intergenerational community was the most sustainable solution for that site.

Urban Design

With the site close to downtown and next to shopping, we saw the opportunity to contribute to the walkability of both the neighborhood and the city of Grass Valley. That compelled us to define the street, define the outdoor room, and facilitate a life between the buildings on the street

Wolf Creek Lodge Vision Statement

We at Wolf Creek Lodge are a group of independent, active adults who have come together to create a supportive community in which we can age safely and live fully with dignity and humor.

Inspired by the splendid serene and natural setting in which we live, we strive to be responsible stewards dedicated to sustaining our physical environment.

While acknowledging that each of us holds dear our personal views and beliefs, it is our individual commitment to the core values and goals we share that unite and guide us. In a community fostered by patience, open-mindedness, respect and trust, we enjoy a cooperative, harmonious way of living, full of laughter and joyful community. Together, we learn and grow, sharing a strong sense of belonging and a heartfelt experience of coming home.

Wolf Creek Lodge conceptual street elevation sketch. MDA

Wolf Creek Lodge Amenities Prioritization

The following list is from the Fifth workshop of Study Group II. It took four hours to establish the group's design priorities beyond the original site plan, common house plan, and private house designs.

December 1, 2006

1. Extra Quiet Package $1,000/unit
   - Extra thick gypsum board
   - Quiet plumbing
   - Solid-core doors
   - Cast iron piping
   - Enhanced caulking and gasketing

2. Energy-Efficient Package $3,000/unit
   - Super insulation
   - High-quality windows
   - Radiant barriers
   - Extra thick gypcrete

3. Hydronically Heated Floor $2,000/unit

4. Low Toxicity Materials $800/unit
   - Paints
   - Glues
   - Carpet pads

5. Sustainable Lumber ....$2,000/ unit

6. Low-Toxicity Cabinets $500/unit

7. "Awesome" Countertops ....$1,200/ unit

more than anything else, has to do with the activity *between* the buildings. There's a place there — an outdoor "room" for conviviality and community. You don't find people sitting in the middle of a suburban street; they gather in cafés along narrow streets because there, it feels like *somewhere*.

We designed the Lodge, the senior cohousing component of the larger Wolf Creek Village, as one building, with parking below grade and an elevator. It has an overt emphasis on "holding the corner." In other words, the building will give the street corner obvious definition. In this particular place, with parking lots along the street and shopping centers behind, where no other buildings define the street, the planning officials asked us: "Why hold the corner when nobody else does?" Our response: "Let it start with this corner." As the area is re-developed, others will see the importance of stitching this area back into the historic fabric of this exceptional small town.

The single corner building also serves the goals of energy efficiency — embracing the sun like an arcology. For this group of people, many of whom are moving from 2-20 forested acres, this project, with people they know, means lots of opportunity for community and living lighter on the planet. The residents won't have to drive to be with other people (one

side, as well as the common side of the building. On the street side, that meant "holding" the corner.

Sustainability starts with smart urban design. The classic architecture book *Life Between Buildings*, by Jan Gehl, discusses how definition of a street, future resident estimates an 80% reduction in driving), and collectively they will encumber less than 1% as much land as they do now. We project the cumulative energy bills will be less than 5% of the group's current, collective bills. The project employs an array of energy-saving strategies including tightening the building envelope, optimizing natural daylight, and solar preheated hydronic heating. Careful shading, super insulation, and ceiling fans provide passive cooling and about thirty five other line items that contribute to the energy efficiency of these houses. After much discussion, the community decided they would not install air conditioning except in the common house.

In all 30 units, we employed Universal Design principles (see Appendix D). Adaptations for accessibility are offered as individual packages, or they can be installed later. An elevator allows equally convenient access among all the units, the street level, and the common terrace. The Lodge outdoor area will include many amenities, such as a terrace, lawn, garden, fire pit, BBQ, hot tub, and petanque court.

Interview with future Wolf Creek Lodge Residents
Interviewer: Laurie Taylor, McCamant & Durrett Architects.

A few of the group's goals that influenced the site design were:

- Living with nature.
- Tending gardens.
- Finding time alone for sitting on the property.
- Creating a tranquil and peaceful feeling.
- Living lighter on the planet.
- Sunshine and shade.
- Campfire.
- Usable year-round.
- Trails.
- Ecological responsibility.

Activities to be enjoyed together will be:

- Cooking.
- Eating.
- Dancing.
- Croquet & petanque (French bocce ball).
- Planting.
- Relaxing.
- Horseshoes.
- Spending time together.
- Yoga.

Lodge members: Wina Simpson (66, retired corporate human resources administrator), Virginia Thresh (69, retired school administrator), Butch Thresh (69, retired Quaker school teacher, gas station owner, and air force veteran).

Laurie: How do you define senior at Wolf Creek Lodge?

Virginia: Here, we start at any age that anyone wants to come in.

Butch: We're making the kinds of agreements that are friendly to our age group. Common meals will be structured according to our needs as active adults. We hope that we will have a wide range of ages. Someone in their 40s might want to move in. But we also have a suite for a caregiver because we anticipate that some of us may get too active and need some assistance.

Wina: We offer an alternative for families with children in the adjacent cohousing community.

Laurie: And the lifestyle you see?

Butch: We will be downsizing and putting ourselves into our new community. We don't see big changes. I just won't have to be spending hours and hours cleaning a large shop. There will be hot tub, yoga, exercise, a crafts room, a patio for minor repair jobs. With downsizing, we won't each need many power tools unless someone wants to do furniture refinishing or something. That type of thing would be done in their garage anyway.

Wina: We've all agreed to have one only car for each household at a maximum. Several of us have said, "If you need to have a car, you can borrow mine." That's one of the advantages of community. As we get older, a lot of us may like to be driven around, at night especially. We might have a van and we will probably get a shared electric car.

Butch: Because we're moving into cohousing, we'll be doing away with our four vehicles and only having one.

Laurie: Are you looking forward to moving into cohousing?

Wina: Yes I am. I'm just so excited. I've been kind of afraid to get so excited about it. I've been kind of leery because it's been just on paper, but now we're talking about the groundbreaking and we're talking to builders, so it's really feeling like it's going to happen.

Laurie: Why cohousing?

Wina: Bob and I knew we wanted to get away from living on three acres of property and we've always been interested in living in community. This was a different kind of community than we thought we would one day be in, but it just felt like we would get the support we'd need as we got older. Others would be around us, and we could communicate easily.

Laurie: How did you know that this would be a group that you would want to live with?

Wina: We didn't.

Virginia: We had no clue.

Wina: We just met with each other each month.

Butch: By the time we were getting into the design workshops, we had people in nine households. Now, as we prepare for construction, we're up to 17 households [for 30 available units].

Virginia: Ten years ago we wouldn't have wanted to live in this area because

The Group's Prioritized Core Values:

- Humor
- Lifelong Learning
- Cooperation
- Affordability
- Good Food and Drink
- Health
- Nature
- Open-Mindedness
- Patience
- Responsibility
- Simplicity

it's too near shopping centers. Now, we're looking at how the same area has become very attractive because we will be able to walk to the bank, grocery store, restaurants, gym, among many other things — and have the bus right at the corner. We wanted to change our lifestyle. We wanted to become more ecologically responsible, and the location spoke to both of us.

Butch: We were looking at another project with the concept of trying to design the houses to where neighbors were in touch — putting up porches in the front instead of garages. What pushed us into cohousing was this location and the real community concept — more community than we would get anywhere else.

Laurie: Why is cohousing attractive to you?

Butch: The location, the emphasis on community, active participation in the design, and community meals.

Wina: Our thought had been to live in a ranch style house, but the more we looked at the condo style of housing, the more we liked the idea of easy living.

Butch: The location is outstanding. The only other place that would have a similar location is San Francisco, near the Ferry building. The accessibility is outstanding.

There really is not another place as friendly as The Lodge. We're on the corner of two separate shopping

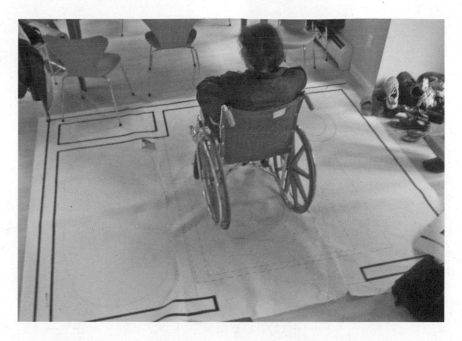

Planning for an adaptive bathroom design at Wolf Creek Lodge.

centers. We can walk to them both on sidewalks and no significant hills. No major streets to walk across. You're right in there. You walk out and you're at street level. We have an elevator if we have enough stuff to bring in.

Wina: In the house where I'm living now, if I fall off the ladder, who's going to know?

In cohousing, even if you're in your own house, you're going to know if you don't see somebody.

Virginia: And you'd better get dressed every morning, because if you don't, somebody's going to knock on your door! They're just wanting to check on you — and that's good. You want someone to knock on your door if you're lying flat on the floor.

We did our regular six participatory design workshops (which range from 4 hours to 3 days) also referred to as Study Group II.

Study group II workshop with future Wolf Creek Cohousing residents.

Butch: I know people in assisted living who are isolated from the outside world.

We're not wanting to go into assisted living. They're warehouses for old people.

Virginia: There are other retirement communities, but they don't have common meals three and four times a week.

Laurie: What do you see as the difference between a retirement community and cohousing?

Wina: It's what I want my life to be about. Those kinds of places are just a place to play together. It's not really a support system. Those places are into materiality. All those little things. Things. It's like where I'm living now. Everybody is into things. Nobody is really into the concepts of "green" or "small footprints." We're going to emphasize the issues of how we age. How we get along. Aging in place. People coming from the same place as you. Living lighter on the planet.

Virginia: Another thing is that we are all committed to developing this community from scratch.

Butch: We're actively creating a community. You're not just buying into a place to live. You're buying a place in the community. You need to learn about the community before you move in, because you're going to have a certain responsibility to that community. In cohousing you meet the people first, then stitch together a community one agreement at a time.

Laurie: Is it perhaps the idea of caring about people more than caring about things?

Wina: Most certainly.

Butch: There's also the aspect of developing a lifestyle around people who think a lot like us. We're not moving in here to get old. There will just be some point in our life that our present home won't make sense. What we are trying to do is make an active choice before we reach that point, an active decision about moving to a community of our choosing, to where we can fit in, be happy. We are choosing a place not because we have to, but because we want to. If you have to move because your kids are telling you it's time to move, you have to move to somewhere that you don't want to move to. We're making a proactive choice about where our life goes from here.

Wina: We're moving into an extended family. Just like an extended family, you're going to have people who you're closer to and others who you'd just as soon just say hello to. We're still all there to support each other.

Butch: Not everybody is going to be everybody's best friend. And that's OK. We already have a lot of good friends. But what we do want is an active community that is self-supporting. Common meals and common areas are a big part of it because they force you into cooperating and interacting with each other.

Wina: And we are certainly growing. We try to think of not arguing with someone but instead listening to the other person without judgment. We are already starting to learn to do this. That's why we have community long before moving in. It has given us the opportunity to grow together and learn how to interact together before we're thrown into living with each other.

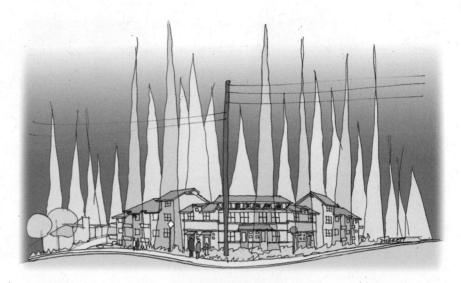

Wolf Creek Lodge early conceptual street corner perspective sketch. MDA

Laurie: Is your new home large enough?

Butch: Yes, and that's the beauty of the common areas — with that, there's plenty of room.

Virginia: I'm excited to be getting rid of stuff. It's almost like a new beginning.

Wina: That's what people who are moving into cohousing know — that things are not going to make them happy.

Laurie: What surprises you most about the anticipation of moving into cohousing?

Virginia: I'm sometimes surprised that I'm even considering it, because I lived for 16 years in a private boarding school with teenagers and staff members, and I thought I would never live that close to people again. It was a great experience, but I thought I'd had enough of that kind of closeness. But

Chuck and Katie present to the Grass Valley city council on behalf of the Wolf Creek project. It was approved because of its positive impact on the neighborhood. Cohousing has traditionally provided notable contributions to the surrounding community.

that was with 16 teenagers. Now this will be with 16 sort-of teenagers.

Laurie: What happens now when you are sick or have had surgery? And how will that change when you are in cohousing?

Wina: When Bob was sick, I had shoulder surgery and that meant neither one of us could drive. And we lived out in the country. It was very, very hard, to try to get him back and forth to the hospital, to try to get him back and forth to the doctor because we had to rely on other people to come and take us somewhere. I felt very guilty having to ask people to help out. But in The Lodge people are going to just be right there.

Wina: In the middle of the night, we can just knock on the neighbor's door and say, "Take me."

Butch: One of the early agreements that we made is that we are not obli-

gated to care for each other. We deliberately made it to where it's not an obligation. But we're hoping that because of the strength of the community you'll want to help others.

Virginia: Oh yes. You'll want to help others. There's a big difference in having to ask for help and living close enough to know that there's a need.

Laurie: How long do you plan to live in cohousing?

Wina: Until I go.

Butch: That's the hope. To age in place. If you live by yourself, not in cohousing, and you break your hip, you're going to have to go someplace or hire someone. Really, you don't need a lot of care. You just need someone to do a little shopping for you and get your meds and maybe get you to the doctor once a month, but you build that community in cohousing, and someone can come check on you and help you. Someone in community can bring meals. But a lot of situations can drive people to an assisted living, and they never come out.

We have designed it so that someone can come in to help, but if you are going to need skilled nursing facilities, you might have to move on.

Laurie: Cohousing seems to be a huge secret that not many older adults are aware of.

Butch: There's a lot of truth to that. There are a lot of adults who are looking for a life that they should just stop and help create. This is good for the person who doesn't just want a few people making all the decisions. In cohousing you have a say in what happens. That's one of the nice parts of cohousing. You're doing it with other people.

Laurie: What happens when someone comes into the group and they are very definite about wanting something in particular set up in a certain way?

Butch: There were a lot of definite ideas, but you just need someone who is very good at facilitating the workshops. They are able to allow people to get over that hump. "Give us a compelling reason for saying what you want." When we were doing our design workshop, we had someone who wanted a meditation room instead of a workshop, but then we looked at our list of priorities and found that a meditation room was way down on the list. There

are some things we can't do now, but we can plan for it after we get in. One or two people can't just stand up and say, "This is what we want." The decision must go through consensus. And that's how we seem to get to the best decision over and over again. As people come into the group, someone from the membership committee lets a prospective person know the decisions that we've already made and understand why we decided what we did.

Laurie: Will privacy be an issue for you?

Butch: What's unique to cohousing is that, although we have common kitchens and common rooms, we also have our own private kitchens, living rooms, dining rooms, in our own homes. These are complete homes. There is a balance of private space (home), semi-private (front porch, gathering nodes), and public space (where you get your mail, the common areas). So there's a balance that you can pick and choose the kind of space you need at the time. Cohousers have developed ways of communicating if they want privacy or are open to company. Some people even have signs on their front doors saying if they want privacy or not.

Laurie: So the nature of it is designed for community?

Butch: Yes. It's set up so that you will cross paths, but also have privacy when you want it.

Laurie: How do you think living in cohousing will influence you as an individual?

Wina: I think it's already given me a great opportunity to look at me. Because I know that if I'm upset with someone else I need to look inside of me to see what's going on. It's helped me to become a more aware and trusting individual of other people. It's becoming easier for me. It's made me more aware of other people because I've become more aware of myself. I think I can be more tolerant and less judgmental.

Butch: I've gone through quite a bit in the last three or four months, and I've found that I'm having to make a lot of adjustments. It takes everybody working together.

Conceptual site plan for a Senior Cohousing and Artisans Plaza in San Juan Bautista, California. MDA

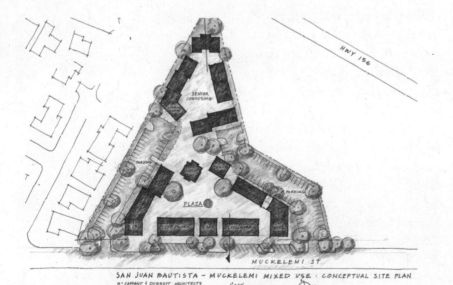

San Juan Bautista Senior Cohousing
San Juan Bautista, California
24 units
Architects: McCamant & Durrett Architects
Status: Pending
Tenure: 24 ownership units

In early 2006 Tod duBois put an option on a 4.25 acre site in historic and sleepy downtown San Juan Bautista, California (population 1,500). He lives just two blocks from the site. Tod was dismayed that his grandparents, sage members of the community, had to move out of town after many years of residency. Their 5-acre ranchette, appropriate for so long, had become impractical. And there were virtually no supportive accommodations for seniors in town. These folks had been valuable, contributing members of the community, and there was no longer a place for them. Tod did not want to see that happen to his parents or to the other folks he grew up with.

San Juan Bautista is everything you'd want in a small town. It's comfortable and very walkable. It's old and charming (settled in the 1700s by the Spaniards) and obviously a community — you can tell that by how many people know and recognize each other walking along the sidewalks. But there is not a place for seniors, and this is true for too many towns in America.

Tod contacted me to discuss building a senior cohousing community as part of a larger, arts-oriented mixed-use project that would have several benefits for the town. San Juan Bautista is not an easy place to build a house, much less a 20- or 30-house community. In San Juan Bautista, the growth ordinance, designed to preserve the historic character of town, requires a public vote to build more than three houses. A public slide show about senior cohousing and this project in particular kicked off the campaign. There was not much time for marketing the event at the Orient Express Restaurant, the only venue in town available to host the numbers we hoped for — though we feared that only 15 people would show up. Unfortunately, Tod had to pay in advance for the restaurant's required minimum of 60 dinners. We figured we'd be eating Chinese for the next month.

Ninety-five people showed up. There was standing room only — and barely that. We saw and heard from that assembly that a lot of people were fed up with inadequate possibilities for the elders to stay in town. This independent-minded, semi-rural population became excited about the prospects of an arrangement in which they had some say, not just a place that you buy, but something much more personal than that. It became clear that only a participatory

effort would make this development happen. Some locals had helped in getting a church and a fire station built, so they had seen what could be created if folks stepped up to help push something through. And they saw that there was a lack of good,

San Juan Bautista residents gather to hear Chuck's presentation on the prospective project.

Fortunately or unfortunately, getting Senior Cohousing built in America means a lot of public presentations.

respectable accommodations for seniors. When the vote came in with 205 in favor, 114 against, it was clear that the proposed senior cohousing in Tod's mixed-use community looked like a fine solution to the needs of many residents to age in town.

Now Tod had a mandate. He garnered other development partners to build the Artisans Plaza, which would include senior cohousing complemented with artists' studios, live-work housing, commercial facilities, a small inn, the city's information center, and a wine tasting room. He proposed restoring a very dilapidated historic house on site as a museum, a café, or art gallery. The project would be a real neighborhood center just blocks from downtown.

Tod is a new developer who saw a real local need and was ready to make it happen. Unfortunately, real estate prices were high and Tod overpaid for the site, and, since the vote, the housing market turned down precipitously. Investors became hard to find, even for such a well-supported, low-risk venture with a clear demand (because senior cohousing comes with future residents, risk is reduced). With conceptual design completed to date, this project is still in the investor-seeking phase.

Whether or when this community gets built, the San Juan Bautista development demonstrates that good senior cohousing sometimes can come from a partnership between a developer who spearheads a project that local folks support, organize, and publicize. This project is indicative of the need and opportunity for cohousing as an alternative for seniors in small towns, rural areas, and counties across the country.

Perspective sketch of the newly proposed plaza adjacent to artists live/work units and new senior cohousing community in San Juan Bautista.

CHAPTER II

Where Do We Go From Here?

The Legacy of Cohousing

The legacy of cohousing in America will be much more than cohousing itself. The same is true in Denmark. More than 30 years after the first cohousing community was built in Denmark, less than 1 percent of the population lives in cohousing. However, the full spectrum of the housing market has seen its influences. Almost no Danish multi-family housing project is designed today without at least a focus group involved, which morphs a project toward a more livable end. In a single family neighborhood, responding to ideas pioneered in cohousing, residents on a street might vote to park all of the cars at the end of the block and have folks walk the half block to their houses. This scenario even has a formal name, a Chapter 44 Street (named after the law that formally set up the possibility for neighbors to vote to close or otherwise alter their

Living room of a one bedroom unit in cohousing.

street to facilitate community.) You can imagine what walking past front porches and children playing does to facilitate community and relationships on a street.

Cohousing is as much a new *process* for developing housing as it is a new housing type. The innovation is in the concept that ordinary people should help build neighborhoods that incorporate what *they* feel are important people-friendly, child-friendly, senior-friendly, and earth-friendly qualities.

The effects of cohousing can already be seen in US housing. Our architectural firm, McCamant & Durrett Architects, has worked on many developments modeled after, but not identical to, cohousing (so we don't call them cohousing). For example,

Typical nursing home in America.

Windsor rentals, with 41 units and ample common building shown to the left.

we designed a new neighborhood for single-parent households on government assistance. The parents (all mothers) had to be in school. Childcare, shared cooking, and other shared facilities were on site. The point was that the moms would take turns cooking so they would have the time and energy to do their homework on the other days. We insisted on working with the future residents because neither Katie nor I is a single mom; we didn't want to decide what the moms would share and what they wouldn't. The moms got housing that responded to their needs, and Catholic Charities, the developer, finds that, of all their subsidized housing developments, this is the easiest to manage by a huge margin. The residents' participation created emotional ownership; they were invested not only in their own success (and survival, really) but the success of everyone there.

Since then, we have designed many multi-family housing projects with input from future residents. We also have worked on many developments modeled after senior cohousing. A good example is Casa de las Flores, a 21-unit senior housing project in Oakland, California. Originally a 1920s, three-story building designed and built to accommodate phone switchboard operators, the renovated structure became a five-story senior residential apartment building by adding a common house on the roof and excavating a basement for common facilities such as laundry, personal storage, mechanical, recycling, and garbage. To reuse this complicated brick-clad concrete and steel structure (already damaged by several earthquakes), we had to physically stitch it together to make it stable. Lots of shotcrete on the interior walls took care of that.

What presented an even more interesting challenge was stitching the resident seniors (18 singles and 3 couples) together into a stable social community. About a month after move-in, I went around to all 21 apartments, asking folks if they were going to come to the workshop that night — the first of three. I also asked them how they liked living there. They all said more or less, "fine, the others leave me alone."

We started the first of the three community-building workshops by asking: "What activities might you do together that would make your life easier, more convenient, more economical, more safe, and even more fun than doing them alone?" I had a Chinese and a Spanish interpreter, so it took time to make sure each suggestion was clear. They generated a list of 19 possible activities that could be done as a group.

The second night was spent prioritizing the 19 suggestions. To my surprise, number one was walking to the grocery store together (number two was bingo). It turned out that Paratransit (public senior van transportation) for the elderly was located over a mile from the building. Individual residents were calling them to come and drive them the two blocks to the grocery store, not feeling safe to walk in that part of town; but there were lots of problems with calling Paratransit. They would ask you to wait in the lobby, then they'd be an hour late. Then they'd take you to the store, but not wait. Residents would then have to call them again from the store. It wasn't fun.

Before the third workshop, I stopped by everyone's apartment again to ask them to join us for the evening. The purpose of the third workshop was to define the high-priority activities. Exactly what would going to the store together look like? Would residents meet in the lobby every other day at a set time, or would there be a grocery shopping phone tree, or would they find another system? In the week that lapsed between workshops, the residents had already started walking to the store together. So again, I asked them individually, "How is it living here?" and they answered "Great, they come and get me when its time to go to the store." Pretty much the opposite of the "Leave me alone" response. When you don't know people, you

Homesafe, in Santa Clara, California. This project consists of twenty four homes, childcare and social services for women. Designed for 24 women and children coming out of abusive households. Again, support, childcare, common cooking, and community, while not exactly new, cohousing has reestablished it as an acceptable means of accomplishing quality of life and in this case, social repair.

Winter creek, a non-profit housing community.

want to be left alone; when you know them, you want to be included.

Building a community like this, finding ways for people to work together to solve their problems, is not just about building more housing

Seniors having fun at Nevada City Cohousing.

Entertaining the folks in the common house in Nevada City.

for people — this is the legacy of senior cohousing. Cohousing teaches us the potential for working together. Then we use this skill elsewhere. Contrast this with another senior housing project. I asked the manager, "How do you manage the social life here?" She said, "Some things get upside down from time to time. Someone starts making trouble, and then I just kick one or two people out every year or two. Then everyone is on their best behavior until I have to do it again." This is not how you build community.

The Legacy in Denmark

The senior cohousing movement had a turbulent start in Denmark. Determined seniors were desperate for more humane housing options, but despite adversity and setbacks, they kept on trying, never gave up, and

Petaluma Avenue Housing, Sebastapol, California.

finally realized their dream. Their lack of a deliberate method meant a lot of agonizing, frustrating, and sometimes dead-end experiences. No one believed them in the beginning — or took them seriously. However, the senior cohousing movement fundamentally changed the general perception of seniors in Denmark. Seniors taking responsibility for their own future led to this change. The somewhat condescending and patronizing way that seniors were treated before has since been replaced by a new kind of respect and attention. The energy and the drive of the first Danish senior cohousers also helped create the picture in Denmark of the active senior — one who faces the challenges and opportunities of his or her retirement life openly and consciously.

Perhaps even more importantly, the Danish government has all but stopped building traditional assisted-care homes and has started building senior housing as assisted-care senior communities, where the seniors have their own moderately sized units and carefully designed common facilities. While this is not senior cohousing per se, it is strongly inspired by key features from cohousing.

Making It Happen in the US

Similar trends in senior housing have been seen in the US, but senior housing here still rarely meets the Danish standards. For cultural, psychological, and even physiological reasons, we simply have not figured out how to care for older people. Ironically, the problem with assisted living here is not necessarily economic — we spend plenty of money on taking care of our elders, but as Lennon and McCartney said, "money can't buy me love." Since, with rare exceptions, we Americans can't as a nation seem to care for our aged with honor and decorum, people have to figure it out for themselves. Physician and author William Thomas notes that senior housing as currently practiced in the US presents us with a three trillion dollar deficit. We can't afford it, and seniors in the future will have to figure out a new means to accommodate themselves. Ironically, this dilemma presents us with a way to enhance the quality of life for ourselves as we age.

Creating senior cohousing in the US does not have to be a go-it-alone experience. The difficult preparation work is done. The path is open. All groups have to do is take the first step.

After designing or co-designing over 50 projects, and developing several of them, we have learned a few things that make the process

Margaret Hall in her kitchen in Doyle Street Cohousing.

Casa de Flores, a five story senior community in Oakland which is modeled after cohousing.

Depot Commons is a thirteen home community for mothers on welfare with one or two children which was modeled after cohousing. According to one of the mothers, "Nothing makes life easier for single mothers than sharing an old fashioned community."

better — much better — less costly, and faster. Our job has become making cohousing available to more and more folks. Katie and I have figured out how to complete the necessary site planning with a resident group in four days, the common house in two days, and the houses in three days (the group will make hundreds of decisions each day). This seems to be a perfect tempo, and it gives the group all the input they want.

Many professionals in the US are not comfortable and not organized enough to build cohousing. As a result, they rush the process (especially the group design work) to get it out of the way. And, of course, there

are others who would just like to build a cohousing-*looking* development, and ignore the social-building aspects of the process. These developers tend to design elements in such a way that they compromise community — like making the common house too small. These developers, well meaning as they may be, want to Americanize cohousing into "fast cohousing." There is no soul in fast food, and there is no soul in "fast" community. Although building cohousing appears to be a slow process to the untrained eye, I'm convinced it is much faster than a typical project. A 30-unit cohousing community plus commercial in Cotati, California took us three years to complete. Three comparably sized and new neighboring developments each took about seven years to complete. That's not atypical in areas with existing neighbors.

On the positive side, developments created to *look* like cohousing typically do provide greater community than do boxes set equidistant across the landscape (otherwise known as sprawl). As stated earlier, the greatest legacy of cohousing is not that everyone is living in cohousing, but that it has had — and will continue to have — such a deep impact on other type of housing developments. When you walk by a cohousing community, you see a profound way to live, and it's palpable and it's heartening that many

A facilitator for a senior housing development in Florida told me that because senior housing preferences vary locally, she spends two days minimum with local focus groups discussing private houses for seniors. In other words, our process to custom design senior cohousing takes just one extra day of work (on private houses) versus speculative senior housing. I mention this because people often think that building cohousing has to be exhausting for those involved. In fact, with good organization, the opposite is true. Building cohousing can be much faster than building a traditional, speculative housing project because the guessing and second-guessing aspects of the process are eliminated. With help, the residents can express what they want and need; then it's up to the professional to realize those desires and realities. As a result, building cohousing can be extremely gratifying. It can also galvanize the larger community. Building cohousing takes energy, but it gives back much more in return.

people involved in housing would like to emulate it as much as possible.

We do have a simple request: If it isn't cohousing; if the resident group does not participate in a meaningful way to build the community; if the common house is poorly designed such that it thwarts community; if cars creep into the spaces that should be reserved for people; if residents don't have anything real in common; then please do not call it *cohousing*. Because it isn't. It is something else entirely.

Next Step: New Industries

I'm hoping for the beginning of an entire new profession in the US: Study Group I Facilitators and Advisors. I expect these advisors to come from the ranks of the many people who have been assisting seniors for years; they will have the experience and knowledge about senior issues that will enable them to sit with a group of 20 seniors and help them figure out how to age in place — gracefully and with dignity. The only way to do this is with preparation; Study Group I is all about getting ready.

Study Group I advisors have to be prepared to patiently walk people through the issues of aging in place and the possibilities of cohousing. It is not a weekend endeavor. It takes an evening a week for a couple of months to successfully raise the consciousness of participants to decide either "A:

Study Group I Workshops

A real economic growth opportunity will go to whoever starts the best Study Group I franchise. After someone has run several groups themselves, working with twenty employees, they can begin to educate the 78 million seniors about the many possibilities for aging successfully. Only 40% of the Study Group I graduates join a senior cohousing group. Like everything else in business, it's all about the numbers.

Building the Market by Building Consciousness

People are already starting to hold senior cohousing development workshops. Soon, however, there will be more people to produce senior cohousing than there are ready to live in it — i.e. not enough market. That's where SG I comes in — building the market by building consciousness first. The yearly National Cohousing Conference is an excellent place to see how others are making new neighborhoods a reality.

This is for me," or "B: This isn't for me." Someone who is entrepreneurial and motivated could start a very healthy business helping seniors turn over the rocks, grapple with the issues, and embrace a scenario for

To qualify to live at Depot Commons, moms must be enrolled in school or a training program. Doing homework is impossible for single moms but with the benefit of shared cooking, on-site child-care and community, it is possible.

Common dinner at the East West House on Baker Street in San Francisco, California.

themselves for aging successfully. The biggest misconception of senior cohousing is that you start with a site. We have worked with groups who had a site and were ready to go. However, it is so much easier if the group starts the process with Study Group I and then finds a site, or at least doesn't work on the site until after Study Group 1.

What to Do?

If you are interested in moving into senior cohousing — or starting a new community — the best thing to do is to contact The Cohousing Association of the United States (www.cohousing.org). It has information about cohousing groups starting up as well as existing cohousing units for sale and rent. You can also post a classified ad on their website that describes what you're looking for (especially handy for people who want to start a senior cohousing group). We at McCamant & Durrett Architects have a growing national list for folks interested in finding others who want to create community in their area. Call, send, or e-mail your contact information to us. Our contact information can be found in in the "Links" section.

Cohousing may seem overwhelming if you don't know anyone in your area who shares your interest, but don't give up. Spread the word! Try to find people who could be interested in

FRONT ELEVATION

LIVING AREAS:

1-13 PRIVATE ROOMS
A. COMMON KITCHEN
B. COMMON DINING ROOM
C. LIVING ROOMS
D. LIBRARY
E. GUEST ROOM

SUPPORT AREAS:

F. MANAGER'S OFFICE
G. COMMON STORAGE
H. LAUNDRY

REAR DECKS

Plans and Elevation of the East West House.

starting a cohousing group. Contact your local senior center, church, AARP branch, College of Older Adults, and so on. It is a lot easier to get something off the ground if you have a few folks working together. Senior cohousing groups are currently forming all over the US, and there might be one in your area that you haven't heard about. There are also conferences about senior cohousing that are now being held on a regular basis.

Be realistic, and try to imagine what you want your life to look like in two, five, ten, and 20 years. What are the senior housing options in your area? How would you ideally like to age? Discuss it with your family and ask them how much they will be able to assist you. It can be uncomfortable to try to predict how your life could look if one day you no longer want to drive as much as you do now, and want to have fun (but self-directed) activities nearby. Maybe senior cohousing is the right solution for you, maybe not. It doesn't matter how old you are — there is nothing like having a forum in which to discuss these issues. Someday you'll be grateful that you deliberately faced these issues before they grew into unmanageable problems.

The Future

The American senior cohousing movement is off to a good start. Since

my first slide show about senior cohousing in Boulder, Colorado in 2000, there has been an inordinate amount of interest in senior cohousing; three communities have been built and many more are being planned. (As well, the closely related trend of *intergenerational* cohousing is going strong. Today there are over 110 projects built in the US, with 100 more being planned, including 20 under construction.)

The 21st century will be an entirely new era in respecting the possibilities for quality of life in its fourth quarter. More and more people will be getting older on their own terms, not in denial, but with the clarity of consciousness. The 20th century made education almost universal in this country, and the 21st century will bring a renaissance to aging gracefully and respectfully in

Don't get me wrong, seniors in intergenerational cohousing have a great time, but sometimes seniors prefer to live only with seniors.

LA QUERENCIA COHOUSING - COMMON HOUSE
FRESNO, CALIFORNIA
©2006 McCamant & Durrett Architects

Fresno Cohousing common house. When this community changed from family oriented to elder rich, the common house design changed from two stories to one.

Fresno Cohousing from the sun's point of view at 1:30 PM on June 21st. Notice that nearly all windows are shaded. This should be the law in this hot climate. Why should we be able to heat the planet so we can cool our homes with air conditioning when it is not necessary if designed correctly.

NOTE: FUTURE SOLAR PANELS ON SOUTH FACING ROOF SHOWN

ALLUVIAL AVENUE

LA QUERENCIA COHOUSING
FRESNO, CALIFORNIA

©2006 McCamant & Durrett Architects

The interior of Pleasant Hill Cohousing's common house ventilation tower. This provides passive cooling for the building.

Dense vegitation in the courtyard space reduces the urban heat island effect typically caused by large expanses of concrete and asphalt, and even homes.

place. There's a lot of work to do, but the potential for enhanced lives is enormous. Never before have there been opportunities for seniors like this in America. The era of creating housing *for* seniors has to end, and the era of creating housing *with* seniors has to emerge and flourish.

Senior cohousing is where people live — "housing with goods in it," as the Danes would say — not warehousing. Our elders are a critical part of our society, highly under-considered in modern times. The time to change is now. And while this book can be information overload — the key thing is to get going and get organized. Sure, it will take two years, but as a resident of Korvetten said, "I think now that I have moved into senior cohousing, I will live ten years longer." Not because it's a magic medicine, but because it's fun to be alive.

Like cohousing itself, this book will evolve (in later editions). So, if you think I've omitted some compelling information, please send me a letter (yes, a letter — and hand-written is fine). I'd also appreciate hearing what you thought was really important for you as well as if you see information that you do not consider essential.

FrogSong Cohousing.

Cohousing celebrates transition away from car culture and towards bike culture.

The future will see lots of folks getting together and asking themselves, "Are we ready to get together and figure out how to best live our lives in a way that allows us to experience life at its highest potential?" Too lofty? I think not. Achievable? Very! Go forth and be one with your own future.

ECO - FRIENDLY
NEVADA CITY COHOUSING

COMMUNITY = SECRET INGREDIENT IN SUSTAINABILITY

In the design of a cohousing community, there is a great deal of opportunity to live in a considerably greener architecture. This example (Nevada City Cohousing) is just one of many. Preliminary data shows at least a $100 a month decrease in energy usage per house. That is just one of a couple dozen ways the project treads lighter on the earth.

- **passive solar heating:** increased thermal mass; 90% recycled cellulose super insulation; perimeter foundation insulation; efficient windows; radiant barriers; buildings oriented for optimum solar gain
- **passive cooling:** no air conditioners in homes; increased thermal mass; whole house fans; radiant barriers; ceiling fans, cross ventilation
- **active solar heating:** water for radiant floor heat and domestic hot water is preheated by solar panels and fed to a single boiler that serves 3 to 6 units

low electricity use: almost all lights are fluorescent; energy-efficient refrigerators; photo-voltaic solar panels (36 kw); projected $30/mo. winter energy bill per household vs. typical household in the area of about $150/mo.

reduced asphalt: 900 S.F. per house vs. the typical 3,000 S.F. per house. (these values include street area needed to access home, driveway and garage area)

low toxicity materials: bamboo flooring; cellulose insulation, low-toxicity paint; low formaldehyde materials; recycled and wool carpeting; marmoleum flooring

responsible water use: low water use per house fixture (such as: savings of 4,000 gallons per toilet per year alone) 100,000 gallons of water used per household per year for the first five years projected, 75,000 gallons per year per household after that. City average is about 164,000 gallons per year per household

responsible forestry: almost no clear cut lumber (FSC certified); advanced framing; 25% to 40% less lumber used to build the same square footage; less than half the lumber used than for a typical new house

responsible waste stream management: no vinyl flooring; refinishable marmoleum floors, (marmoleum is made primarily of cellulose & linseed oil and composts into landfills)

responsible resource use: recycled paint; low construction waste; recycled cellulose; sustainable ceiling tiles; average house size = 1,250 S.F. compared to the average of new American houses of 2,300 S.F.

- **air quality:** there are no wood stoves in any of these 34 homes; and no auto garage attached to houses, a common cause of indoor air polution
- **walkable to downtown:** goods and services (dentist, store, church, bus stop, work places) are available without getting into a car; pedestrian/child friendly site design
- **minimum impact:** minimum grading and tree removal; 60% of site has been preserved as open space
- **responsible landscaping:** planting more than 100 new trees; indigenous grasses & wildflowers; minimum water use and other key permaculture attributes; minimum grading and tree removal; on-site drain water management at densely planted bio-swale; water retention on site
- **workforce housing:** allows for more affordable housing than other new houses built in the area; creates housing for a diversity of incomes
- **reduced driving:** studies show that folks who live in cohousing drive 25% less and own fewer autos
- **urban ecology:** replaces Nevada City housing stock that has been lost to recent commercial development
- **preserves rural Nevada City community feel:** by building where services exist (sewer and water) county wide sprawl is reduced
- **handicap accessibility:** exceeds state and national requirements
- **appropriate architecture:** architecture that fits with the cultural heritage of the area
- **community:** this intergenerational community allows for sharing resources, such as autos, camping stuff; education regarding using less water; less resources; less energy; and just less. Community facilitates environmental stewardship

Appendix A:
Why Aging in Community?

Anne P. Glass, Ph.D.

It's everywhere! Advertisements for aging-related products (or — more often — *anti-aging* products!), images of active grandparents having fun with their grandchildren, and an 80-year-old shown running in a marathon. Why are we seeing so many more older adults in the media? Well, in part, we have the baby boomers to thank for this increased presence.

More people are living longer than ever before in history. Americans living in the early 1900s had an average life expectancy of only 47 years. Since then, we have added an amazing 30 years to our life expectancy. People born nowadays can expect to live to 78[1] or beyond. From 1900 to 2006, the United States has seen the percentage of those aged 65 and over triple, from 4.1 percent to 12.4 percent, while the actual numbers have increased 12 times, from 3.1 million to 37.3 million.

Add to that the baby boomers — those born between 1946 and 1964: in 2011 the first of the boomers turn 65 years old and the last in 2029. The result? The so-called "graying of America."

So what does this mean to American society? You name it, it will be affected. Businesses and organizations are beginning to work feverishly to prepare for this huge influx of "elders." To give you an idea of the magnitude, a few statistics may help explain:

- By 2015 — less than 10 years from now — we'll have more people aged 60 and above than children![2]
- And, as far as American centenarians are concerned — those who have reached the 100 year mark and who receive birthday greetings from Willard Scott on the *Today* show — the number is projected to grow from about 70,000 centenarians now to as many as *one million* by the year 2050.[3]
- The 85 and above age group is 43 times larger now than it was in 1900.[4]

No wonder aging is "suddenly" a hot topic. The world as we know it will look a lot different in the coming decades. Picture as you walk down the street. One in five of the people you pass could be age 65 or over. More older will be working — from bagging groceries to leading corporations — and products and services will adjust to meet the demands of this market. Now we need to create new and satisfying options and ways for elders to live out the gift of these years.

Complicating the picture is the recognition that the older population is the most diverse of any age group. No assumptions can be made based merely on knowing a person's chronological age. The use of the age 65 to designate the "older population" is itself simply an arbitrary, artificial cut-off point. People can be fit and active at age 90, or disabled by a chronic condition at age 50. Genes, personalities, health behaviors, education, career choices, and family networks — all these aspects and many others result in wide variation among older adults. While a small percentage of families headed by a 65-plus householder have incomes lower than $10,000, more than 20 percent report incomes over $75,000.[5] The older population is becoming more diverse as far as color, ethnicity, and sexual orientation, as well. In addition, the various life paths that elders have traveled and the life stories they can share make them the most interesting of all age groups.

Active and Engaged

If you reach age 65 today, you are likely to live another twenty years or even longer. With better health and lower rates of disability than those experienced by past generations,[6, 7, 8] many older adults are living in high contrast to the outdated stereotype of "retiring to the rocking chair." There are stories every day of older adults with new accomplishments that were never imagined by our grandparents, such as "Banana George" Blair[9] of Florida, who holds the world record for skiing barefoot at the age of 91, and Bill Hargrove of Georgia, aged 106 and still bowling. Many more

"Banana George" Blair of Florida, who holds the world record for skiing barefoot at the age of 91.

Bill Hargrove of Georgia, aged 106 and still bowling.

elders are enthusiastically participating not only in personal fitness activities, but also in competitive sports, with many senior athletes ultimately competing at the national level. According to the National Senior Games Association (NSGA), for example, there is a 100+ age group in the individual, doubles, and relay competitions, and an 80+ age division for three-on-three basketball.

Among their advantages, today's elders are increasingly likely to have higher levels of education than past generations. Census data demonstrates this increase even within the current older population, as seen in Chart 1. Almost half of those aged 85 and above did not complete high school, but the percentage drops to less than a third of those who are in the "young-old" group, aged 65 to 74.[10] Among all older age groups, including the 70-plus, labor force participation is increasing slightly for men and even more significantly for women.[11] Rates are highest among those age 65 to 69; in this age group, one out of three men are employed and one of four women.

Older adults are also actively engaged in civic and volunteer activities. About one in four elders is currently volunteering[12] and 14 percent of all volunteers are 65-plus. Almost half of all those age 55 and above volunteered at least once in the prior year, including over 40 percent

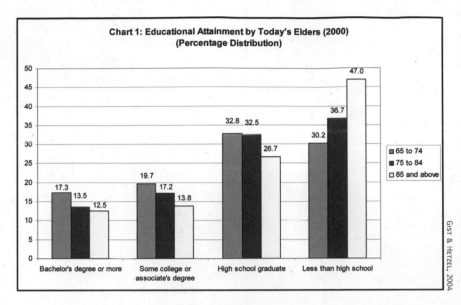

Chart 1: Educational Attainment by Today's Elders (2000)
(Percentage Distribution)

Legend: ■ 65 to 74 ■ 75 to 84 □ 85 and above

Bachelor's degree or more: 17.3, 13.5, 12.5
Some college or associate's degree: 19.7, 17.2, 13.8
High school graduate: 32.8, 32.5, 26.7
Less than high school: 30.2, 36.7, 47.0

of those 75 and above.[13] Older adults also contribute twice as many hours annually to community volunteering, compared to the median of 52 hours.[14] They are helping everywhere, in a wide variety of ways, from working with underprivileged children in the schools, delivering Meals-on-Wheels to homebound elders, and serving in their churches, to monitoring water quality of local rivers and streams, just to name a few examples.

Such activities have been proven to improve physical and mental health,[15, 16] particularly for older adults.[17, 18] Volunteering offers opportunities to meet and socialize with others. Participants take satisfaction from knowing that they are continuing to contribute to the community and gain a sense of accomplishment through learning new skills. There is awareness among many elders of the importance of "giving back." As some contributors have eloquently voiced in a Harvard School of Public Health/MetLife Foundation initiative, *Reinventing Aging*[19]:

> I feel that the majority of people over 60 … are giving back …. Most of us have had some success, are now retired and are eager to give back what we can. We are excited about having the opportunity to help others …. In the mornings as we get up we say to ourselves, "what can I do for someone today?" It's just a quiet feeling. So we do what we can and we do it quietly. We really don't need our deeds in the paper or on the airways
>
> — Ted Andrewlevich

"I'm thrilled that I'm in this stage of life. Confidence comes late, but it's solid, and confidence is self-nurturing"

> — Margot Doohan

"The things that give meaning to this period of life are relationships, spiritual connections, inner reflection and concern for others."

> — June Chapko

As these individuals indicate, service to others becomes a priority for many older adults. Interestingly, it turns out [20] that elders who support others may actually gain more themselves in health benefits than those who receive. Maybe that old adage, "it is more blessed to give than to receive" is true. All in all, most elders will have many years to be active in the ways that they consider most important.

Challenges

The majority of older adults — nearly three quarters — consider their health good to excellent. Almost 30 percent of the oldest old (age 85 and above) are among those reporting themselves in the best health — "excellent" or "very good."[21] Of course, some of this positive self-reporting may be due to the principle of relativity, as reflected in the example of the older adult who says, "My joints hurt, I've had cancer, and my hearing is not what it used to be, but I can still get up and go, unlike poor Beatrice, bless her heart. Compared to her, I'm doing pretty good!"

The latter stages of life do include challenges, however, with chronic conditions and aging processes eventually catching up with most individuals. The following facts may be useful as fodder for Study Group 1 discussions. While many older adults will remain active (even those who are dealing with a disability), over 40 percent report having a long-lasting condition or disability. The percentage increases with age to almost three-quarters of those aged 85 and above. One in five reports some difficulty with going outside the home, again with the percent increasing with age to almost half of the "older-old."[22] People may begin to have trouble first with things like getting groceries, doing housework, and preparing meals, the tasks that are referred to as the "instrumental activities of daily living" (IADLs).

The basic "activities of daily living," commonly referred to as ADLs in healthcare lingo, include bathing, dressing, eating, getting in and out of bed/chairs, using the toilet, and getting around inside the home. See Chart 2, which displays the functional status of elders still dwelling in the traditional community compared to those who have moved into housing that offers services (not including nursing facilities). While only a handful of the "young-old" group report needing help with personal care, the number increases to about 20 percent in the later ages (see Chart 3).[23] Even this number is still rather low and may surprise you, compared to our stereotypes of old age. This statistic means that fully *80 percent* of all those aged 85 and above still living in the community continue to be able to provide for their own personal care needs.

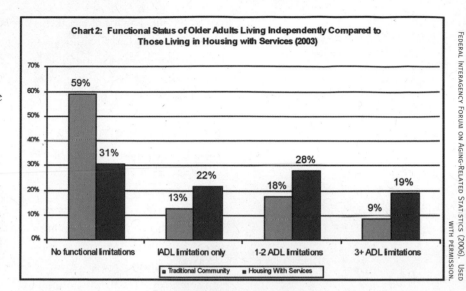

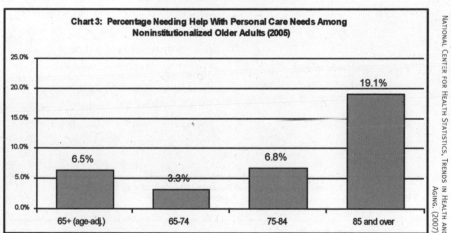

FEDERAL INTERAGENCY FORUM ON AGING-RELATED STATISTICS (2006). USED WITH PERMISSION.

NATIONAL CENTER FOR HEALTH STATISTICS, TRENDS IN HEALTH AND AGING. (2007).

If still living in the community, once you've reached the age of 65, most of us can expect to eventually spend a year or more having some difficulties and needing some help.[24] Where will this help come from? What does the future hold? Even with optimistic projections that disability rates will continue to decline for older adults, the number of older individuals with disabilities will more than double by 2040, from about 10 million now to 21 million.[25]

The Family's Role in Caregiving:

Contrary to popular belief, most older people *do not* live in nursing homes! In fact, less than five percent of the 65-plus population are residing in nursing facilities at any one point in time. Again, this reality may surprise you. While families are *not* abandoning their elders (the parents often rely on them for their very survival), not all families can provide anywhere near real companionship, but they do the best they can to be adequate caregivers. For every nursing home resident, there are four times as many individuals with similar needs who are remaining in the community.[26] Of those who receive care at home, over 90 percent rely primarily on family and friends for some or all of their care,[27] with two-thirds depending completely on family and friends to provide this help, as shown in Chart 4.

We place such a heavy emphasis on the value of independence in our American society that many older people express concerns about "not wanting to be a burden" to their children. There is nothing wrong with having some dependency on your family, and we as a nation need to rethink our views on independence as we age and the need for help becomes increasingly inescapable. Many families willingly and lovingly take on the role of caregiving, and in fact, they sometimes carry it to extremes by refusing support for themselves. We all know people who have burned themselves out trying to provide care for a family member. Family caregivers are often guilty of thinking and insisting that they can do it all (an obstinacy that goes back to that independence thing again!). As a society, we are greatly indebted to all those families who freely put in so many hours to help their loved ones. Our government could never afford to pay for all the care that families voluntarily supply.

Despite the substantial and comforting amount of caregiving that families provide to their older members, everywhere I go, the idea of elder

Data refers to Medicare enrollees who live in the community who receive personal care from a paid ("formal") or unpaid ("informal") helper.

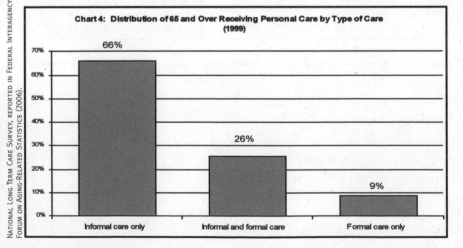

Chart 4: Distribution of 65 and Over Receiving Personal Care by Type of Care (1999)

NATIONAL LONG TERM CARE SURVEY, REPORTED IN FEDERAL INTERAGENCY FORUM ON AGING-RELATED STATISTICS (2006).

cohousing seems to resonate with people. An increasing number of people are thoughtfully pondering the question, "Who's going to take care of me when I need help?" They may be wondering because they have no children to call upon; one-fifth of older Americans currently have none.[28] The facts are, childless older adults have reason to be concerned, especially frail elders who are unmarried. They are substantially less likely — 31 percent less likely, according to one study[29] — to receive in-home help from family and friends, compared to elders with two or more children. They are also at higher risk of nursing home placement if female (not so for older men).[30] This concern will grow, as the fertility rate has slipped by about 50 percent in the past century.[31] With lower fertility rates among the baby boomers than among prior generations, the number of older adults who are childless will continue to increase. It is projected that by the time the boomers reach age 65, one in three will have no children.[32]

Other elders who have children may not wish for them to take on this role for assorted reasons. For example, older adults may prefer to stay in their longtime community rather than relocate to another state where their children are living, or they may feel their children are already stretched too thin by taking care of the needs of their own children and the demands of their jobs. Also, baby boomers are more likely to have only one child, which means as these parents age, that child will have no siblings to share the care. Additionally, while the older population will double by 2030, the population of traditional caregivers — generally women in the middle age ranges — will increase only slightly during the same period.[33] Chart 5 shows the projected growth in numbers of women aged 20 to 44 compared to the numbers projected for the population aged 65 and above. As we shall see later, living in community and building interdependence can be the answer for many elders, as the supply

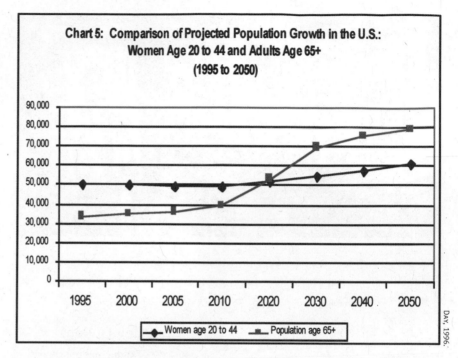

Chart 5: Comparison of Projected Population Growth in the U.S.: Women Age 20 to 44 and Adults Age 65+ (1995 to 2050)

DAY, 1996.

Residents and planners of Silver Sage Senior Cohousing enjoy the newly completed project.

of traditional caregivers wanes in comparison to the increasing number of older adults.

Current Housing Options

The majority of older people own their homes, but the percent decreases with age, from 81 percent in the youngest group to two-thirds in the oldest.[34] Obviously many people feel strong attachments to their homes. One choice for older adults is simply not to make a choice and just remain in their longtime residences; arranging for help at home when needed. This assistance may be provided by family or friends, by the "gray market" — aides who are hired and paid directly, rather than through an agency — or by taking the more formal route of hiring help through a home health agency or personal care services provider. Some long-term care insurance policies will cover such

care, but it is often paid for out of pocket, which can amount to a considerable sum, as the average charge for home health aides is currently about $19/hour[35] in urban areas.

Aside from the cost and the difficulties of finding qualified, reliable help, remaining in the longtime residence raises other issues. For example, there is the burden of continuing the maintenance of what is often an older structure, as older people tend to live in older homes compared to other householders,[36] and five percent of these homes have physical problems. Over 40% of those aged 65-plus had significant housing challenges in 2005,[37] when adding in consideration of high cost burdens and crowded or inadequate housing. Then there are the ongoing challenges of the mundane regular upkeep like mowing the lawn and cleaning the house. The house may also feel too large now for just an older couple or an individual living alone. The design may not be ideal for aging bodies either; it may include lots of steps or other inconvenient aspects not well suited for this stage of life.

Older individuals can also become quite isolated in their homes, especially as they reach the more advanced ages and it becomes harder to get around. Marital status, too, plays a substantial role in living arrangements. As you may have already noticed, women tend to live longer than men, so it may not surprise you to hear that three quarters of older men are married, compared to less than half of the women.[38] If you are a man, you are more likely to be able to remain in your home. Those who are married generally live with their spouses, equaling over half of all elders living in the community. Only 11.8 percent of all older adults were divorced or separated in 2006, a relatively low percentage, but this figure has been growing, more than doubling from 5.3 percent in 1980. Significantly, 42 percent of older women are widowed compared to only 13 percent of older men.

Thus, women are far more likely to live alone, and this likelihood increases with age. Thirty percent of community-based elders live alone, comprised of 7.8 million women and 2.9 million men, including almost half of all women aged 75 and above. Living alone obviously contributes to the likelihood of isolation, particularly for the oldest old.

Other choices are to live with the children (see potential problems noted earlier), to move to another house or apartment, or to relocate into "senior housing." The image of retirees moving en masse to Florida conjures up the idea that moving is common for older people. The reality is that compared to other age groups, older adults are actually less likely to

change residence. Fewer than one in twenty moved in the period from 2005 to 2006.[39] When they moved, they tended not to stray far. Of the older movers, half remained in the same county and over three-quarters in the same state; less than one in four moved out of state. Of course, there are always those who see such moves as an adventure!

About five percent live in self-described senior housing of assorted types; many of these arrangements include some level of services. As noted earlier, even fewer live in nursing facilities. The number of nursing facility residents overall has actually decreased by 5 percent in the years between 1998 and 2004[40] as more alternatives become available. Some of these options stem from the rise of assisted living and the increasing availability of home and community-based services. In order to have a better

The Wolf Creek Commons planning group and their completed site layout.

basis to consider elder cohousing as a choice, it is worth spending a few minutes to clarify some of the various housing options currently available, what they offer, and their costs.

Independent or congregate living apartments, sometimes called "active adult communities," are available in many areas and take many forms. Typically, residents are still able to take care of all their activities of daily living, but they might have one meal together daily and perhaps have services such as light housekeeping and maintenance. These facilities can be feasible choices for some elders, but if the residents' conditions deteriorate, they will be forced to give up their homes and move out.

"Assisted living" has grown from more humble beginnings of what used to be called adult care homes or homes for adults (among other terms varying from state to state). Assisted living facilities now are often quite attractive … and expensive. Nationally, the average private pay monthly base rate is about $3,000, translating to $36,000 annually,[41] although it can run much higher. You must pay completely out of your pocket for assisted living, unless you had the forethought to purchase long term care insurance that specifically covers this level of care. In assisted living, there is presumed to be an emphasis on independence and autonomy, but help with the basic

activities of daily living is available as needed. Sometimes a resident may only need supervision and reminders to take medications.

If an individual reaches a point of near or total dependence in the activities of daily living, the nursing home is an option, although generally not a popular one. There are many nursing facilities that are well-managed and provide excellent care, and many hardworking and caring individuals are employed in this setting. Despite heavy regulation over the past several years, however, serious concerns about quality continue to plague many of these facilities.

In addition, what many people do not realize is that Medicare — the federally-run health insurance program for older people and those with disabilities — pays almost nothing for the kind of long term assistance with the activities of daily living that most nursing homes provide. Medicare pays only for limited stays for "skilled nursing facility" care, typically for rehabilitation after surgery, or for designated "skilled care needs" such as wound care. Even though many facilities now label themselves as "skilled nursing facilities," this name should not be confused with the kind of nursing care — help with the activities of daily living — that most residents require. In this latter situation, Medicare pays nothing. You must again pay out of your own pocket — to the tune of an average of $206/day, or $6,266 per month, equaling $75,190 annually for a private room, to $183/day, $5,566 per month, or $66,795 annually for a traditional semi-private room[42] — unless you have long term care insurance or are low income.

In the latter case, Medicaid will step in. Medicaid is a federal/state-run program that is income-based, and it will also step in if you "spend down" your personal funds below a certain limit. Medicaid varies from state to state, but it is now the primary payer for many nursing facility residents nationally.[43] Chart 6 shows the sources of payment for all health care services for all Medicare enrollees in 2003, while Chart 7 shows, in sharp contrast, the source of payments for nursing homes/long-term institutions.

Furthermore, nursing facilities are institutions and generally operate on a medical model. The number of residents and the challenges of finding and keeping staff make it difficult, if not impossible, to promote and provide individualized care. Residents typically are placed with a person previously unknown to them, and expected to share a room. They must get up, eat meals, and go to bed on a schedule set by the institution, based on the most economical patterns of staffing. With an often insufficient number of aides struggling to meet too many demands, even the most well-intentioned and

"Health care services" includes physician/medical, inpatient hospital, hospice, home health care, short and long-term institutions and nursing homes, out-patient hospital stays, prescription drugs, and dental care. "Other" includes private insurance, Department of Veterans Affairs, and other public programs.

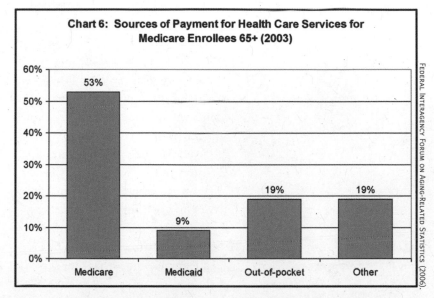

Chart 6: Sources of Payment for Health Care Services for Medicare Enrollees 65+ (2003)

FEDERAL INTERAGENCY FORUM ON AGING-RELATED STATISTICS (2006).

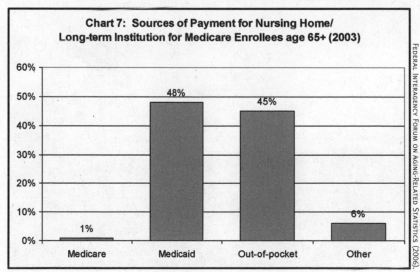

Chart 7: Sources of Payment for Nursing Home/Long-term Institution for Medicare Enrollees age 65+ (2003)

FEDERAL INTERAGENCY FORUM ON AGING-RELATED STATISTICS (2006).

caring aide may not be able to spend quality time with the residents. The stage is set for what Bill Thomas, M.D. and long-term care advocate, calls the three plagues of nursing homes: loneliness, boredom, and helplessness.[44] Thomas and others have advocated for changes in the traditional nursing home model. Without the development of alternatives to nursing facilities, some projections forecast the number of nursing facility residents will double by 2030, even under the most optimistic scenario.[45]

Another option is the continuing care retirement community (CCRC). The CCRC brings together multiple levels on one campus — with individuals typically initially moving into houses or apartments and living independently, except perhaps for some light housekeeping and maintenance services. There are usually wellness and activities centers and public dining areas. If and when the need for more services and help with activities of daily living arises, CCRC residents can move into the assisted living or the nursing facility right on the same grounds. Living on the same campus makes it easier for a spouse and other CCRC friends and neighbors to visit. Moving into a CCRC can also serve as a form of long-term care insurance, depending on the type of contract offered. Residents generally pay a hefty entrance fee, ranging from less than $100,000 to more than $500,000, and then must pay a monthly maintenance fee, generally in the $1,000 to $5,000 range. CCRCs can be very attractive for some older individuals, but again they include the traditional nursing home model, and require a certain level of income.

The Case for Elder Cohousing

Remembering the diversity of the older population, we clearly must have a variety of options to satisfactorily fit the needs and priorities of different individuals. One size does not fit all, and not everyone is satisfied with what they have observed of their current choices. A growing number of older adults and baby boomers are rebelling against the threat of spending their final years lonely and bored, wondering who will take care of them, and ending life in a conventional nursing home.

A small gathering in a Glacier Circle living room. One resident said, "Living here I can be a better friend to my friends."

Thus, creative new models are emerging, including intentional communities in the form of elder cohousing. All over the country, interested groups of older adults are beginning to gather, eager to learn more about this exciting new option.

The ElderSpirit Community in Abingdon, Virginia, is one of the first elder cohousing communities in the United States. Some observations from personal interviews I conducted with the first residents illustrate the problems elders may experience before moving into elder cohousing. When asked how older adults are viewed in our society, participants responded with comments such as "older people are invisible." Many said it was more difficult to make friends when they moved to a new area.

Living in self-managed communities of peers, as in an elder cohousing community, can give people an entirely new positive experience in this period of life. Respondents reported feeling affirmed through the sense that they are valued and capable of being productive, worthwhile, and important to others, no matter what their condition. Being able to self-govern instead of having someone tell you what to do is also a radical idea for this age group in our society, when you look at other senior housing options. One of the founders of ElderSpirit Community said:

I think it's a holistic approach to aging, and we have figured out a way where people keep their money and keep their independence, which is a big deal, because the resident management means that they get the control.

At ElderSpirit, there is also a focus on mutual support. Even as residents' conditions worsen, with the support of concerned friends and supplemental home care, many will be able to remain at home, and out of institutions. This scenario could provide a better and more satisfying experience for the residents. At the same time, elder cohousing provides the twin opportunities of being able to easily engage with others, but also being able to return to your own place for time alone. Likewise, there is the choice and responsibility to cook for yourself, but there are often community meals, and always a neighbor handy to help out if you are having a bad day.

One of the residents at ElderSpirit Community described a series of health problems that forced her to realize she had to move from her isolated country home and eventually led her on the path to ElderSpirit Community. She visited an independent living apartment building in Florida where she would have paid $2,100 a month and received only food and light house-keeping. She described it this way:

> The people were just there.
> They were warehoused. They
> were walking around but they
> were still warehoused. They
> would come in and eat and
> kind of drift away. I don't think
> I heard a single person laugh.

In trying to decide what to do, she felt she "was really sinking down badly." After moving to ElderSpirit Community, however, she says she is eating better and exercising.

> This has been a real answer to
> a prayer... I say to myself
> everyday, you know it's amaz-
> ing... And it's such a secure
> feeling. The laughter here is
> wonderful, it just makes you
> want to cry. I don't know what
> other older people are going to
> do, but I hope there can be other
> ElderSpirit Communities. I am
> lucky... I am happy, I am peace-
> ful... I don't feel like the rug is
> going to be pulled out from me.
> I am comfortable and secure.
> And secure I think is one of
> the best words I can think of.

In addition to security, living among your peers in such communi-ties can also make it easier to adapt to the inevitable changes that sooner or later accompany the aging process for each individual. My early interviews have suggested some evidence of such "communal coping."[46] For example, two women who had hearing impair-ments each told me separately how they found humor in comparing notes and laughing over what they thought they had heard!

Those who wish can still work with children in the larger commu-nity, but enjoy the pleasures of living among peers. "It's very comforting to be among those your own age group... [with a] shared history. They lived in the same world and have many simi-lar memories in that way" stated one resident. Another said,

> Intergenerational is nice, but
> younger people are interested
> in their own thing and ... I
> think they tend to shove us to
> the back. They don't mean to.
> They are full of life, vitality,
> and they can still run down
> the trail while I walk. It's nice
> to have somebody to walk
> with and not feel that I am
> holding them back.

It is also not too farfetched to imagine that living "in community" has the potential to help residents age "better" on many levels. One level is simply through the cohousing design, which promotes interactions. An elder cohousing community naturally facil-itates informal sharing of information as a sense of community develops. Topics such as trips, volunteer opportunities, medication problems, best doctors, gardening tips, yoga, good recipes, dealing with grief, and a host of other life experiences can be discussed, with a likely resultant improvement in residents' quality of life. Having neighbors readily available to walk with, talk with, and eat with can also promote better mental and physical health.

Community and interdependence can be even more important for older people than for other age groups. One resident described "sense of community" as:

> It means a wholeness. It means we will be eating and sharing, if we want to, meals, three and four times a week. It means that we have a buddy system and when my friend across the way is ill, one of the two of us here will be there for her. It means I can pick up the phone... and say "hey, I need help." Or it means we will just walk together and laugh.

Conclusion

As this book explains, cohousing communities are specifically designed to promote social interaction through living "in community." The cohousing model directly attacks the three plagues identified by Thomas: loneliness, boredom, and helplessness. Making the choice to develop and reside in an elder-only cohousing community is becoming increasing popular as an alternative to the options described above. Even among these intentional communities, however, there will be much variation.

Those who choose elder cohousing will face the challenge of living together and continuing to be actively engaged in their own lives as well as that of the cohousing community. One resident stated,

> I think we are a self-growth model, where you can't just say "well, I have done everything, so now I am just going to sit here and vegetate." You know and even if you want to, living

Nevada City Cohousing.

in a community, there's going to be a challenge to do that...I mean you are going to have to change and grow."

And we'll let another resident of ElderSpirit Community speak for her neighbors as we close this chapter:

We don't feel our age. We don't sit around and talk about our operations. That's a big difference. We've got too much living to do. We can live and be aging.

References

1) Greenberg, S. (2007). *A Profile of Older Americans: 2007*. Washington, DC: Administration on Aging (AOA), US Department of Health and Human Services.

2) United Nations. (2005). *World Population Prospects: The 2004 Revision*. Washington, DC: Population Reference Bureau. Retrievable from prb.org/

3) Dollemore, Dong. (Updated 2007). *Aging Under the Microscope*. Washington, DC: National Institute on Aging. Retrievable from nia.nih.gov/ HealthInformation/Publications/ AgingUndertheMicroscope/

4) Greenberg, S. (2007). *A Profile of Older Americans: 2007*. Washington, DC: Administration on Aging (AOA), US Department of Health and Human Services.

5) Ibid.

6) Manton, K.G., & Gu, X. (2001). Changes in the prevalence of chronic disability in the United States black and non-black population above 65 from 1982 to 1999. *Proceedings of the National Academy of Sciences*, 98, 6354-6359.

7) Martin, L.G., Schoeni, R.F., Freedman, V.A., & Andreski, P. (2007). Feeling better? Trends in general health status. *Journal of Gerontology, Series B: Psychological Sciences and Social Sciences*, 62, S11-S21.

8) Waidmann, T.A., & Liu, K. (2000). Disability trends among elderly persons and implications for the future. *Journal of Gerontology, Series B: Psychological Sciences and Social Sciences*, 55B, S298-S307.

9) bananageorge.com/

10) Gist, Y.J., & Hetzel, L.I. (2004). *We the People: Aging in the United States*. Washington, DC: Census 2000 Special Report CENSR-19, US Census Bureau.

11) Federal Interagency Forum on Aging-Related Statistics. (2006). *Older Americans Update 2006: Indicators of Well-Being*. Federal Interagency Forum on Aging-Related Statistics. Washington, DC: US Government Printing Office. Retrieved May 19, 2007 from agingstats.gov/agingstatsdotnet/main_ site/default.aspx.

12) Bureau of Labor Statistics. (2006). *Volunteering in the United States, 2006*. Washington, DC: US Department of Labor. Retrieved May 30, 2007 from bls.gov/news.release/volun.nr0.htm.

13) Experience Corps. (No date). *Fact Sheet on Aging in America*. Retrieved May 25, 2007 from experiencecorps.org/ images/pdf/Fact%20Sheet.pdf.

14) Bureau of Labor Statistics. (2006). *Volunteering in the United States, 2006*. Washington, DC: US Department of Labor. Retrieved May 30, 2007 from bls.gov/news.release/volun.nr0.htm

15) Luoh, M.C., & Herzon, A.R. (2002). Individual consequences of volunteer and paid work in old age: Health and mortality. *Journal of Health and Social Behavior*, 43, 490-509.

16) Morrow-Howell, N., Hinterlong, J., Rozario, P.A., & Tang, F. (2003). Effects of volunteering on the well-being of older adults. *Journal of Gerontology, Series B: Psychological Sciences and Social Sciences,* 58B s137-S145.

17) Moen, P. & Fields, V. (2002). Midcourse in the United States: Does unpaid community participation replace paid work? *Ageing International,* 27, 21-48.

18) Musick, M.A., & Wilson, J. (2003). Volunteering and depression: The role of psychological and social resources in different age groups. *Social Science and Medicine,* 56, 259-269.

19) Harvard School of Public Health — MetLife Foundation Initiative on Retirement & Civic Engagement. (2006). *Reinventing Aging: What Would You Call the New Stage of Life Between 60 and 80?* Retrieved May 28, 2007 from reinventingaging.org./.

20) Brown, S.L., Nesse, R.M., Vinokur, A.D., & Smith, D.M. (2003). Providing social support may be more beneficial than receiving it: Results from a prospective study of mortality. *Psychological Science,* 14, 320-327.

21) National Center for Health Statistics, Trends in Health and Aging. (2007). *Perceived Health Status: Respondent-Assessed Health by Age, Sex, and Race/Ethnicity: United States, 1982-2005.* NHIHS05. Retrieved May 23, 2007 from cdc.gov/nchs/agingact.htm.

22) Gist, Y.J., & Hetzel, L.I. (2004). *We the People: Aging in the United States.* Washington, DC: Census 2000 Special Report CENSR-19, US Census Bureau.

23) National Center for Health Statistics, Trends in Health and Aging. (2007). *Needing Help With Personal Care Needs by Age, Sex, and Race/Ethnicity: United States, 1997-2005.* NHIN05. Retrievable from 209.217.72.34/aging/TableViewer/tableView.aspx?ReportId= 378.

24) Crimmins, E.M., Kim, J.K., & Hagedorn, A. (2003). Health expectancy: An indicator of successful aging and a measure of the impact of chronic disease and disability. L.W. Poon, S.H. Gueldner, & B.M. Sprouse (Eds.), *Successful Aging and Adaptation With Chronic Diseases* (pp. 7070-82). New York, NY: Springer Publishing Company.

25) Johnson, R.W., Toohey, D., & Wiener, J.M. (2007). *Meeting the Long-Term Care Needs of the Baby Boomers: How Changing Families Will Affect Paid Helpers and Institutions.* Washington, DC: The Urban Institute.

26) ILC-SCSHE Taskforce. (2006). *Caregiving in America.* New York, NY: International Longevity Center. Retrieved April 17, 2007 from ilcusa.org/media/pdfs/Caregiving%20in%20America-%20Final.pdf.

27) Federal Interagency Forum on Aging-Related Statistics. (2006). *Older Americans Update 2006: Indicators of Well-Being.* Federal Interagency Forum on Aging-Related Statistics. Washington, DC: US Government Printing Office. Retrieved May 19, 2007 from agingstats.gov/agingstatsdotnet/main_site/default.aspx.

28) Gironda, M., Lubben, J.E., & Atchison, K.A. (1999). Social networks of elders without children. *Journal of Gerontological Social Work,* 31, 63-84

29) Johnson, R.W. (2006). *In-Home Care for Frail Childless Adults: Getting By With a Little Help From Their Friends?* Washington, DC: The Urban Institute.

30) Aykan, H. (2003). Effect of childlessness on nursing home and home health care use. *Journal of Aging and Social Policy,* 15, 33-53.

31) National Center for Health Statistics. (2005). *Birth Rates and Fertility Rates*. Retrievable from cdc.gov/nchs/data/statab/t001x01.pdf

32) Gironda, M., Lubben, J.E., & Atchison, K.A. (1999). Social networks of elders without children. *Journal of Gerontological Social Work*, 31, 63-84

33) Day, J.C. (1996). *Population Projections of the United States by Age, Sex, Race, and Hispanic Origin: 1995 to 2050*. US Bureau of the Census, Current Population Reports, P25-1130. Washington, DC: US Government Printing Office.

34) Gist, Y.J., & Hetzel, L.I. (2004). *We the People: Aging in the United States*. Washington, DC: Census 2000 Special Report CENSR-19, US Census Bureau.

35) Houser, A., Fox-Grage, W., & Gibson, M.J. (2006). *Across the States: Profiles of Long-term Care and Independent Living*. Washington, DC: AARP.

36) Greenberg, S. (2007). *A Profile of Older Americans: 2007*. Washington, DC: Administration on Aging (AOA), US Department of Health and Human Services.

37) Federal Interagency Forum on Aging-Related Statistics. (2008). *Older Americans 2008: Key Indicators of Well-Being*. Federal Interagency Forum on Aging-Related Statistics. Washington, DC: US Government Printing Office. Retrieved September 29, 2008 from agingstats.gov/agingstatsdotnet/main_site/default.aspx.

38) Greenberg, S. (2007). A *Profile of Older Americans: 2007*. Washington, DC: Administration on Aging (AOA), US Department of Health and Human Services.

39) Ibid.

40) AARP. (2005). *Reimagining America: AARP's Blueprint for the Future*. Washington, DC: AARP.

41) MetLife. (2006a). *The MetLife Market Survey of Assisted Living Costs*. Westport, CT: MetLife Mature Market Institute.

42) MetLife. (2006b). *The MetLife Market Survey of Nursing Home and Home Care Costs*. Westport, CT: MetLife Mature Market Institute.

43) Federal Interagency Forum on Aging-Related Statistics. (2006). *Older Americans Update 2006: Indicators of Well-Being*. Federal Interagency Forum on Aging-Related Statistics. Washington, DC: US Government Printing Office. Retrieved May 19, 2007 from agingstats.gov/agingstatsdotnet/main_site/default.aspx.

44) Thomas, W.H. (2004). *What Are Old People For?* Acton, MA: VanderWyk & Burnham.

45) United States Administration on Aging. (2004). *Aging Into the 21st Century*. Washington, DC: Department of Health and Human Services. Retrievable from http://www.aoa.gov/prof/Statistics/future_growth/aging21/health.aspx.

46) Lawrence, A.R., & Schigelone, A.R.S. (2002). Reciprocity beyond dyadic relationships: Aging-related communal coping. *Research on Aging*, 24, 684-704.

Anne P. Glass, Ph.D., is the Assistant Director of the Institute of Gerontology and an Assistant Professor in Health Policy and Management, in the College of Public Health at the University of Georgia.

Contact information:
aglass@geron.uga.edu, 706-425-3222

Appendix B:
Frequently Asked Questions

Until people have experienced life in a cohousing community, they often have questions and concerns about the details of daily living. But once they have moved in, they find their concerns mitigated by the trust, respect, and commitment neighbors feel for one another. In this atmosphere, long discussions of policy give way to human interactions.

What is senior cohousing?

Senior cohousing is a lifestyle choice for folks 50 years or older, where people get together and make a neighborhood that suits their particular needs from an economic, physical, social, practical, and emotional point of view.

Why live in cohousing?

When describing cohousing, most people search for words like "family" and "village-living." Many elderly people I interviewed in Denmark cited the word "hyggelig" — cozy, pleasant,

Preparing common dinner at FrogSong Cohousing.

homelike, in terms of quality of life. In Holland they use the word "gezellig," which has the same approximate meaning. For others, it's a decision to make life more practical, more convenient, more economical, more interesting, and more fun. Many say that it is the best and easiest way to live lighter on the planet and enhance quality of life at the same time.

How is senior cohousing different from a condominium or a cooperative?

Condominiums are a type of ownership where residents own their own houses and they own any common facilities together. Cooperatives are a type of ownership where everyone owns an interest (shares) in what amounts to a corporation. Cohousing is about cooperation rather than type of ownership. And, as it turns out, cooperation transcends ownership type. Cohousing has worked well as ownership (condos), rental, and as cooperatives.

I'm a healthy, able-bodied 55-year-old. Why would I want to live in senior cohousing now?

Moving into a senior cohousing community when you're a healthy, able-bodied 55-year-old is like putting money aside from each of your paychecks into a 401k plan. You're saving surplus money while you're young because you plan to use it later — when you're older and will need it most. Seniors who move into a senior housing community when they're younger are essentially doing the same thing. Over time (day-by-day, project-by-project, year-by-year), they cement the personal relationships, community routines, and expectations from a group of peers that allows everyone involved to live longer, healthier lives. They know their community will be there for them when they are needed most (like tapping that 401k account). But you can't tap that account if you haven't contributed to it.

Yeah, but who takes care of whom?

In senior cohousing, you only help someone if you want to. It's an individual choice. Nobody has to take care of anyone unless you have made that agreement. This individual choice in terms of co-care is a fundamental aspect of a senior cohousing community that works. But experience shows that you probably will want to provide care for others, just as you probably will welcome the aid you receive — it will just be how things are. No big deal. If you are the person who is sick, who would you prefer to take care of you? A visiting nurse just making the rounds, or your close friend who also happens to be your next-door neighbor?

How does cohousing differ from other kinds of living arrangements?

In cohousing you have as much privacy as you want and as much community as you want. In your private house, you get as much privacy as you want and as much privacy as you want. Or later, in assisted living, you get as much institutionalized cajoling as you want or as much isolation as you want. In cohousing you realize the benefit of sharing with your neighbors — the advantages of cooperating as a means of enhancing quality of life.

What are some of the unique design elements in senior cohousing?

First and foremost, unlike traditional senior housing, a great deal of attention is truly paid to the success of the social aspects of the community. Kitchens are placed to the front of the house so you can wave to a neighbor passing by. Houses are placed in close physical proximity to each other. Individual houses are smaller, but have more attention paid to good design detail. More attention is paid to present and future mobility challenges. Sustainable design and low-toxicity materials are given more consideration. Finally, the entire community is designed with conscious consideration paid to the life between the buildings and every other nuance that affects social success. There are many differences between senior cohousing and intergenerational cohousing, for instance, seniors often plan for emergencies with emergency supply storage, and they plan for folks to come stay long term.

If I live in cohousing, will I have my own kitchen?

You won't believe how many times I've been asked this question by reporters standing in my kitchen!

Why cohousing just for seniors?

I've visited close to 300 cohousing communities now, several dozen of them senior cohousing. Seniors in their own cohousing community live among people with whom they share the most: a common bond of age, experience, time, and priorities. The relationships that inevitably develop provide purpose and direction in residents' lives and are as meaningful as any they have ever had. Seniors will probably end up living with mostly seniors anyway. The only question is when and how. Will it be on their own terms or on the terms of others?

Because residents plan their community to specifically meet their own needs, they prioritize their goals to fit their budget. If the generations are mixed, so are the priorities. It is unlikely for a reasonably priced project to provide a soundproof kid's room, a playground, and a baby pool as well as a hot tub, meditation room, labyrinth, grab bars, railings, an elevator, and a caretaker's suite, and to provide for all of the differences.

Are people in senior cohousing isolated from children?

People assume that senior cohousing is taking the elder away from intergenerational contact, but this isn't true. Grandchildren visit often — lots of people visit. And because everybody has a relationship with everyone, they end up visiting with everyone. Rarely is there a meal in the common house that does not include children or younger adults. I don't think there was a single dinner that I went to where there weren't grandkids visiting, playing, and interacting with the senior residents. This is in contrast to what occurs in the usual neighborhood, where a 17-year-old would rarely interact with a senior neighbor. Senior cohousing, with its separate guest quarters, encourages visits of parents with children who might not otherwise stay under the same roof with grandma.

Is there a screening process? Who decides who can join the community?

Some groups do have vetting and interview procedures for new members. But these are rare and not that successful (a person may just be a good talker).

Most established groups now agree that nothing works better than self selection. They invite prospective new residents to a common dinner or two, to a workday, and to a common meeting. Spending some time this way gives prospective residents the chance to see if they think cohousing is right for them, if this particular group is right for them, if they really think cooperating with their neighbors is the way to go, and whether they can handle the responsibilities expected of them. People recognize that if they are not into the whole cohousing concept, then other, more conventional options may be better for them, and for the group they were considering joining.

How do planners and city officials respond to senior cohousing?

Most city officials recognize that new, positive housing options are necessary, but few ever get to put forward positive solutions — they just edit mediocre possibilities. When cohousing comes along, those officials who have the best interests of the community in mind really come forward to support it. Unfortunately, some city officials seem to be there just to further their own needs. When a cohousing group runs up against such an official, it's often best for the group to find a way to get support from the public-at-large. Large-scale support ultimately prevails at city hall. After almost 50 projects, we've only had one project declined by city or county officials.

What is the ideal size of a senior cohousing community?

There are lots of theories, but after interviewing hundreds of residents of cohousing, the answer seems to be somewhere in the range of 15 to 25 houses. Too big, and discussions begin to sound more like politics than consensus building. By their own admission, seniors often want and need more time to discuss issues of mutual concern than do intergenerational cohousers. The advantage of larger-sized communities however, is that it increases the chances that each person will have something in common with several people, and will make more close friends — a very satisfying experience. A larger group also helps amortize the cost of a larger common house. The smaller the community is, the more community/social and financial responsibilities each household will bear.

How often do people eat in the common house?

It varies, from infrequently to most nights. Usually, there are common dinners between two and five times per week, and on average, about half the community participates in each meal. After interviewing hundreds of cohousing residents, the vast majority said that they ate in the common house about twice as often as they thought they would before moving in. (That is, unless the common house was designed poorly. See Chapter 8: Study Group II for design best practices.)

How does the community deal with differences in food tastes and requirements?

Sometimes there are formalities around food — you have to make a vegetarian entrée if you make a meat entrée, and so forth. But usually, the residents of a community care about one another enough that they will accommodate each other. "Oh, Joe is coming to dinner and he can't have lactose. We'll just whip up a cheese-free pizza to go with the other homemade pizzas we're having tonight."

How is a community managed?

By the residents, with discussion, by consensus. Therefore, people cooperate when it makes sense, but consensus has back up, super-majority voting for time-critical issues.

What about pets?

Pets mean a lot to people, and to seniors in particular. People worry about others having too many unruly pets, however, much more than is warranted. I'll never forget (while planning the 12-unit Doyle Street Cohousing) one woman exclaiming, "Yes, but what if everyone has two cats? We'll have 24 cats!" That's about as likely as being hit by a meteorite. The residents moved in with 12 cats, and interestingly, ten years later they had none. When the cats died they weren't replaced. It turns out that having real people to talk to made the cats less essential. (Since then a cat or two has been replaced.) Ultimately, it is up to the group to formulate their own pet policies during the Study Group III phase of the project.

How do cohousing prices compare to other kinds of housing?

It depends on a lot of factors. Some say that you can expect to pay the same amount per square foot as for other multi-family condominiums. But it varies. Cohousing can initially cost as much as other kinds of new-built housing (sometime more, sometimes less). Cohousing may cost more when the project is not well planned or organized, or not made to fit optimally into production construction (versus custom construction). Cohousing can cost less, even when the group asks for more accessibility and more ecological design features (custom construction), if, in order to keep

costs down, these "custom" features are made to fit into a standard design.

Where the real savings are to be made is after move-in. The increase in disposable income can be $200 to $1000 a month for each house in senior cohousing because of the things that people do for each other as a natural part of a normal day, rather than having to pay a stranger for it.

Do I need big bucks to move into cohousing?

Not really. What you do need is a bit of entrepreneurial spirit. An advisor (a key participant in the development of a senior cohousing community) will help the resident group to find the resources available in order to make a senior cohousing dream a reality. There is another way to look at this question: Getting older is expensive. Hired help, home remodels, or (most expensive of all), assisted-care facilities, all cost. So if you can get your senior cohousing project designed and built in such a way that you can more easily live there for the rest of your life, then you will save considerable amounts of money and effort over the other options.

What about rentals?

When nonprofits develop cohousing in Europe, they tend to be rentals. In ownership cohousing, it is up to the group to decide how many units can be rented. Not that renters harm the social dynamic at all, but it's the absentee owners who hesitate to make timely investments that make having rentals in cohousing a little more complicated. However, there were one or two rentals in the 12-unit cohousing community we lived in, and there were no problems; the renters were great contributors to the community.

How does resale work?

Theoretically a house is for sale on the open market and again there is very little vetting by the community at-large. But usually folks who buy into a project that has already been built are quite familiar with it. Most groups ask prospective members to come to a couple of common dinners, to participate in a common workday, and to attend a common meeting. The key thing is to help people make sure that cohousing is for them. Since supply is far short of demand, even in Europe, it's best that the folks who can really appreciate the benefits of cohousing, and who are best able to contribute, be the ones to move in. Empirically it has been proven to work best if prospective residents are fully apprised of the development of the community to-date. The best data to go through is the site plan program (every community will have this on file) which explains why the buildings were placed where they stand, what

common facilities there are, why the houses were designed the way they were, etc. All of the agreements the group has made to date and details of the active committees will be available for review. And the "buddy" who's showing a prospective resident around will probably also describe some of the nuances of the subculture — who appreciates it when you come to dinner on time, who's a good organizer, and who it's best to talk to about whatever you might be interested in, like landscaping or such.

How much participation is required?

While building a community, that is to say the social and developmental side of the equation, most groups meet twice a month for about a year.

Do I have to be an extrovert to live in cohousing?

When I lived in a single-family house it was hard to get away from the neighbor once a conversation got started. It happened so rarely I didn't want to seem rude. Cohousing is different. People know you, and when you say, "Can't talk — gotta go," they assume you mean you can't talk — you gotta go. You can be honest. However, introverts thrive in cohousing, possibly because they don't have to be an extrovert just to have good social relationships. And if it happens that you're married to an extrovert, s/he always has someone to chat with, and you don't have to drive somewhere to be with others and then subtly nag them that it's time to go home.

Yeah, but what if there's one, you know, jerk that lives there?

An interesting thing about cohousing is, if you know you are grating on others, you will probably move out.

Who are these cohousing people anyway?

People ask this question all the time. Who does this? Do they have some previous connection or a spiritual connection or what?

Usually they are just folks who have figured out that their own personal lives will be more practical, more economical, and more enjoyable if they give cooperating with their neighbors the benefit of the doubt. Many also have ideals they wish to live: If we can't solve problems with those that we can talk to — such as our neighbors in cohousing — then how can we solve problems with folks across town or around the world? People give many reasons, and the fact that cohousing sustains each member's continued participation means that it serves that individual day after day, year after year.

For example, when Katie and I lived in the 12-unit Emeryville cohousing, each household had one car and shared a 13th vehicle. That meant that our household didn't have to own a second car. It fulfilled many individuals' goals about living lighter on the planet, cost savings, and more. It also fostered our community, because it gave us practical stuff to organize around. At one point, one of the cohousers wanted to co-purchase a pick-up truck with his neighbors. He went around to everyone's home and announced, "I'm going to buy a pick-up; do you want to co-own a pick-up?" No, no thanks, and no were the answers he got. Can you imagine doing that in a regular neighborhood? It might take 30 minutes before someone would call the police. The point is, cohousers cooperate when it makes sense — and don't when it doesn't.

How do I get started?

E-mail The Cohousing Company at coho@cohousingco.com. Let us know where you live. The Cohousing Company, and others firms and organizations in the US, have worked hard to figure out how to make developing cohousing as easy, economical, and successful as possible.

Appendix C:
Economic Structures

Pooling Equity: The LLC

The difference between cohousing and a typical development is that cohousing communities either develop the project themselves or co-develop it with an industry professional. Prospective members usually pool their equity and form a Limited Liability Corporation, or LLC. The LLC assumes the role of developer, negotiates with the lender, buys the land, and hires the architect. When the project is completed, each individual resident then "buys" their house from the LLC, and assumes responsibility for their own mortgage. The benefits of the LLC system are enormous:

• By cooperating to build a large number of units (comparable to a suburban subdivision), cohousing residents take advantage of economies of scale that are usually available only to large developers. Also, by participating in the process from start to finish, residents avoid paying realtor fees, excessive developer fees motivated by risk, as well as extra expenses for things they don't need or want.

• The addition of the common house usually means that residents do not need their own private units to be as large as the industry-standard "McMansion." Instead, by pooling resources, they get the amenities afforded by a larger house at a much lower per-household cost.

- By initiating the project as future homebuyers, cohousing residents can guarantee that each unit will be sold (to themselves) at the end of construction. Risk is reduced, and loans are easier to secure. This is an advantage to the developer participant as well.

- Because cohousing residents plan their neighborhood from the start, rather than buying individual units piecemeal from a developer, they get a better-quality product. Developers are typically uninterested in future equity, and as a result generally pay less attention to quality construction. With resident involvement, a developer will be held accountable for work quality. Moreover, a well-planned neighborhood results in a predictable increase in property values, a consideration that appeals to most lenders and buyers.

All of these advantages are also available to the participant developer — the developer that chooses to develop a project with the future residents.

Legal Agreements

Bylaws for a building association or a development partnership are drawn up with the assistance of an attorney, and generally include provisions for:

- The group's general intentions.
- Membership requirements.
- Decision-making procedures.
- Financial liability (individual and joint).
- Who can legally represent the association.
- Members leaving the group.
- Settling financial accounts when someone withdraws.
- Amendment procedures.

If a group joint ventures with a developer, the development agreement will reflect the nature of that relationship. Once construction is completed and the construction loan is transferred to individual mortgages, a permanent homeowners' or residents' association and its bylaws replaces all previous legal arrangements. Organizations like The Cohousing Company and Cohousing Partners have sample contracts. Our company can be found online at www.cohousingco.com.

Before a group can proceed very far into the Study Group II planning process, it must consider its legal organization and shared liabilities. Luckily, the many professionals involved with cohousing have now turned this daunting task into standard fare.

Legal agreements serve several purposes besides settling questions of liability. Requiring members to sign an agreement, even in the initial stages, clarifies who is able or willing to commit to the project, thus sorting out those who are serious from those who are still curious observers. Becoming a legal entity also inspires confidence among members and consultants alike.

When the group is ready to purchase property and/or hire consultants (architect, lawyer, etc.) for extended services, a more extensive legal agreement is necessary. At this point, the group typically incorporates as a building association, which functions through the construction phases. It is at this stage that members are generally required to invest a minimum amount toward the down payment on their house.

Cooperative Ownership

Most cohousing groups, at some point in their discussions, bring up the possibility of organizing their community as a cooperative. In this ownership structure, the entire community is owned by all of the residents as a nonprofit corporation, and each household buys a share in the corporation equivalent to the price of their home. Philosophically, a cooperative seems to be an ideal structure for a cohousing community. As one resident put it, "In a sense, I own everybody's unit. I'm responsible for everyone's unit working. It has a different feeling."

Although cooperatives are a proven form of home ownership, American banks are generally wary of financing them. Even the National Cooperative Bank (NCB), which was created to support cooperatives, will not provide complete construction financing and offers only a limited range of loans. As a result, most cohousing projects have been set up as condominiums, a structure that banks and city officials already understand. Structuring the project as a condominium development doesn't seem to have any effect — negative or positive — on the success or failure of community building.

COOPERATIVES: LIMITED-EQUITY VS. MARKET-RATE

For those groups determined to form their community as a cooperative, they should know that in the US cooperatives come in two basic flavors. One provides limited-equity returns; the other provides market-rate returns. In a limited-equity cooperative, owners agree to limit the return on their investment, generally in line with the consumer price index. When they sell their share, the price they ask may be increased only up to a limited amount over what they originally paid. Typically, a limited-equity co-op is formed with special government funding designed to make the project more affordable to residents whose income is required to fall within certain government guidelines.

A market-rate, or stock, cooperative provides that a home's price be based on the market value of housing, equivalent to other housing options. This preserves the investment value of the home, allowing the owner's equity to be treated as the available asset it is, just as it would be with non-cooperative ownership schemes.

There are generally three stages at which legal agreements need to be drawn up, reflecting the needs of each development phase. These agreements are:

1. An initial pre-site acquisition agreement (partnership).
2. A "building association" or development partnership (LLC).
3. A definition of the final ownership structure and management association (Home Owners Association/HOA DOCS).

The initial agreement, drawn up before the group is ready to purchase a site, generally outlines the group's purpose, decision-making procedures, membership recruitment methods and limitations, and fees to cover operating expenses and consulting services.

The Senior Cohousing Business Model

Our books about cohousing have stressed the people and lifestyle and even the societal and environmental benefits of cohousing. Those are critical no doubt. Another key question is finding development partners for a cohousing project: How does a group find them? How do they partner with them, and what are the various development scenarios? From a business perspective, there are about 1.5 million houses built in the US every year. At one percent, that means about 15,000 new houses a year could be cohousing. That's a significant niche. That's 500 new cohousing communities a year (averaging 30 households). We're not there yet. It will require a scaling up of significant measures. Wonderland Hill Development Company of Boulder, Colorado has developed more cohousing communities than any other developer in the United States. Cohousing Partners of Nevada City, California has been very successful in helping groups develop their projects throughout the state.

Nonprofit Model

Senior cohousing is a perfect model for nonprofit developers, using the same development model that we have outlined. The main hindrance is that nonprofit projects usually take much longer to develop, and it's harder for future residents to hold on during the five or six years that it takes to get them funded. Some nonprofits believe that you can't choose the future residents ahead of construction — but you can. We have done so with the help of local congress people and national H.U.D. officials. Unfortunately, over time, nonprofits have forgotten how to develop housing *with* people and focus on developing *for* people. Nonprofits need to believe that success lies in more than production. Success is that palpable feeling you get when you walk through a neighborhood and see people talking, working, relaxing, and managing together, not complaining or demanding, but rather working together to solve problems.

Appendix D:
Universal Design

Examining Code Requirements

The applicable building code in many localities will require that a small percentage of housing units be fully accessible and, in some situations, will also require that other units be of moderate accessibility with adaptable features. These code requirements do not apply to the majority of the units in typical multi-unit dwellings, and they ignore some common areas with potential for increased accessibility.

In senior cohousing communities, the code requirements should, of course, always be met. But it is important that senior cohousing go above and beyond the code requirements. Community interaction and the ability of one neighbor to visit another's home are key elements in any cohousing community. The successful facilitation of community interaction and "visitability" in senior cohousing is contingent upon a completely access-friendly environment and results in greater independence for seniors.

In a typical senior cohousing community with 25 units, many state, local, or municipal codes require that one unit be fully accessible and at least 20% of the ground floor units be adaptable (i.e., convertible into accessible units without great expense).

Common spaces and areas that serve accessible units are generally required to be accessible. At least one of each type of recreational facility on site is generally required to be accessible,

285

and at least one accessible parking space is required. Accessible walks are required between accessible units, accessible parking, and accessible common facilities.

As you can see, the code leaves the majority of units free of any accessibility requirements. Other areas of the site may also be free of any accessibility requirements.

Access-Friendly Design

Access-Friendly Design is a holistic approach to providing the maximum amount of affordable accessibility in every facet of the built and social environment, whether or not it is required by code.

We always recommend that all elements of a cohousing community, if possible, follow the *Principles of Universal Design*, a comprehensive list of guidelines for Universal Design features in housing compiled by the Center for Universal Design at North Carolina State University. The Center acknowledges that not all features can be included in any given home. While many Universal Design features in housing can be accommodated by a conscientious and experienced architect without adversely affecting the budget, some features may increase the cost of the project too much to be included.

It is important that an open dialogue occurs between the future residents of a senior cohousing community and their architect regarding Universal Design principles. One of the key advantages to the self-development process is how future residents themselves are able to weigh the principles of Universal Design against their budget. The future residents are most capable of making informed decisions regarding potential compromises between complete accessibility and affordability. Nonetheless, many future residents may underestimate their future needs. Although cohousing residents can sometimes switch units to accommodate changing needs, this strategy should not be overly depended upon. Following is a list of recommendations for creating an access-friendly environment for any senior cohousing community:

Minimum Standards for an Access-Friendly Community (in addition to code requirements):

1. Accessible paths should connect parking, the primary pedestrian entrance of the community, all common facilities, and all residential units. All paths should be well lighted. Benches should be located regularly along the paths.
2. All common facilities should be completely accessible. The common house should either be single story or have an elevator. There

should be an accessible common kitchen, and garden areas with plants that are easily reached for pruning/maintenance, etc.

3. Entrances to all units and common facilities should be devoid of steps and have low thresholds, doors with lever or other effortless hardware, and maneuvering space beside the door. All entrances should be 36 inches wide and well lighted. House numbers should be a minimum of 3 inches tall, with high contrast between the numbers and their background. All doorbells should be lighted, and doorbell signals should be both audible and visual.

4. If site density requires second-floor units, the entrances should be off a common balcony that is accessed by an elevator. If an elevator is not financially feasible, the stairs to the second-floor units should be built wide enough and have a large enough area at the top and bottom that a platform lift could be added later. An alternative is to include, toward the middle of the unit, a set of closets, one above the other, that could later serve as the shell for a residential elevator. The cab could be added when needed at a fraction of the cost for total renovation. It is preferable that all stairs and balconies be completely indoors.

5. Every unit should have an open floor plan (kitchen, dining, and living areas all planned as one great room).

6. Interior unit doors should provide at least a 32-inch clearance when open and lever handles or push-plate hardware.

7. A 42-inch wide circulation route should exist throughout all units. If possible, every room should include a 60-inch diameter turning space once furniture is in place. If space is limited, the furnished room should at least be laid out in a way that allows a wheelchair to make a three-point turn.

8. Every unit should have at least one first floor bedroom.

9. Preferably, the first floor bathroom of every unit should be completely accessible. Grab bars don't necessarily need to be included, but there should be blocking around the toilet and bathing fixture for installation of bars in the future. Toilets should be at an accessible height (17-19 inches above the floor) and centered 18 inches from any side wall. Lavatories should be at an accessible height with space underneath, and pipes should be insulated to prevent contact with hot or sharp surfaces. Vanities should have removable doors and bases to provide accessible under-sink space. Bathtub sides should

be a maximum of 15 inches above the floor. Bathtubs should have grab bars, an interior rim that will support a removable seat, and a floor that does not slope abruptly so that a shower bench is stable. In addition, other important features to include are hand-held showerheads and controls that are offset toward the outside of the tub that have a pressure-balancing mixing valve. Some units may include curb-less showers. All faucets should have single-lever water controls. Mirrors should start 36 inches above the floor and continue to 72 inches above the floor, so both standing and seated people can see themselves. There should be a 30-inch by 48-inch clear floor space at each fixture. The first floor bathroom should preferably have a 60-inch diameter turning space. If space is limited and a 60-inch diameter turn cannot be accommodated, the room should at least be laid out in a way that allows a wheelchair to make a three-point turn.

10. Kitchens should have a minimum 30-inch by 48-inch clear space in front of cabinets and appliances. Sinks should be at an accessible height with space underneath and pipes should be insulated to prevent contact with hot or sharp surfaces. Cabinets under sinks should have removable doors and bases. All countertops should be at an accessible height and large stretches of continuous countertop should be provided immediately adjacent to appliances and sinks. Raised dishwashers are a real advantage and minimize stooping and bending. Care must be taken when locating the dishwasher so it does not interrupt the necessary workspace. Wall-hung cabinets should have adjustable-height shelves. All appliances should have front mounted controls. Refrigerator/freezers should be of the side-by-side variety or may be the over/under variety with the freezer space in a pull-out drawer below the refrigerator. All faucets should have single-lever water controls.

11. Washers and dryers should be front loading with front controls, and raised 12-15 inches off the floor to make loading and unloading easier. A 36-inch clear space should be provided in front of washers and dryers. The clear space should extend 18 inches beyond the left and right sides of the washer and dryer. Laundry sinks should be accessible.

12. Half of all storage should be less than 54 inches high.

13. Garage doors should be power operated, with remote controls. All parking should be at grade

level and should be connected to the rest of the community by an accessible path. Van-accessible parking should always be provided.

14. A deck should be at the same level as the floor in the common house and for any individual unit.

15. All cabinet doors and drawers should have loop handles.

16. Window sills should be a maximum of 36 inches above the floor (in general) for seated viewing. All operable windows should be crank operated.

17. Lighting should be adjustable. Bright, focused lighting should be provided at all work surfaces. Switches, along with thermostats, should be 48 inches above the floor. Switches should be easy-touch rockers. Electrical outlets should be a minimum of 18 inches from the floor.

Selected Bibliography

Ambrose, Iver, "Looking towards the future: Danish cohousing focuses on seniors," *CoHousing Journal* Fall 1993: 4+.

AARP, "Changes in home-care use by older people with disabilities: 1982-1994." Bofællesskaber for Ældre, *Rapport fra seminar 16-18 september 1994. Conference Proceedings*, Gilleleje, Denmark: Foreningen af 1994.

Brenton, Maria, *We're in Charge: Cohousing Communities of Older People in The Netherlands: Lessons for Britain?* Bristol, England: Policy Press, 1998.

Christensen, Karen and David Levinson, *Encyclopedia of Community: From the Village to the Virtual World*, Berkshire Publishing Group, 2003.

Co-Housing for Senior Citizen in Europe, EU Conference, "Growing grey — in a happier way," *September 1993 Conference Proceedings*, Copenhagen, Denmark: Boligtrivsel i Centrum, 1993.

Dejgaard, Olaf, "Registrant over 42 seniorbofællesskaber," *Foreningen Bofællesskaber for Ældre* September 1997.

Duke University Center for Demographic Studies, *National Long Term Care Survey 1982-1999*, New York.

Durrett, Charles, "A neighborhood that works," *Seniors' Housing News*, NAHB, 2002.

Durrett, Charles, "Senior Cohousing," *Seniors' Housing News*, NAHB, 2004.

Franck, Karen A. and Sherry Ahrentzen, *New Households, New Housing*, Van Nostrand Reinhold, 1989.

Gehl, Jan, *Life Between Buildings*, 1987.

Gerontologisk Institut Publikationer, *Bofællesskaber i bestående byggeri*, Første delbetænkning.

Hyman, Anne Kopp, *Architects of the Sunset Years: Creating Tomorrow's Sunrise*, Central Coast Press, 2005.

Krull, Kim Plummer, "Alternative living choices for older adults: New housing options offer companionship and support," *General American Solutions* Spring/Summer 1998: 10+.

MacMillan, Jeffrey, "Feathering a shared nest: How three groups of seniors created their own alternative lifestyles." *US News & World Report* 12 June 1995: 86+.

Marcus, Clare Cooper and Wendy Sarkissian, *Housing as if People Mattered*, Berkeley: University of California Press, 1986.

McCamant, Kathryn and Charles Durrett, *Cohousing: A Contemporary Approach to Housing Ourselves*, Berkeley: Ten Speed Press, 2004.

Ornish, Dean, *Love and Survival: The Scientific Basis of the Healing Power of Intimacy*, Perennial Currents, 1999.

Pedersen, Max, *Nybyggere — i den tredje alder*, København: Boligtrivsel i Centrum, 2000.

Pedersen, Max, *Seniorbofællesskaber: Hvorfor og hvordan: Evaluering af BiCs model til etablering af seniorbofællesskaber*, Boligtrivsel i Centrum, 1999.

Schachter-Shalomi, Rabbi Zalman and Ron Miller, *From Aging to Saging*, New York: Warner Books, 1995.

Stock, Robert W., "Seniors living independently, but not alone," *The Press-Enterprise* 15 January 1998.

Thomas, William H., M.D., *What Are Old People For?* Acton: Vander Wyk & Burnham, 2004.

US Department of Health and Human Services, *A Descriptive Analysis of Patterns of Informal and Formal Caregiving Among Privately Insured and Non-privately Insured Disabled Elders Living in the Community*," April, 1999.

US Department of Health and Human Services, Administration on Aging, *A Profile of Older Americans: 2002.*

Van Vliet, Willem, "Co-housing the elderly in the Netherlands," *CoHousing Journal* Spring 1993: 4.

Winters, Ben, "Cohousing: Restoring the traditional sense of community." *SeniorBeacon* September 1996: 1+.

Links

Cohousing Partners: www.cohousingpartners.com

McCamant & Durrett Architects: www.mccamant-durrett.com

The Cohousing Association of the United States: www.cohousing.org

ElderSpirit Senior Cohousing: www.elderspirit.net

SilverSage Senior Cohousing: www.silversagevillage.com

Wonderland Hill Development: www.whdc.com

BiC, Boligtrivsel i Centrum (Quality of Living in Focus): www.boligtrivsel.dk (in Danish only)

DaneAge (ÆldreSagen): www.aeldresagen.dk

Adopt-A-Native Elder Program: www.anelder.org

Elder Cohousing Network: abrahampaiss.com/ElderCohousing/

Index

Page locators in **bold** indicate photographs or illustrations.

About the Author

CHARLES DURRETT has designed or consulted in the design of over fifty cohousing communities in North America and has consulted on many more around the world. His work has been featured in *Time Magazine*, the *New York Times*, the *LA Times*, the *San Francisco Chronicle*, *Architecture*, *Architectural Record*, *The Wall Street Journal*, *The Economist* and a wide variety of other publications. He and his wife have received numerous awards for their work including, the most recent World Habitat Award, presented by the United Nations; the Mixed Use, Mixed Income Development Award, presented jointly by the American Institute of Architects and the United States Department of Housing and Urban Development; and the National Home Builders Association Award for energy, efficiency and smart growth. Charles has given many public presentations for groups from the US Congress, the Commonwealth Club, scores of Universities, City Councils and Planning Commissions around the country but most importantly, new cohousing groups just getting going.

He has developed group process and design approaches to meet the tight constraints posed by balancing a budget, providing a high standard of value and design, successful community, and achieving the sustainable design goals and aspirations of cohousing groups. These techniques include architecture with maximum potential for sustainability, architecture that best assures the long-term success of the community, facilitation and group process that incorporates highly valued lifestyle goals, such as natural light, beauty and delight. Architecture that brings together the needs, wants, and desires within budget and balances community and privacy while creating spaces that bring people together.

Charles Durrett has also co-authored *Cohousing: A Contemporary Approach to Housing Ourselves*, the book that introduced the concept of cohousing to the United States. With is wife and partner Katherine McCamant, he currently lives in Nevada City Cohousing in CA in which 21 seniors also reside. He previously lived in Doyle Street Cohousing with his family for 12 years. As credited in the Oxford English Dictionary Charles with his wife coined the word cohousing. He is a reluctant writer and wrote this book because seniors asked him to, "Get that book done Chuck, I don't even buy green bananas anymore". He realized long ago that developing healthy environments requires starting with the culture — and seeing the much wider array of issues than the sticks and the bricks.

If you have enjoyed *Senior Cohousing* you might also enjoy other

BOOKS TO BUILD A NEW SOCIETY

Our books provide positive solutions for people who want to
make a difference. We specialize in:

Sustainable Living • Green Building • Peak Oil • Renewable Energy
Environment & Economy • Natural Building & Appropriate Technology
Progressive Leadership • Resistance and Community
Educational and Parenting Resources

New Society Publishers

ENVIRONMENTAL BENEFITS STATEMENT

New Society Publishers has chosen to produce this book on Enviro 100, recycled paper
made with **100% post consumer waste**, processed chlorine free, and old growth
free.

For every 5,000 books printed, New Society saves the following resources:[1]

44	Trees
3,976	Pounds of Solid Waste
4,375	Gallons of Water
5,706	Kilowatt Hours of Electricity
7,228	Pounds of Greenhouse Gases
31	Pounds of HAPs, VOCs, and AOX Combined
11	Cubic Yards of Landfill Space

[1]Environmental benefits are calculated based on research done by the Environmental Defense Fund and
other members of the Paper Task Force who study the environmental impacts of the paper industry.

For a full list of NSP's titles, please call **1-800-567-6772** *or check out our website at:*

www.newsociety.com

NEW SOCIETY PUBLISHERS